Two Lives in Uncertain Times

Studies in German History
Published in Association with the German Historical Institute, Washington, D.C.

General Editor: **Christof Mauch** is Director of the German Historical Institute, Washington, D.C. and Professor of Modern History at the University of Cologne

Volume 1
Nature in German History
Edited by Christof Mauch

Volume 2
Coping with the Nazi Past: West German Debates on Nazism and Generational Conflict, 1955–1975
Edited by Philipp Gassert and Alan E. Steinweis

Volume 3
Adolf Cluss, Architect: From Germany to America
Edited by Alan Lessoff and Christof Mauch

Volume 4
Two Lives in Uncertain Times: Facing the Challenges of the 20th Century as Scholars and Citizens
Wilma and Georg Iggers

Volume 5
Driving Germany: Landscaping the German Autobahn, 1930–1970
Thomas Zeller

Volume 6
The Pleasure of a Surplus Income: Part-Time Work, Politics of Gender, and Social Change in West Germany
Christine von Oertzen

TWO LIVES IN UNCERTAIN TIMES

Facing the Challenges of the 20th Century as Scholars and Citizens

Wilma and Georg Iggers

berghahn
NEW YORK · OXFORD
www.berghahnbooks.com

Published in 2006 by
Berghahn Books
www.berghahnbooks.com

© 2006, 2013 Vandenhoeck & Ruprecht
Reprinted in 2013

All rights reserved. Except for the quotation of short passages for the purposes of criticism and review, no part of this book may be reproduced in any form or by any means, electronic or mechanical, including photocopying, recording, or any information storage and retrieval system now known or to be invented, without written permission of the publisher.

Library of Congress Cataloging-in-Publication Data

Iggers, Wilma.
   [Zwei Seiten der Geschichte. English]
   Two lives in uncertain times : facing the challenges of the 20th century as scholars and citizens / Wilma and Georg Iggers.
     p. cm. — (Studies in German history)
   "Many sections have been modified to make them more meaningful to a non-German readership; others … have been thorougly rewritten"—Pref.
   Includes bibliographical references.
   ISBN 1-84545-138-4 (hardback : alk. paper) — ISBN 1-84545-140-6 (pbk. : alk. paper)
   1. Iggers, Wilma. 2. Jews—Czech Republic—Bohemia—Biography. 3. Iggers, Georg G. 4. Jews—Germany—Hamburg—Biography. 5. Refugees, Jewish—United States—Biography. 6. Jewish college teachers—United States—Biography. 7. Germany—Ethnic relations. 8. Czech Republic—Ethnic relations. 9. Reconciliation—History—20th century. I. Iggers, Georg G. II. Title. III. Series.

DS135.E89I34 2006
305.892'400922--dc22
[B]
                                                                         2006013190

British Library Cataloguing in Publication Data

A catalogue record for this book is available from the British Library.

Printed in the United States on acid-free paper.

ISBN 978-1-84545-138-7 hardback
ISBN 978-1-84545-140-0 paperback

Contents

Preface — vii

Chapter 1
From Bohemia to Canada (1921–1942) — 1

Chapter 2
From Hamburg to Richmond (1926–1944) — 23

Chapter 3
Graduate Studies in Chicago and New York (1943–1949) — 44

Chapter 4
The Struggle against Racial Segregation: Little Rock and New Orleans (1950–1960) — 61

Chapter 5
Return to Europe (1960–1962) — 88

Chapter 6
Turbulent Years in Buffalo (1962–1970) — 103

Chapter 7
The Seventies and Eighties (1970–1990) — 121

Chapter 8
Our Contacts with East Germany (1966–1990) — 143

Chapter 9
Private Life and Ties to Bohemia (1970–2006) — 168

Chapter 10
After the Cold War (1990–2006) — 181

Chapter 11
Conclusion — 200

Index — 205

PREFACE

The idea of writing a joint autobiography emerged gradually. On numerous occasions, Georg had been asked to write about his youth and emigration. In 1996, Klaus Bade, the director of the Institute for Migration Research and Multicultural Studies in Osnabrück, Germany, asked us to deliver a lecture at his institute about our early lives and emigration, then published our lectures in a handsome, illustrated issue of their journal and urged us to expand it into a full-fledged autobiography. In 2002, a German edition of our autobiography was published.[1] We had a two-fold purpose in writing these memoirs. One was to convey the experiences of our lives and what we sought to achieve to our friends and to our children and grandchildren. The other was to offer a document of the times across national, religious, and ideological borders, as they affected our lives.

Our lives began in Czechoslovakia and Germany respectively, before the Nazis gained power. We both fled from Europe with our parents in the fall of 1938 to North America. We were soon confronted with segregation in the American South, where we taught at two African-American colleges between 1950 and 1963, and were active in the civil rights struggle. Beginning in the early 1960's, we spent increasing time in West Germany. In spite of initial apprehensions, Göttingen soon became a second home for us. Crossing ideological lines after the mid–1960s, we established contacts with many people, not only scholars, in East Germany, Poland, and Hungary; Wilma befriended people in Czechoslovakia. Since 1980 these contacts have been extended to East Asia. Just as we have been active in seeking reconciliation between Germans and Jews, Wilma has also been involved in the reconciliation of Germans and Czechs. We are pleased that a Czech translation of the German edition of our autobiography has appeared this year.[2] The autobiography, moreover, has generated interest from historians, and the Chinese Academy of Social Sciences in Beijing is publishing a translation into Chinese.

---

[1] Wilma und Georg Iggers, *Zwei Seiten der Geschichte. Lebensbericht aus unrugihen Zeiten* (Göttingen: Vandenhoeck & Ruprecht, 2002).

[2] Vilma a Georg Iggersovi, *Dva pohledy na dějiny. Svědectví o životě v neklidných dobách* (Praha: Nakladelství Lidové Noviny, 2006).

We are grateful to Marion Berghahn for having made the English publication of our book possible. This version is not a literal translation of the German book. Many sections have been modified to make them more meaningful to a non-German readership; others such as the chapter on Georg's experiences as a student at the University of Chicago, have been thoroughly rewritten on the basis of information that was not accessible to us when we were preparing the German edition. We both employed different approaches in writing this book. As is to be expected, we have relied largely on our memories in discussing our personal experiences; Georg has been more concerned with placing them in the context of the time and included written correspondence, and even archival sources to supplement his narrative.

We are grateful to a large number of people who read and commented on parts of the German manuscript, and have listed them in the foreword to the German edition. We consulted Gerald Diesener about the fate of the historians at the University of Leipzig after unification. Hans Schleier, Werner Berthold, and Wolfgang Küttler read the English version of the chapter about East Germany after having previously read the German version. We were able to fact check parts of our Little Rock chapter with Linda Pine at the archive of the University of Arkansas at Little Rock, and with Lee Lorch, a survivor of the Little Rock crisis. We want to thank Marilyn and George Majeska for having read Wilma's chapters for style, and our son, Daniel, who did a momentous job in not only reading the entire manuscript promptly, and correcting stylistic infelicities, but also for making valuable comments on content before we submitted it to the publisher, and once more reading it carefully after it was copyedited. Karl Sieverling at the Max Planck Institute for History in Göttingen deserves thanks for his continuous support with our computer problems, and we wish to thank Sandra Ernst, also at the Max Planck Institute, for having gone carefully through the entire manuscript before we sent it to the publisher.

Chapter 1

FROM BOHEMIA TO CANADA (1921–1942)

WILMA

I was born on March 23, 1921, in the village of Miřkov/Mirschikau, in the Bohemian Forest. The house was built for my parents when they were married in 1919. It was on a farm rented from the formerly noble von Trauttmansdorff family. On the house facade were my parents' initials. My sister Marianne was born there two years later.

My mother Elsa, née Ornstein, came from Waldmünchen in Bavaria, two miles beyond the border. Her parents were Bohemian Jews, her mother more German, her father more Czech. They had moved to Waldmünchen as a young couple, but returned to Bohemia in 1933 and then lived kitty-corner across from us in Horšovský Týn/Bischofteinitz until we all had to flee in 1938. My mother and her sisters attended the only girls' school in Waldmünchen, a convent school. My mother was such a good student that the nuns urged my grandparents to let her join their order and become a teacher. My father Karl Abeles was descended from Jews who farmed in the West Bohemian countryside. The members of my family mostly spoke to each other in High German, and with the servants and villagers in the Egerland dialect.

I was born into the "Kompanie Abeles and Popper," and it was only long after we had to emigrate that I came to realize how unusual our Kompanie was. It was as important to me as my family. The Kompanie came about long before I was born. In 1887 my grandfather Richard Abeles from Vysoká Libyna/Hochlibin near Královice, married Mina Popper from Rejkovice, a Chodish village near Domažlice. The Chodové were a Czech tribe who lived near the German border, spoke a distinct dialect, and had preserved many colorful folkloric traditions. This date is engraved on my grandmother's wedding ring, which is now my wedding ring. My grandparents lived with my grandfather's parents in the village square of Vysoká Libyna, in a house that is still standing. Soon after their marriage, my grandmother wrote her parents and siblings that she was lonesome for them, and so her brother Pepi (Josef) made a magnanimous offer. He offered his less well-off brother in-law a partnership: everything would be owned jointly by the two families. Richard and Mina agreed, and moved to the Hamr farm, not far from the Poppers, where their first child Olga was born.

While each partner was in charge of a separate farm, all major decisions were made jointly. The partners shared the same values, were thrifty and industrious and supported poor relatives, and wasted nothing. Fortunately the two families grew symmetrically: each had a daughter who had to get a dowry, and two sons to whom to pass on the farms.

Before my father's birth in 1896 the Kompanie rented the farm Lazce/Hlas from the town of Horšovský Týn/Bischofteinitz. My father and uncle Leo were born at the farm, which was two miles from the town. The day my father was born, my grandfather gave his workers the rest of the day off and treated them to a barrel of beer. I remember a coffee mug with a German rhyming inscription celebrating my father's first birthday.

My grandmother Mina was remembered in our extended family with affection and respect. Three of her granddaughters, I among them, and one grand niece were named after her. When she was diagnosed with tuberculosis in about 1903, she frequently went to spas such as Karlovy Vary and Merano, and as a result her children were sent to live with relatives. Aunt Olga was raised by relatives in Horažďovice, and at the age of ten my father and his brother Leo were sent to live with uncle Siegfried in Prague. Four years later my father entered an agricultural high school in Kadaň/Kaaden that was to prepare him for university. In 1919 Kadaň was the scene of deadly clashes between police and German nationalists.

My father was the first of the sons of the Kompanie to marry. In the chaotic immediate post-war period, he smuggled my mother across the Bavarian border. About a year later his cousin Hugo Popper married my mother's sister Martha, and my father's brother Leo married Ida Eckstein from the neighboring village of Blížejov/Blisowa. The last to marry were Alois Popper, Hugo's brother and Hedda Eckstein, Aunt Ida's sister. The marriages again resulted in symmetry. Each of the four couples was responsible for one farm, but everything was owned jointly. Generally this arrangement worked well, although sometimes one could detect a division between the Eckstein daughters and the Ornstein daughters. My father made all major decisions, but there was never the slightest suspicion of favoritism.

In 1925, when I was four years old, we moved to Horšovský Týn/Bischofteinitz. The Trauttmansdorffs, who also owned other large estates in Bohemia and in Austria, had lost Miřkov in the land reform of 1924–25. It was given to a coal dealer who during the First World War[1] had been a member of the Czech Legion and thus supposedly had contributed to liberation "from the Habsburg yoke." In the land reform all of our machinery and cattle was taken without compensation. During that time my grandfather Richard died. Although we soon rented another Trauttmansdorff farm, Nový Dvůr/Neuhof, we could not live there, as it had no suitable house for us. Hence we moved to my grandfather's house in Horšovský Týn, to Nádražní/Bahnhofstrasse 75, where we would live until we had to emigrate in 1938.

There were many expropriations during the mid-1920s, and tenant farmers and nobles alike turned to my father for advice. I do not know how much property he was able to salvage for those people, but they gladly paid for his advice. By 1931 he had a million Czech crowns, enough for a down payment to buy Nový Dvůr.

In the following years many new buildings went up at Nový Dvůr. First the Kompanie built a large barn with a vaulted roof, then three pigsties made of pressed straw and fitted with blue glass windows to deter flies. These buildings attracted a lot of attention. Next the Kompanie built a house with two apartments. Although my family did not move to Nový Dvůr, as there was no school nearby, my maternal grandparents Ornstein and other older relatives spent their summers there.

Most of the milk from Nový Dvůr was shipped to Plzeň/Pilsen, which was for us "the city." My parents often went there to meet with friends. Our pediatrician Dr. Vogl also lived there. With him my father hit upon the idea of pasteurizing our milk, which was previously unknown in our area, and selling it in attractive glass bottles decorated with a picture of a mother and child. Yoghurt and apple juice were also bottled in the Nový Dvůr dairy.

On our premises in Bischofteinitz/Horšovský Týn big, round loaves of rye bread were baked once a week by Mrs. Wondrasch. She lived with her husband in a small apartment attached to our house. The Wondraschs took care of our large garden and slaughtered poultry for us. She helped with the laundry and Mr. Wondrasch also went on errands. In the thirties, when grain prices were low, my father decided to avoid the middleman. He converted one of the former farm buildings into a bakery and hired a baker, Mr. Kitzberger, a fun character who probably contributed to the popularity of our bread with the locals. I recall that an old man used to bring us a basket full of crawfish from a nearby brook and would receive a loaf of bread in return.

Fish was a regular part of our diet. We always looked forward to fishing in the ponds in Hlas, at the farm run by Uncle Hugo. Once a year the ponds were drained of water, and men with boots up to their hips waded in the mud and threw the fish into large tanks. The fish were then transferred to large wooden cages in the Radbusa river, which flows through Bischofteinitz.* We took fish from the cages

---

[1] A Czech who deserted from the armed forces of the Central Powers and joined a Czech unit which faught with the Allies.

*I am referring to my hometown by its Czech, German and abbreviated name—just as was customary at the time with which I am dealing.

whenever we wanted to eat them or give them away. The fish were mostly carp, but there was also pike and sometimes an eel. We ate fish every Friday evening, undoubtedly in part because of the servants who were Catholic.

Pork was also part of our diet. Every year a butcher slaughtered a pig in our farmyard in Bischofteinitz. It was not until much later, when I met Jews from outside Bohemia, that it occurred to me that there was anything unusual about our eating pork. I knew of course that pork was not kosher, but that did not concern us. After the pig was slaughtered, pieces of meat, blood sausages and liver sausages and headcheese were boiled in a large kettle over an open fire. Some of the sausages were given to people in town and the rest was smoked.

Our house in Bischofteinitz had a magnificent garden. On the left side of the garden were asparagus beds, on the right vegetables and strawberries. The fence was hidden under lilac bushes and beneath them violets bloomed. Most of the garden was taken up by an orchard. The gravel path that divided the left from the right was lined with currant and gooseberry bushes. Halfway up the path was a gazebo with a table and benches and walls made of wooden planks, through which the sun peeked. The path and the orchard ended in a small park filled with leafy and coniferous trees, with a four-seated swing under one tree. At the entrance to the park was a deep well, covered with stone slabs. As a young child, I was convinced that the well and the large vases that crowned the pillars on both sides of the gate to our property contained treasures from the Thirty Years' War. At the end of the garden was a two story stone tower that my mother called the "Luftschloss" (castle in the air). The first floor was full of old garden furniture and tools. On the second floor we children played and tried to frighten people who passed on their way from the train station. Again and again we were offered much money for the garden, but we never considered selling it.

In front of our kitchen and living room windows was the small flower garden. The most beautiful thing there was the little almond tree, when it was in bloom. On warm evenings we would sit with Mrs. Wondrasch on the little wall that enclosed this garden and listen to her stories about the childhood of people who lived long ago.

Our maids were with us for many years. Kaiser-Mari and Marchet had come with us from Mirschikau. Mari was obsessed with medical matters, memorized medical journals word for word and convinced herself that she had diseases; these all eventually healed of their own accord. When Marchet married after being with us for twelve years, Leni came. In our yard was also the "garage" where the machines from all of the Kompanie's farms were repaired. In charge was Mr. Tichopad, a very talented and versatile Czech from Moravian Silesia who eventually followed us to Canada. With him worked a German mechanic and an apprentice, also German. Across the yard worked the baker Kitzberger, a Czech, Leni, a German, and the Wondraschs. She spoke only German, he mostly Czech. Mr. Zwetschkenbaum, a Polish Jew who performed the function of a rabbi, although he did not have the required formal education, also worked for us part time as a bookkeeper. Nobody addressed him as "Rabbi", but he was highly respected nevertheless.

In one corner of our yard a small stable housed bulls that were owned by the town. Since cows were brought there regularly, my mother insisted that a fence be built to obstruct the view. A fenced-in area also held our doghouse; our last dog was an Irish setter called Troll. The rest of the yard held a milk cooler, an outhouse for the employees, a water pump, the Wondraschs' apartment and two poplar trees.

Once an old man came to our house and told us that he came from America and that he had lived in our house before my grandfather had bought it. We let him go through the garden alone. Then he thanked us and left. After he left, I tried to imagine what reason there could be for leaving our house and garden. Later the Nazis made our house into an administration building, and where the large garden used to be, there is now the ruin of a dairy that was built by the Germans. There is nothing left that reminds us of what my home used to be.

The day when most people came into town was the feast of St. Anne, in July. The church of St. Anne was a mile from the town on a wooded hill, and was reached by a road marked by sandstone statues depicting "the way of the cross." Under high leafy trees was a statue of a group of sleeping apostles. There was a bench where one could read undisturbed and where I also had French conversation lessons with a woman who had worked in Paris as a maid. On St. Anne's Day, thousands of people came from the villages, many in regional costumes. There were stands and booths where anything from Turkish honey to salt pickles was sold. Most of the visitors had to pass our house. For days before St. Anne's Day, the women had been baking the traditional koláče which were filled with poppy seed, cottage cheese and plum jam. The koláče lay in rows on boards in the pantry and in the cellar, and we would give them away whole or cut in wedges. We were not aware that the occasion was actually a pilgrimage; undoubtedly many German Catholics who were more religious than most of the Czechs were aware of the significance of the day.

My parents were a very important part of my life. My mother was an upright, intelligent woman, with more education than the average of her generation. She was very much concerned that my sister Marianne and I should receive a good education. My mother's Czech was very good, although she was born and raised in Bavaria, and she spoke French with Aunt Martha when she did not want others to understand. She made sure that we had piano lessons, but she seldom played the grand piano, a wedding present from my grandfather Richard, out of concern that passersby might think that "this Jewess has nothing else to do than to play the piano in broad daylight." She could imitate voices of people and of animals and knew by heart parodies of German classical poems and poems by the satirist Fritz Löhner about Jews who did not want to be known as Jews.

Mother had a great sense of humor, which unfortunately did not extend to situations when she was jealous of my father. It was clear that he was very much admired by men and women, but I of course do not know how far his relationships with other women went. My mother often felt neglected when my father engaged in lengthy, lively conversations with women. I understand better now than I did seventy years ago that she was hurt when she was left at home to take care of the accounts of Herr Ubl, who shipped the Kompanie's milk to Plzeň, while my father amused himself with friends from his youth at the Thalermühle, the swimming area at the river, which even had cabins for swimmers to change. The fact that there was nothing secret about this arrangement did not make it any easier for my ambitious mother. Nevertheless, I think that my parents had a good marriage and appreciated each other very much.

How can I describe my father without giving the impression that here is an old woman who has a crush on her daddy? Someone who knew him could perhaps make plausible, why he meant so much to so many people. There is nobody with whom one could compare him. Meanwhile, I also see his faults, and that because of him my life has not been easy. His intelligence was remarkable, and he could immerse himself in other people's problems like no one else, and he did that often. We felt safe with him, even when we had to emigrate. He enabled many people to emigrate and so saved their lives.

As long as we lived in Teinitz, he drove every day the eight miles to the farm. During the summer we often went along to swim in the Suchana pond. (Many names of bodies of water in Bohemia had Celtic origins. Surely that was also the case with Radbusa and Suchana.) Often our friends or friends of my parents came along. Near the pond my father had a cabin built in which we could change. Half a century later it was still there.

I learned from my father that we were well off and we should be grateful. He wanted us to observe the people who were working hard in the fields. During the last two years we were there he wanted Marianne and me to work for a week in the fields tying sheaves of grain, from six in the morning until six at night, for the same wages as the laborers. During the two-hour lunch break, the women who worked alongside us went home, cooked a meal and took care of their families. My father had no sympathy for the women from our circles who suffered from depressions which for some reason were quite common. "Look at the workers," he would say, "they have no time for such nonsense".

Many people came to my father for advice or help. On Sundays our kitchen was like a waiting room. Some wanted to know what to do when the insurance company did not pay, others wanted to borrow a team of horses, such as when a daughter was about to be married and needed to transport her possessions. I remember young women considering marriage and asking my father to look at the young man and his small farm, and give his opinion. One of the women, Olgerl Oesterreicher, was a Jewish orphan who lived in the village of Muttersdorf, where all women contributed to the family income by making bobbin lace. We sat around a table with Olgerl and her relatives, my father had a conversation with her intended and soon the wedding was celebrated.

All of the family, except for uncle Alois and aunt Hedda, who lived in the hops growing area of Žatec/Saaz belonged to the Bischofteinitz/Horšovský Týn Jewish community, which consisted of about twelve families. Except on the Jewish New Year and Yom Kippur, most of the families went to services only on the anniversary of the death of a close relative. The "temple," as it was called, was the second floor of a house in Bräuhausgasse. On the ground floor lived the Klaubers, the only poor Jewish family in town, and Rabbi Zwetschkenbaum during his bachelor days.

More than to the Jewish community, we belonged to the German bourgeoisie. Most of the Czechs living in town were officials who had come relatively recently, and kept to themselves. I doubt that even they knew that until the seventeenth century this had been a Czech town. There were also many German officials in our time, from the head of the district down. Until the thirties there seemed to be no problems between the nationalities.

Our standard of living was very much like that of the German doctors, officials and merchants. Perhaps we ate somewhat better as farmers and because the Abeles' thought they knew a lot about good food.

My father sometimes met friends at a bar in town, and my mother saw ladies at Jung's, the best pastry shop in town. During carnival everybody, including my relatives who lived in villages, went to the masquerade ball and the firemen's ball. Relatives came to visit frequently, often for days or weeks. My parents' sisters who lived some distance away, came with their families for the whole summer, and after 1933 some Jews came from Germany. Aunts, uncles and cousins came. My father often invited people and forgot to tell my mother who found out when they appeared with their luggage. On Sunday other Jewish farmers much like ourselves came to visit from some distance away, as did the Salzs, owners of a brick factory. Their uncle Artur, my grandfather's card playing partner during his cures in Karlsbad, was a professor in Heidelberg, and was the only professor any of us knew.

My father's best friend was Friedl Rudofsky, the manager of one of the two local banks. He was a member of the most respected family in town, which had lived there since at least the seventeenth century. He proved to be a real friend. When we had to leave in 1938, he advanced us enough money for all of us—four families—to live on in the following weeks. For this generosity he was persecuted by the Gestapo. My father and Friedl remained friends, and my father sent the Rudofskys care packages from Canada.

In September of 1927 I started school. The day before school started I sat on the swing in the garden feeling sorry for myself because I saw school as the end of my freedom. I went to the German girls' grade school where the first three grades were taught together by the somewhat old-maidish Fräulein Quitterer. While she concentrated on one grade, another class read and the third did calculations on the blackboard, all in one classroom. Being impatient, I read ahead in the reader. Fräulein Quitterer solved the problem by having me read to the class from a reader about Emperor Joseph II, an idealised portrayal that must have been published in the days of Emperor Francis Joseph, or from another book about the history of our town since the Middle Ages.

All of my friends were Gentiles; the few Jewish children in the school were either a little older or younger than I. The Jews of my parents' generation were mostly either unmarried or had moved away. Only much later in gymnasium did I briefly have a Jewish classmate. On Thursdays, which the Catholic children had off we had religious instruction. Mr. Zwetschkenbaum taught all the Jewish children from town and from the villages in one group, which meant that we had to listen to the same stories year after year. He had come from Galicia as a 14 year-old refugee and stayed when the other refugees returned to Galicia at the end of the First World War. He impressed everybody as a very intelligent man with high moral principles. The salary that the Jewish community paid him was not enough for him to live on, so he earned money on the side buying and selling feathers for bedding and furs for tailors and furriers. Apart from my great-aunt Sophie Popper, he was the only Orthodox Jew I knew.

I always liked to read. Among the earliest books I read were the Dr. Doolittle books. In grade school I read stories about knights in the Middle Ages and legends from Greek antiquity. Many of the stories were read to my sister and me by our father. One of my favorite authors was Karl May, who wrote dozens of adventure novels about American Indians and about Arabs and Kurds, without ever having seen the places he described so vividly. In my teens I devoured three kinds of literature: German books written for teenage girls, novels that mother bought from the Social Democratic Gutenberg book guild (some of them contemporary best sellers translated from various languages) and Czech and Russian classics which were required reading at the gymnasium.

My favorite book was *Modche a Rézi* (Modche and Resi) by Vojtěch Rakous, which I read in German, undoubtedly on my mother's advice. Rakous was a Czech-Jewish author who dealt with the lives of Czech country Jews in the second half of the nineteenth century. Despite the idealization he can be accused of, *Modche a Rézi* has remained a favourite of mine and was the starting point of my scholarship. My favorite place to read was in an apple tree in the garden where I could not be easily found. Why a hiding place to read? Reading was a leisure time activity to which one was entitled only after one had practiced the piano, done homework and darned all the worn stockings.

I did experience anti-Semitism on the part of the boys who went to the German school which was located next to our house. On my way to school, I met dozens of these boys, and they sometimes really gave me a hard time. When I was in first grade, a boy hit me and cut my upper lip so badly that it bled. When mother complained to the boy's teacher, he told her that her daughter was not exactly a peaceful little dove.

Even before I was of school age, I associated with Inge Pelzer, the daughter of a bank official. At her house, we attended annual masquerade parties for children from "better" families. The same children also met at other events, such as a ballet performance at the Hotel Traube. (The building continued to house the town's only hotel until 2003, although changing names reflected the changing political fate of the region.) During my five years in grade school my best friend was Ilse Haberzettl. She was the only Protestant child in the school, and as we both were "freed" from Catholic religious instruction, we spent those hours together.

Ilse and I were almost seventy years old when we found each other again. Her family had been expelled in 1946 along with most of the Germans. I remember very vividly how Frau Haberzettl, Ilse's mother marched past our house with the only other remaining Social Democrat on the first of May, 1938 behind the procession of hundreds, perhaps thousands, of Nazis. Later I found out that Ilse's older sister Erna had hidden an anti-Nazi parachutist in her room in Vienna, was arrested by the Gestapo in 1944, and committed suicide. After many years apart Ilse and I still had much in common. I am especially pleased that her son Ernst Michael Böhm, who was born in Teinitz, illustrated my 1993 edition of Josef Seligmann Kohn's *Der jüdische Gil Blas,* a picaresque novel of 1837.

In 1932 I enrolled in a Czech high school, which I attended for a year to learn Czech before going to gymnasium, There I mostly associated with Hilde Liebscher. Her family serves as a good illustration of the much discussed and little understood question concerning the nationality of officials in the First Czechoslovak Republic. Hilde's father, a German, was head of our political district, but his daughter attended a Czech school. The Liebscher family was also expelled to Germany in 1946. I have been in touch with Hilde and so have Czechs, including a recent mayor of Horšovský Týn.

After fifth grade I was supposed to go to the Czech gymnasium in Domažlice, as there was none in Teinitz. During my year in the local Czech high school, I had private lessons in Czech with slečna (Miss) Koptová, a retired teacher from one of the few old Czech families. The facade of her little house in the Czech section of town was just large enough for a window flanked by portraits of Božena Němcová and Karolina Světlá, the greatest Czech women writers of the nineteenth century. Slečna Koptová's methods were old fashioned, but I learned with her very quickly. She regularly gave me pages with texts full of grammatical and spelling mistakes, written in her beautiful handwriting, which I then had to correct. On my first three essays at the school I had grades of satisfactory, good and very good.

To get to school I normally would have had to take a roundabout way through town, but we devised a short cut. Diagonally across from us lived our friend enginéer Beck, and his property ended at the Radbusa. My father had wooden beams and boards brought, and together we built a bridge across the river, beyond which a swampy area extended almost all the way to the Czech school. In wet weather I crossed it with high rubber boots. I am sure that no permission was required to build the bridge.

About that time I had my braids cut off. The reason was that I was in love with a young man who, to please my mother, had told me that he would never love me as long as I had the braids. He of course never noticed that I had cut my braids, but my former teacher from the German school Steinbach did and said: "Now you no longer are a German girl." He had been teaching us in fourth and fifth grade. He spoke much about being the son of a poor widow in the village of Pollschitz, and about having become a teacher through hard work. His favourite writer was Peter Rosegger. For me he and Rosegger merged into one, and probably contributed much to my idealization of country life.

My sister Marianne and I exercised twice a week at the Social Democratic Workers' Gymnastics Association. For us it was the only possible choice, as both the German nationalistic club and the Czech Sokol were out of the question. We were Social Democrats, but I was not allowed to march with them on the First of May, because my mother did not consider it appropriate for the daughter of the most visible employer in town to identify to that extent with the workers.

The rest of our athletic activities were not organized. We played tennis, swam, canoed, bicycled, skied, skated, tobogganed, and in Hlas we sometimes rode work horses into the pond, where they cooled off after work. I often think of the many opportunities we simply had at our disposal, while elsewhere people had to pay for them.

More than occasionally, I caused disagreements between my parents. To my mother, good manners and appropriate clothing, including bras and hairdos were very important, while to my father these were superficialities. The fact that I took seven years of piano lessons, despite my teacher Herr Schlesinger's absolute lack of pedagogical talent and my lack of interest, was a result of my mother's attitude that in the right kind of circles playing the piano was expected.

We often visited my grandparents in Waldmünchen. They formerly had a larger general store, but after they lost much of their fortune through war loans and inflation, they had moved and lived above a smaller store across the street from a church. When Marianne and I visited there with my Mother for a week or longer, we went to the convent school, and were taught by some of the same sisters who had taught Mother and her sisters. We received colorful pictures of saints made of cellophane when we did well. Grandmother used to send the sisters samples of her cooking and baking, and the sisters repaid her in kind. After the war she sent Sister Jakobea care packages from Canada.

At first living in Waldmünchen does not seem to have been easy for my grandparents. Was it simply because they were newcomers, or because they were Jews, the only ones far and wide? I remember being told the story about a Mr. Fuss, who considered my grandparents his competitors. Grandfather saw him on the other side of the street; crossed the street, extended his hand to him, and said: "I think there is room here for both of us. I think we can help each other." This ended all of their problems. I often thought of applying this philosophy in my own life, and decided that it is easier said than done.

Grandfather sometimes went to the local tavern to be sociable, but did not like beer and watered the potted flowers from his glass. Grandmother was more sociable and associated with the wives of officials, the pharmacist's wife and Mrs. Silberhorn who had a fabric store a few houses from my grandparents'.

For the High Jewish Holy Days they went to synagogue in Cham. Their daughters had religious instruction there, the same as Karl Stern who also emigrated to Canada and became a well-known convert to Catholicism.

Waldmünchen was only one hour by car from Teinitz, but the atmosphere was quite different. There the Catholic Church played a much greater role, and Waldmünchen seemed more old fashioned. Both towns still had night watchmen in my childhood. The Waldmünchen one went from door to door on New Year's Eve, singing for tips. At my grandparents' home he sang: "I wish Herr Ornstein and his wife and his three virgins a blessed New Year.

Grandmother seems to have been disappointed when her daughter came back with a knowledge of North German cooking, which we all considered far beneath ours, even though we did not know much about it. Therefore Aunt Martha was sent to Fraeulein Kleeblatt's finishing school in Regensburg. I am sure the pursuit of a career other than marriage was never considered; when during Wold War I Aunt Irma wanted to take a job at the post office, my grandparents consented only on condition that she not accept a salary.

Mother was sent to the Lyzeum in Pilsen, graduation from which entitled her to attend university. After graduating from commercial academy in Prague, she became engaged to my father.

I was an adult when I came to realize that my status as my father's favorite child was very hard on Marianne. I remember that when Marianne became an outstanding swimmer during our teens, I was not used to all the attention being paid to her. When in the spring of 1939 she dropped out of high school in Hamilton after only a few weeks, there was no way one could have predicted that she would become an outstanding economist and a role model for younger women far beyond her field of specialization.

From early childhood on I had certain attitudes that came from my father: life is better in the country than in the city; dialect is better than High German, casual is better than formal, and friendships with people below the bourgeoisie are better than with people from the higher classes. My mother saw things differently. For example, she would not allow Marianne to associate with a certain girl because she was illegitimate and because her grandfather was the town gravedigger.

My father had a very high opinion of me, and despite my mother's criticisms, she seems to have shared it. However, she convinced all our relatives that I was difficult and that I always hurt her feelings. Actually, all our conflicts were trivial. One Sunday afternoon, for example, we were going to go to Hlas for coffee. Because the road was muddy, I decided to wear sturdy walking shoes with my blue party dress. A big argument followed, since of course those shoes don't go with a silk dress. But they go with the muddy road. Mushrooms were to be sliced with a knife, not with a cucumber slicer. Another time we were sitting in the gazebo darning stockings with my aunt and my cousin, who were spending the summer holidays with us. To keep the work from being too boring, I had thought up a decorative pattern. The response was, "Where does she get these crazy ideas?" and "You will turn out just like Martha Arnstein", a divorced relative who supported herself in Prague with a bridge salon. In our circles such an occupation was little more respectable than prostitution. But in the end I think that my father's exaggeratedly high opinion of me did me more harm than my mother's criticisms.

By contrast, Marianne was a normal child, and my cousin Hanna who sometimes lived with us, was always pointed out to us as an example. Relatives often appealed to my conscience, especially Grandmother. When Grandfather, of whom

I was especially fond, also began to preach to me, I decided to run away from home. I must have been about twelve. I packed a lot of apples into my briefcase and walked some distance past St. Anne's Church, sat down on a slope, ate my apples and read until Mother came to look for me, accompanied by a number of relatives.

When I went to the Gymnasium, I had to take the train at five thirty in the morning. School began at eight and normally lasted until one pm, unless we had physical training or stenography in the afternoon. I did much of my homework along the way. In summer we shortened the trip by bicycling to Blízějov and by catching the train there. On the way back we visited our relatives along the way.

In those years my best friend was Anita Krucká. She was two grades ahead of me in the Gymnasium and an excellent student and athletic. She was beautiful and still is, at the age of eighty-seven. With her I sometimes went home on foot, which was faster than taking the circuitous train ride, but was strictly forbidden. We waded in the brook, baked potatoes on an open fire, stole cherries from the orchard that was rented to the owner of a small fruit and vegetable store, played cards with homemade cards with the boys who also commuted.

For several years Professor Zástěra was my homeroom teacher. Before he came to Domažlice, he had been teaching at a Hebrew Gymnasium in Carpatho-Ruthenia, the easternmost province of Czechoslovakia. I do not know why he taught there, as he was not Jewish. In fact I never knew a Jewish teacher, apart from Mr. Zwetschkenbaum. He taught mathematics, in which I was not particularly good, and German. It was customary for parents to meet with their children's teachers and to inquire how they were doing, and so my parents met Zástěra. He and his wife Míla had married a few years before, after she had graduated from the Gymnasium. With her dark red hair she looked very chic and reminded me of characters in Eliška Krásnohorská's novels for teenage girls who married their teachers. My parents and the Zástěras struck up somewhat of a friendship and exchanged visits, but I was much too shy to show up on such occasions. One generally had an impersonal, very respectful relationship with one's teachers. To this day some of the feeling of not being a very well prepared student comes back to me when I have dealings with Czech professors.

In October 1938, after we had fled from home and waited in Prague to emigrate, I learned that Professor Zástěra had committed suicide after the Munich agreement. More than thirty years later I met his wife again. After the war, when Czech universities reopened, she had received a doctorate in Byzantine studies, became the editor in chief of the journal *Byzantinoslavica* at the Czechoslovak Academy of Sciences, and was in the United States to do research. After her visit in Buffalo we remained in touch until her untimely death.

I thought highly of Professor Zástěra, but my favourite teacher, the favorite of all of us, was Professor Lochman. We had an hour of Latin with him everyday. When he explained the word *polyhistor* (polymath) to us, we knew that we had one in front of us. We considered this short, middle-aged man with thinning hair extremely intelligent, well educated and above all a man of principle. I wanted most of all to impress him. Once he spoke about an early play of Ibsen's about the

Roman politician Catiline. I announced that I would bring a copy of the play to class the next day, but to my embarrassment, our edition of Ibsen was not complete. In May and June of 1938 my fellow student Franta Hruška and I had private lessons in English, which was not taught in our gymnasium, with Professor Lochman, which he of course gave free of charge.

When I saw my friend Anita again for the first time in 1966, she told me that she had visited Lochman in the hospital shortly before his death. Although he was a Communist, he spoke about the wrongs that had been inflicted on the Sudeten Germans by the expulsion. His idea of communism had been different from the one he experienced.

I also have fond memories of Professor Klečková, who taught us Czech and history. In those days one had to memorize innumerable dates and facts. Those did not interest her very much, but in her class we became well informed about the history of architecture since the Middle Ages. When during the crisis of the fall of 1938, a huge exhibition of "Czech Baroque" opened in Prague, I was prepared. When the Sudeten crisis reached its climax, the demonstrations took place against the grandiose background of the *son et lumière* of the exhibition. I was not the only one to experience the exhibition as the grand finale of Masaryk's Republic.

By no means did all of our teachers merit respect. There were also the inconspicuous, the ridiculous, and the sadistic. Some were unfair and others simply boring. Frantisek Nepauer, who taught German, when he first met our class announced that there was a Jewish student in the class, and that either she or he would have to go. He insisted there were mistakes in my assignments where there were none, and was also peculiar in other ways. Not only was he the only strict Catholic among our teachers, but he also talked about it during class. He was convinced that he had a sixth sense and could predict events. What could he have meant when he said: "You all hate the Germans, but you will come to love them"?

My concern for social problems, which I shared with my father, was actually superficial. I never thought about the fact that the maids and the schnorrers, the Jewish beggars who mostly came from Galicia, ate in the kitchen. That the maids' room had no window, but only a glassed in square at the top of a shaft, and that in the room there was a wardrobe with our clothes to which we had access at any time, caused me no sleepless nights. I did think that it was nice of Mrs. Wondrasch to make up a place for the schnorrers to sleep on hay in the barn, but it did not occur to me that we should have done more. I was sad, when our maid Marchet left us after twelve years to get married, and accompanied her to the station. Decades later it occurred to me that the whole family should have accompanied her.

Starting in the early thirties Mr. Zwetschkenbaum worked for the Kompanie as a part-time accountant. We had long conversations about Orthodox Judaism and about Zionism. He used to tell me that if one kept all the commandments, faith would come by itself. This did not make sense to me, and so I never tried it. He was not a good teacher, either in class or in the office. Although he spoke enthusiastically about Palestine, he, like many other Zionists, made no plans to go there.

Zionism made sense to me. I saw it as a movement striving for a place Jews could consider their own, free of all the evils of big cities and industrialization. All of the photographs from Palestine showed healthy tanned young people in sandals and without ties. I was sure that Arabs, in case there were any there, would of course be part of that society.

One Jewish girl from Teinitz, Kahler-Gretl, was the only person I knew who went to Palestine. She went around 1930, against the wishes of her parents, and lived in a kibbutz. I met her and her two little daughters, who only spoke Hebrew, during her only visit to Teinitz and we continued to correspond until we had to leave in 1938.

In the mid-thirties I became friends with Hans Stein, a young Viennese who wanted to learn agriculture from the Kompanie and then to go to Palestine. He was one of the idealistic young people who wanted to have nothing to do with their fathers' businesses or factories. Hans, who had just finished the Gymnasium, was assigned to Uncle Leo. For me he was a window to the outside world. After some time, however, he was transferred to Uncle Alois' much more distant farm. I suspect that my mother felt uncomfortable about us reading Freud together. We were still corresponding when I was in Canada and he was guarding sheep on the Dutch island of Texel. There Hans married a Romanian Zionist. She and their child survived, but Hans died of tuberculosis in a concentration camp in Poland shortly before the end of the war. He had talked to me about lyric poets such as Bialik and Rachel, not about problems one might encounter in Palestine.

My thoughts about Palestine were vague. In 1938, when our plans to emigrate were becoming more concrete, I did not want to go to Canada. To stay where we were out of solidarity with the Czechs made sense to me, regardless how the Sudeten crisis might turn out. Going to Palestine was also a possibility, but not Canada. I wanted to at least graduate from the Gymnasium before leaving. But, to be honest, I would not have stayed against my father's will.

It was after the Anschluss of Austria on March 13, 1938 that we began to worry about National Socialism becoming a problem for us. My parents had decided to convert part of one of the former farm buildings adjacent to our house into a room for my sister and me. On Monday after the Austrian Anschluss, the work was supposed to begin, but it was called off. In May, Mother sent our silver flatware to relatives in the interior of Bohemia for safekeeping. She always tended to be pessimistic; my father, on the other hand, had automatic drinking fountains installed for the cows on our farm about the same time.

Emigration was first seriously discussed concretely in June. Emil Lederer, a friend who lived in northern Bohemia, told us about a friend of his, a Sudeten German Social Democrat, who had emigrated to Nova Scotia in Canada, who urged him to follow. Our Kompanie decided that my father should take a trip to Canada together with Karl Schleissner, a relative who lived in our town, to gain a firsthand impression of the country. My father contacted the Canadian Pacific Railway, which was in charge of the immigration of farmers to Canada. The official who was sent to our farm was enthusiastic about my father and about the farm and recommended that Ottawa issue immigration permits to our mostly Jewish group of prospective immigrants, which had grown to thirty-nine persons. Jara, the wife of our cousin Hugo Abeles, was Catholic, and Arnold Schmoker, the son of our Swiss cattle breeding expert, was Protestant. Most of the others were Jewish relatives, although some very distant.

My father decided to pair each family of farmers with a family that had hard currency abroad, something that was actually illegal in Czechoslovakia. The pairing was necessary because, in addition to paying for passage, every family had to have $1000 in Canadian currency for a down payment on a farm. None of the farmers had money abroad. Our partner was Alex Lustig, a young lawyer from Prague and his wife Marianne and little daughter. My father succeeded in smuggling a few Persian rugs to England, the sale of which netted $300 for each pair of partners. He gave his $300 share to the partners, I am sure so he could say that he started in Canada without a cent. Mother objected: what if one of us needed an appendix operation? My father assured her that this would not happen, and once again he was right. That one of us could become seriously ill never crossed our minds. We were strong, healthy people. When both of my parents died at an early age, our sadness was mixed with anger at such an injustice.

My father did not feel like emigrating to Canada. It was far from home, and unlike Mother he was very attached to our corner of the world. When he heard that France needed farmers, he decided to make an exploratory trip to France at the end of August with his cousin Walter.

In September 1938, with the new school year, I began again commuting to school in Domažlice. Our little group of commuters saw an increasing number of Czech and Jewish families with trunks, bales of bedding, and baby buggies heading toward the interior of Bohemia. My mother was afraid to let me ride on the train, because there were rumors of clashes with Germans, but I had my way. The attitude of the German population toward us was changing. One day the wall of our garden was defaced with swastikas. Another day when I sat down on a bench in the railway station, one of the girls from a poor family that had been given lunch at our house several times a week got up and spat on the ground in front of me. On our farm one night, forty newly planted cherry trees were broken.

In Domažlice my friend Iva Běláková and I walked in the park while eating our lunch, when we had classes in the afternoon. We idealized the simple life as propagated by Tolstoy and as depicted in Kaethe Kollwitz's art. Iva sympathized with me when I had conflicts with my mother, because I did not want to wear a bra or a permanent wave in my hair. Like many Czechs, we talked about our allies, the French who, in contrast to the Germans, were a cultured people who would not leave us in the lurch. We were glad, and I still am, that we had grown up in Masaryk's Republic.

During this time Marianne was sent to a gardening school in Krč near Prague. The decision had been made under the pressure of the prevalent opinion that Jews should turn to practical occupations.

My father returned from France with great enthusiasm. He and Walter had been offered the rental of a farm in Calvados on very good terms. They also liked the apple brandy that was produced there. "And when Hitler is finished, we can be at home in an hour." However, this time he was outvoted, and Canada remained the destination.

Our actual flight came suddenly. Strangely, none of us remembers the exact date, but it may have been on September 15th, when Joe (then "Pepi") Loewith, a member of our group who was in the Czechoslovak army, knocked on our window about 4:30 am to tell us of a rumor that the Nazis were planning something against the Jews that day. It was clear that Mr. Stirba, the only local policeman, would not be able to protect us. We hurriedly packed everything we could take along in our little Praga Piccolo. I had my last Teinitz fight with Mother that morning, because I wanted to take along all my photo albums and books, while she thought warm clothing was more important. We drove to central Bohemia, to Walter's farm in Svinaře near Beroun. My most vivid memory is the last trip made with my father to Nový Dvůr, our farm. After he said his goodbyes to the workers, he stopped the car outside the farmyard, put his head on the steering wheel and cried.

When we arrived in Svinaře about seven o'clock in the morning, other relatives were already there from the border area and from Vienna, and more came. At least five families had to be housed and fed. I slept on two easy chairs.

My father had to obtain airplane tickets to somewhere beyond Germany. We could not travel through Germany because a 10,000 Reichsmark reward had been promised to anybody who would deliver my father dead or alive. I don't know why the Nazis considered him so important. Why did a small child, when he saw my father shortly after we arrived in Canada, ask if he is a millionaire? Why was my mother sure, when she was dying of cancer, that she would recover since my father wanted her to? The answer is that he had tremendous charisma that inspired confidence and faith, something the Nazis would have seen as threatening.

Then came the Munich agreement. When I look back at the news of 1938, I see clearly that there had been many indications that France, England, and the Soviet Union would turn their backs on us, probably with no pangs of conscience. The Munich agreement was the greatest shock imaginable for my belief in the decency of the world. From then on, I knew that one could not rely on treaties. The memory of Munich and of the Vietnam War pull me in different directions. Is war ever the better alternative? I can still see the people who at the time wanted Czechoslovakia to fight alone against Germany if necessary. From the flowers that were left around the statue of St. Wenceslas, it seems that as time goes on, an increasing percentage of Czechs think that they should have fought.

In the first ten days in October, when the border area and also Teinitz were occupied by the German army, my father returned one last time to pick things up from our house. Through Arnold Schmoker's father, he met people from the Swiss embassy, who got us airline tickets to Zurich. About the middle of October, a few of us actually boarded a small airplane, but before it started we had to give up our seats to Swiss citizens. We left the plane, but part of the baggage wasn't returned to us, including the briefcase with all my treasures. On October 24 we flew with part of our group to Brussels. High above the clouds we unpacked the food packages Walter had handed to each of us as we boarded.

At the Brussels airport the immigration officials looked at our documents, and one said "vierundzwanzig Stunde heraus" (twenty-four hours out), but we were able to stay in Belgium for a week, mostly in Antwerp. My father went alone to London to find money to continue our journey. Hugo, my favorite cousin from my parents' generation, a Bohemian who remained a good friend of mine until his death, had arrived earlier and did much to take our minds off the sad reality we were experiencing.

I think many members of our group of my generation felt as I did. We were sad that the life we had known had ended, but we did not really worry. It did not occur to us that my father would not find a way to take care of things. There were new things to be explored, and this is how it would be for a long time. In Brussels, Hugo took me along to a coffeehouse where he met a native English speaker. At Antwerp harbor I for the first time saw Africans, probably from the Belgian Congo. From Antwerp the thirty-nine of us then took a boat across the channel to Harwich, England.

In England we took a train through the Midlands, and saw Manchester and Liverpool. I had never seen streets in which all the houses looked so alike, gray, dirty and barren. What we saw of the countryside looked equally depressing. In England I came to realize how beautiful home had been.

On the channel crossing and during six days on the ocean, from October 4 to 11, most of us were seasick.

In Montreal, the Lederer family left us to go to Nova Scotia, and the rest of us took the night train to Hamilton, Ontario. Most of our group went to the Wren farm (named after the previous owners), which my father and Karl Schleissner had rented during their trip in the summer. Our family and the Lustigs stayed at a small hotel. We paired with the Lustigs because Alex Lustig was the only one who knew enough English to serve as my father's interpreter. The first day we drove out to the farm, where we stuffed straw ticks and gathered apples and potatoes that had been left on the ground by the previous owners. We cooked the potatoes and apples in large kettles for our noon meal. I think everybody remembers that meal.

A few days later we moved with the Lustigs to the Van Sickle farm, about nine miles from Hamilton. The former owners, who had gone bankrupt, stayed on for some time "to teach us the ropes."

The time with the Lustigs was very pleasant. Both were in their early thirties, had a great sense of humor, sang songs from their student days, and knew how to find humor in our situation.

Ever since the editor of the newspaper in my home town in Czechoslovakia had to leave town because he was bankrupt, I had thought bankrupcy was terrible, but the bankrupt Van Sickles didn't seem to suffer at all. For breakfast there was always bacon, eggs, toast, orange juice, jam, large bowls of stewed fruit, and coffee. The quality of the other meals, and of Canadian cooking generally, on the other hand, was disappointing. My mother, who had been used to household help, now had to do the cooking and laundry for the family and for one or two hired men and for John, the good-for-nothing son of Mr. Colley, our liaison to the Canadian Pacific Railroad.

One day Mother decided to make things easy for herself and to "cook Canadian." She took a head of cabbage, boiled it in water with a little salt and brought it to the table. My father rocked his head from side to side, and nobody touched the thing, not even the Canadians who had become spoiled by her cooking. Mother turned red in the face, jumped up and dumped the unfortunate vegetable in the dog's bowl. Rex sniffed at it, and "as truly as I am alive," as my grandmother would say in German, shook his head and slowly walked away. This was the end of Canadian cooking in our household.

We knew practically nothing about Canada when we arrived. Ontario was emphatically Anglo-Saxon and Protestant. Although Canada did not want to admit many immigrants and least of all Jews, the population was friendly, mostly in a superficial way, and few people had the slightest notion of why we had come. How anti-Semitic Canada was at that time and how few Jews had succeeded in immigrating there is documented in the book, *None Is too Many* by Harold Troper and Irving Abella. The title is the literal answer that the Canadian director of immigration F. C. Blair gave to the question as to how many Jews should be admitted.

The first question we were generally asked was, "How do you like this country?" and the second was, "What church do you go to?" Before the outbreak of the war in 1939, more of our people came to Canada, many with my father's help. Many denied more or less emphatically that they were Jews. Some pretended to be Catholic, not realizing that in Ontario Catholics were not very popular. At that time I had little tolerance for these efforts to "pass." Now I understand that they knew little or nothing about Jewish religion and history, and wanted to spare their children the experience of anti-Semitic prejudices. Those who remained Jewish attended, at first occasionally and then more and more regularly, the Hamilton Reform synagogue.

On January 3, 1939 I started going to classes at Central Collegiate, a high school in Hamilton. For three dollars a week, Marianne and I shared a room with a Jewish family. Many years later I found the notebook in which I had written down how much I spent on food: five cents for sardines, a little more for cream of wheat. We brought milk, fruit, and potatoes from the farm, where we spent our weekends.

Canadian bread was terrible; the "Jewish" bread that one bakery carried was somewhat better, although "Canadianized." Day old bread was shipped to a silver fox farm up north. We soon discovered that we could buy this bread for half price.

When Marianne lost interest in school, she returned to the farm, where she was put in charge of the chicken coop. I stayed in school. Unlike the situation in the Gymnasium, here one could choose one's subjects. Except for English, I did not have to work very hard. When I arrived, the class was engaged in a very detailed study of *Macbeth*. In the school edition, half of every page of the text consisted of notes. So every night from 6.00 to 10.00 p.m. I read four pages, looking up almost every word in the dictionary. I know that nobody would think of recommending that method of learning a language, but I learned English very quickly. In the spring I received a letter from McMaster University. I was accepted for the fall semester, regardless whether I would pass the "senior matric" that students in Ontario took at the end of high school. Besides, I was offered a full scholarship of $150.

History courses in Czechoslovakia had generally consisted of memorizing names, facts, and dates—our Professor Kleckova had been an exception—and students were expected to know almost the entire slender text book by heart. In Canada, on the other hand, we would read a large, illustrated, well written book from which we would be expected to pick out what we considered important. The instruction was problem oriented and we were expected to think.

Probably all students who came from Europe to Canada found school very easy. I was the first student at McMaster, who, to paraphrase Chamberlain, "had come from a distant country which nobody knew." At first the attitude of us refugees toward Canadians was condescending, especially toward their taste in clothes and food, but eventually this changed.

In the summer of 1939 I was invited by the YMCA to attend a summer camp on Lake Erie. I helped the counsellors and I think the reason I was invited was to provide a glimpse at a different world for the campers, twelve-year-old girls. Before going there, I had asked my parents to visit me on the following weekend with my grandparents, who were due to arrive from Europe. They could not make any promises, because they expected my grandparents, who were 69 and 79 years old, to be very tired.

On Saturday I suddenly had the feeling that something bad had happened to my grandfather. I had always rejected the idea of premonitions and yet could not stop crying. On Sunday parents who came to visit the camp brought the Hamilton Spectator which contained a front page article about my grandfather. He had waited outside the Gestapo office in Prague day after day for many months to get an exit permit, and had been so weakened by this ordeal that on his arrival in Canada he had to be carried off the boat. He was brought to the farm, where he still managed to say "Dej Vám Pámbůh štěstí" (May God give you good luck). He died half an hour later.

McMaster at that time was very small and strictly Baptist. Smoking, alcohol, and dancing were strictly forbidden. Professors were required to be "good, active Christians," and many of the students were planning to become ministers. I could not understand how people who had been trained at first-rate universities could talk about their personal relationship to Jesus. Nevertheless almost all of my friends at McMaster were pious Christians. I did not blame them for trying to convert me to Christianity, away not from Judaism but from my lack of any faith.

I would have liked to study medicine. As a doctor, I thought, one could really do something to help people. But that was not possible, not only because McMaster had no medical school and going elsewhere was out of the question for financial reasons, but also because my father could not see me or perhaps any woman as a doctor. I was also not particularly good in the physical sciences. So I majored in French and German and in addition to the compulsory courses in the humanities registered for as many courses as I could fit into my schedule. The university allowed me to finish the four-year course in three years. Apart from my German professor, the teaching staff was excellent, and I profited much more from McMaster than later from the famous University of Chicago.

McMaster had 500 students and 40 faculty members. The administration consisted of the Chancellor, the Dean of Arts and Sciences, the Registrar, the Bursar and the Dean of Men and the Dean of Women.

Freshman initiation was confusing. It was customary for freshmen to be pulled out of their beds at night and tied to a tree, or asked to push a small coin around the gymnasium with their nose or tongue. I was very conscious that I was different from my fellow students. I participated in class discussions, but on social occasions I was very shy. I only had a few dates with a theology student with whom I mainly talked about religion, and we remained in touch when after my graduation. I worked in Ottawa in the Department of Postal Censorship, and he served in the Royal Canadian Air Force during the war. Since I had sent him a package, I remember that I had enclosed Pascal's *Pensées,* I was notified that he had died when his airplane was shot down over the channel.

When I came to McMaster, I had *au pair* jobs with several families in succession, but none were very enthusiastic about my work in the household. But then I was lucky: my father had met Mr. Bray, the owner of large chick hatcheries, who invited me to live with his family. I was expected to teach his children French and to help in the kitchen when the maid was off. The Brays soon realized that the children were totally disinterested in French, but permitted me to stay nevertheless. Mrs. Bray has remained for me the personification of "a lady." It was a good, peaceful time for me. I remember a discussion about ethnicity with Mr. Bray, who could not understand why I insisted on identifying myself as Jewish, since Canadians associated something very different than me with Jewishness. He said I was only hurting myself.

Most of the Jews in Canada in my parents' and grandparents' generations were immigrants from Poland, Russia, or Lithuania. Most were traditionally religious and spoke Yiddish, or English with a Yiddish accent. With them as later with Jews in the United States, it struck me that unlike people from Czechoslovakia, they were not interested in their countries of origin.

When we arrived in Canada we were discouraged by the authorities from having contacts with Canadian Jews, probably out of concern that this might lead to further Jewish immigration. One of the Jews in Hamilton, Morris Silbert, discovered our group and always gave us useful advice when we needed it.

The majority of the Canadian Jews found it strange that we did not eat kosher and did not speak Yiddish. Once some Canadian Jews came to a "Czechopeople" farm to visit just as a pig's head was being boiled in a kettle in preparation for making headcheese. The incident certainly did not contribute to mutual understanding.

I think that many German Jews would be shocked about some of the things that were amusing to us, such as the story about the pig's head or the stories about Jews who denied their Jewish background or about Dr. Vogl, our former pediatrician who claimed that in all of St. Catharines he was the only person who did not know that he was Jewish.

At the end of the academic year the Brays decided that it would be better for me to live on campus, in order to assimilate more quickly. Until I received my B.A. in 1942, the Brays paid for my room and board in the girls' residence hall. During the academic year I worked in the library and helped the Dean of Women prepare for her German examination for her doctorate. I translated with her Friedrich Gundolf's monograph on Goethe, and for both jobs I was paid thirty cents an hour. At that time professors who taught in Canada did not always have Ph.Ds. In the evening I often babysat, washed dishes after dinner parties in the neighbourhood, or was paid to sleep in the "annex", a small girls' residence hall, making sure that nothing forbidden took place. In retrospect I wonder why I, who was hardly older than the girls who lived there, was given that responsibility.

After awhile, Marianne tired of cleaning the chicken coop and allegedly because of the impression that I had made was able to gain admission to McMaster without having graduated from high school. She majored in economics and became an excellent student.

Many of the Jewish refugees were critical of our attending university. They felt that Jews should stick to "practical" professions. One day Mr. Colley, our liaison to the CPR, came to the farm and accused my father of breaching his agreement with the CPR because his daughters attended a university instead of working on the farm. When my father told him that he had not sold us into slavery, Colley realized that there was nothing further he could do.

I observed that Canadians who were better off than we were, generally were less willing to finance their children's education than my parents had been. Many years later I met Colley's daughter Louise at the University of Chicago. She was far beyond the normal college student age because she was only able to go to university after she had earned enough money to pay for her education.

In the summer of 1939 I wanted to earn money for the next academic year at university, but it was difficult to find a job, since there was a good deal of unemployment in Canada at that time. For a few weeks I worked in an underwear factory in Hamilton, and then in a candy factory in Brantford where my father was managing a farm. Two of his hired men were German Jews who had been released from an internment camp. A fair number of my co-workers were aboriginal Canadians who had come from the Six Nations Indian Reserve near Brantford. In another job that did not last long, I was to keep house for my father, who was to equip and manage a farm north of Toronto for Mr. Creed, a rich man from Toronto. Creed gave my father notice as soon as the cattle and the equipment had been bought.

The longest summer job that I had was on the farm in Brantford. It consisted mainly of milking twenty-nine cows, partly by hand and partly by machine, together with Frank Eckstein, an old bachelor from Teinitz. I also cleaned up the barn and the milk room and cultivated corn with a tractor. Back home, Frank let me ride to school on his bicycle and gave me honey candy. On the farm, he would recite passages from German classical poetry, especially *Faust,* with the manure fork in his hand. He was fond of the passage "No dog would want to live like this," and other passages that seemed relevant to his condition at the time. He was still hoping that his mistress of many years, who had emigrated to New York and was recently widowed, would marry him, but she had no intention of doing so.

Chapter 2

FROM HAMBURG TO RICHMOND (1926–1944)

GEORG

I was born as Georg Gerson Igersheimer on December 7, 1926, in Hamburg, Germany, in a Jewish family. My ancestors had lived in Germany for many centuries. There is speculation that our Minden ancestors may have come to Westphalia from Poland in the mid-seventeenth century. The genealogical information we have for the various branches of my family go back to the eighteenth century, but genealogies tell us little about the conditions in which these families lived. By the second half of the nineteenth century, we know that they all engaged in commercial activities; unlike Wilma's family they did not live in the countryside and engage in agriculture or cattle trade. Few of them seem to have been very affluent, although all of them appeared to have been quite comfortable They were increasingly acculturated—assimilated would not be the right word–into German middle-class culture, while maintaining a Jewish religious identity. Much has been written about the Jewish upper social strata, a *Bildungsbürgertum*—a term difficult to translate, a bourgeoisie steeped in German classical high culture, which had largely left the Jewish religious community and in many cases had converted. But none of my ancestors belonged to this category. They definitely felt bourgeois *(bürgerlich)*, as distinct from the working and artisanal classes, and cultured on the basis of their education. Unlike the lower social classes, who typically finished school after the seventh grade at age thirteen, it was usual in my family to attend the *Realschule,* which was midway between the working class *Volksschule* and the university preparatory *Gymnasium,* from which they generally graduated at the age of fifteen. A sign that this was officially recognized as an elevated social status was that male graduates of the *Realschule* were only required to serve one year in the military, and not the usual three years. Women in our family generally attended a *Lyzeum,* a female version of the *Realschule,* which came into existence toward the end of the nineteenth century. As far as I know, no one in my immediate family before 1914 attended university, and thus probably not *Gymnasium* either. One cousin of my father, Josef Igersheimer, who became a famous professor of ophthalmology, was an exception as was my mother's brother, Henry Minden, who became a lawyer. It was assumed that the men would enter commercial professions and the women would be housewives, although with their secondary school education they considered themselves members of the cultured classes.

My grandfather, Gerson Igersheimer, was born in 1859 in the medium sized town of Bad Mergentheim in Northern Swabia, approximately two miles from the village of Igersheim. His parents ran a small general store. In 1871 the family moved to Frankfurt, where Gerson married Lina (Carolina) Mela. Her ancestors were Sephardic Jews who had fled the Catholic Inquisition in the sixteenth century. The name Mela—Italian for apple, a Jewish name for which there is no counterpart in Spanish or Portuguese—seemed to indicate that the family came from Italy. By the time she grew up, however, the family belonged to the Ashkenazi (German) Orthodox congregation in Frankfurt. Otherwise I know little about the Mela family.

My maternal grandfather, Max Minden, was born in Hamburg, also in 1859. The Mindens originally came from Minden in Westphalia, and in the eighteenth century moved to Altona on the outskirts of Hamburg. At the time Altona was under Danish rule, and Jews had greater freedom than in the neighboring Hanseatic city of Hamburg. Sometime in the nineteenth century, the family moved to Hamburg. Max's wife, Sophie *née* Feitler, was born in 1867 in Oppenheim on the Rhine. Her parents had moved there from Seeheim near Darmstadt in Hesse where the family lived for generations.

As far as I know, there were no conversions to Christianity, but in the second half of the nineteenth century a man who married into the family converted to Judaism. Increasingly in the course of the nineteenth century, the Jewish religious community in Germany divided into Reform (more frequently called Liberal) and Orthodox orientations. Liberal Judaism, in the tradition of Moses Mendelssohn's Jewish Enlightenment *(Haskalah),* sought to bring Jewish religious practices into harmony with modern culture, insisting that one could be a good Jew and a member of the German cultural community. The religious services were reformed, the liturgy included prayers in German, the sermons were in German, and in many cases there was organ music, which was anathema to traditional Jews. The Liberal service resembled the Protestant in that respect, while seeking to preserve the essential elements of Jewish tradition. Somewhat later there developed a counter movement, initiated by Rabbi Samson Raphael Hirsch, which sought to preserve the core of Jewish orthodox practices. Hirsch insisted on the full observance of Jewish law. Yet he also was convinced that Jewish orthodoxy and German culture were compatible. It is thus striking that for their bar mitzvah (confirmation), Jewish boys received gifts of the German classics, such as the complete works of

Goethe and Schiller as well as Lessing, the eighteenth-century Enlightenment poet and dramatist, who pleaded for toleration of the Jews, and the nineteenth-century, originally Jewish, poet Heinrich Heine. However, the Orthodoxy of Hirsch, which was practiced in many Jewish congregations in Germany from the mid-nineteenth century until the Holocaust, differed markedly from Orthodoxy as it had been practiced in Germany before and as it was still practiced in the shtetls of Eastern Europe. Thus sidelocks *(payes)* were rare among German Orthodox Jews. Dietary laws and the Sabbath were still strictly observed. But Judaism was no longer identified with Jewish ethnicity as it was in Yiddish speaking Eastern European communities. For example, Judaeo-German translation in Hebrew script in the prayer books were replaced by standard German. The Orthodox services introduced solemnity and orderliness reminiscent of Christian services; participants no longer recited the prayers aloud individually while swaying.

Both Liberal and Orthodox orientations were present in my family. My father was brought up in a very observant Orthodox family in Frankfurt, in the congregation that had been founded by Hirsch. That congregation in the 1870s separated from the main Jewish community in Frankfurt, which it considered too Liberal. In 1912 the family forbade his sister, my aunt Martha, from marrying a Liberal rabbi and instead arranged a marriage with a decidedly Orthodox businessman in Hamburg. My mother's father, Max Minden, was the son of the cantor of the central Liberal synagogue, the Temple, in Hamburg. I suspect that my grandmother Sophie also came from a Liberal family in Oppenheim. My grandfather Max seems to have been religiously indifferent but was active in Jewish philanthropy. He helped to resettle Russian Jews in the United States and made at least two trips to the United States to see how they were doing. He became a prosperous businessman, with a firm with branches in Hamburg and Hull, England, that imported eggs and other agricultural products from Russia. There is speculation that his sudden death in February 1914 may have been a suicide due to financial difficulties.

The family lived in Hull from 1894 until 1904, where my mother was born shortly before they returned to Hamburg. Max was cremated in violation of Jewish law and tradition. The children were excused from Protestant religious instruction in school and, as my aunt tells me, had no formal Jewish religious instruction at all. Of the ten of my grandparents' children who grew to adulthood, four married non-Jews and broke all ties to Judaism. Two became Christian Scientists. Others remained loosely Jewish, while the oldest son, Henry, became an observant Orthodox Jew and his children, grandchildren, and great grandchildren remained Orthodox. My mother had two Jewish best friends throughout her school years, and they were socially isolated from their Gentile classmates.

It is my impression that the common picture of largely upper middle-class and religiously assimilated German Jews is not correct. Very few of the approximately six hundred German and Austrian refugees in Richmond, Virginia had been upper middle class in Europe and even fewer were intellectuals or academics. Few were totally estranged from Jewish religion, yet most also felt little at home in the Orthodox congregations in Richmond, which in their Eastern European ethnicity differed from the Orthodoxy they knew in Germany. Temple Beth Ahaba, the largest and most established Reform congregation, however, was also not quite to their liking, as it had abandoned many Jewish traditions. Thus many of the refugees, including my family, joined the Conservative Beth El congregation. In recent decades since the Holocaust, American Reform Judaism has again become more traditional.

In the first years of their marriage my parents kept an Orthodox household. I remember the two separate tables in the kitchen for meat and non meat foods, but at some point the second table disappeared. When it became increasingly difficult after the Nazi accession of power to obtain kosher meat, my parents like others began to eat "new kosher", that is meat from ordinary butcher stores, but avoided those meats that were forbidden by Jewish law, such as pork. My father seldom went to religious services except on the High Holy Days and on the anniversary of the deaths of his parents, but we very frequently observed the Friday evening Sabbath Kiddush service and meal at the home of my father's sister Martha and her family.

My best friend since before I started school was Karl Heinz Martin, the son of the superintendent of our apartment house, even after we had moved to a different more modest apartment nearby. I celebrated Christmas with his family and he Hanukkah with us, without either of us considering this as unusual. I considered it perfectly normal that I was Jewish. On Christmas Day 1932, only a few weeks before the Nazis came to power, my father took me to a children's play. At the end of the play, the leading actress announced that because it was Christmas all the children in the audience would receive a bag of candies. When I got up and loudly announced that I celebrated Hanukkah, she replied that the child who celebrated Hanukkah would receive two bags.

I began school on April 3, 1933, in the neighborhood public elementary school for boys in the Knauerstrasse, two days after the Nazi nationwide boycott of Jewish stores. I had experienced no anti-Semitism before and experienced none in the school. On the other hand, changes soon became apparent after the Nazi accession to power. During the first few months, we regularly greeted the teacher as "Guten Morgen, Herr Lehrer." One day we were told that we should discontinue this and stand next to our desks, raise our right arm, and say "Heil Hitler." I was not excluded from this, nor from the Monday morning assemblies in the schoolyard, where the principal in Nazi uniform addressed the children. The Swastika flag was raised and the German national anthem, "Deutschland, Deutschland über alles," was sung, followed by the Nazi "Horst Wessel" song, honoring an SA (storm trooper) martyr.

My teacher, Fritz Pohle, born in 1904, too young to have served in the First World War, was an ardent German nationalist but no anti-Semite. He glorified the heroism of the German soldiers in the First World War, spoke about the injustice that had been done to Germany by the Treaty of Versailles, and reminded the students that someday they too might have to defend the Fatherland. One wall poster in the classroom spelled out the territories Germany had lost as a result of the First World War. Another wall poster showed how Germany, restricted by the Treaty of Versailles to an army of a hundred thousand men, was encircled and threatened by its neighbors, France, Belgium, Poland, and Czechoslovakia, which were all heavily armed. Another read "Ein Volk, ein Reich, ein Führer." I do not know whether Herr Pohle belonged to the Nazi Party—at this early stage he probably did not, although ultimately he most certainly had to join the Nazi teachers' organization. The fact that he shielded the Jewish students in his class spoke against it. Herr Pohle was deeply inspired by the youth movement. The movement had arisen in the late nineteenth century, a revolt by mostly middle class youths, as yet mostly male, against what they considered the stuffy bourgeois world of their parents. The youth movement was not associated with any one political or religious orientation. The most important group was that of the *Wandervogel* which was nationalistic, generally did not admit Jews, and welcomed the outbreak of war in 1914 as a liberation from existing values, and an opportunity for heroism. But there were counterparts to the *Wandervogel* among other very different ideological groups, Catholic, Jewish, socialist, and after 1919 also Communist. The Nazis emulated the romanticism, the return to nature, and the hiking and campfires of the youth movement, but changed the organizational structure of the youth movement to centralized control. For the most part, the movements were highly decentralized, consisting of small groups, often only a handful of young people led by a charismatic leader, and loosely associated with the larger organization. After 1933, the Nazis absorbed much of the youth movement into the Hitler Youth, and the separate association for girls *(Bund Deutscher Mädel),* retaining the romanticism of the movement but organizing it from the top and centralizing it.

The Jewish youth movements were left untouched because there was, of course, no place for them in the Nazi scheme. There were several Jewish youth movements along political and religious lines that foreshadowed the political parties in Israel. Some of these movements also became established in other, particularly Eastern European countries. These movements were also closely associated with sports organizations such as Maccabi, which existed in Jewish communities throughout the world and for the first time in 1930 held Maccabi Games in Tel Aviv. Zionism was unthinkable without the romanticism of the youth movements and without the kibbutz as a communal alternative to the modern bourgeois society. Herr Pohle communicated a good deal of the idealism of the German youth movement, which made a deep impression on me that easily transferred to my attachment to the Jewish youth movement. I naturally participated in the excursions and hikes on which our class went with Herr Pohle, several of them to the home of Prince Otto von Bismarck at Friedrichsruh near Hamburg.

In retrospect, I am surprised by Herr Pohle's political openness, considering the circumstances in Nazi Germany. I followed the Italian-Ethiopian War in the fall and winter of 1935–36 with intense interest. My sympathies were totally on the side of the Ethiopians whom I saw as the victims of aggression. Astonishingly Herr

Pohle permitted me to talk about the war and to show maps about its course, notwithstanding that after all the Ethiopians were black. At that time Nazi Germany and Fascist Italy were not yet allies and in fact, relations between them were strained about Austria.

My experiences in the Knauerstrasse school were not quite typical of Jewish children of my generation but also not exceptional. Contemporaries of mine in Königsberg in East Prussia and in Vienna even before the Nazi takeover in 1938 were seriously harassed in their schools as Jews. On the other hand Peter Gay and the literary critic Marcel Reich-Ranitzky report in their autobiographical accounts that they suffered little discrimination from fellow students and teachers in their *gymnasiums* in Berlin as did an acquaintance of ours in his *gymnasium* in Göttingen. If there was a dividing line in our class in the Knauerstrasse, it was between bourgeois and working-class children. This division was not very serious. Of the eight children from bourgeois families four were Jewish. There were no Jewish children from the working class. I am now surprised that there were so many children of working class background. The fathers of half of the working class children were unemployed in 1933 and 1934. The school is in a neighborhood, Eppendorf, which was then and still is, largely middle class. However, poorer families lived in the tenements behind the front houses. Some of the children may have come from the other side of the Eppendorfer Landstrasse, very close to the home of Ernst Thälmann, the leader of the German Communist Party. I suspect that many of the children came from Social Democratic and Communist families, which tended to reject anti-Semitism. The boys in the class regarded me as one of them. A new child who had recently come from Flensburg on the Danish border was told to shut up by my fellow students when he made an anti-Semitic remark directed at me. Another new student, Erich Lau, voiced anti-Semitism when we took a walk together. He had not known that I was Jewish and changed his tune when I told him that I was Jewish and we became good friends. In October 1936 when I wanted to transfer to the Jewish Talmud Thora school, already at a very late date, Herr Pohle urged my parents to leave me in the school, naively assuring them that as long as he was a teacher at the school I was perfectly safe. The same naiveté was also expressed by two of my former classmates who completely misunderstood the situation and when we turned ten wanted me to join the *Jungvolk*, the pre-Hitler Youth organization for ages 10 to 14, and urged me not to tell that I am Jewish.

On the other hand I was very soon confronted by anti-Semitism outside the school. There were newspaper display cases along the main streets with the pornographic anti-Semitic *Der* Stürmer, and the hatred against Jews was spread systematically in the media. There soon appeared signs on store windows and on movie theaters "Juden unerwünscht" (Jews not Wanted). I was shocked when I went with friends to the nearby swimming pool to which I had gone frequently and saw a similar sign. The most frightening incident occurred when I was ten, when a bunch of uniformed Hitler Youth accosted me, threatened me with knives, and pushed me down some stairs. Fortunately I was not hurt. A Göttingen acquaintance, who never had problems in his school, told me that he was once beaten so badly by Hitler Youth who did not attend his school, that he still suffers from the injuries today. On the other hand the food shops with which we dealt in our neighborhood had no such signs and remained friendly. The superintendent of the house to which we had moved, Herr Motzek, and his wife would often take my sister and me along with them over weekends to their garden and little cottage *(Schrebetgarten)* at the edge of town.

In reaction to the anti-Semitism that surrounded me, I became gradually more aware of my Jewish identity. For three summers, 1934 to 1936, I attended an Orthodox day camp sponsored by the Jewish community where for the first time I encountered Jewish children from poor families. I was excused from the Protestant religious instruction at the Knauerstrasse school but expected to have Jewish instruction elsewhere. Once a week I attended classes in Hebrew, Jewish religion and Jewish history with a small group of children in the intimacy of the home of Cantor Lieber—who later became the rabbi of the German Jewish congregation Habonim in New York. My reaction to this Jewish instruction was very different from that which Wilma received from Rabbi Zwetschkenbaum in Teinitz, which left her totally cold. What I learned fascinated me and contributed decisively to my later commitment to Judaism. I also had increasing contact with Jewish kids my age, most of whom were observant. I joined the Bar Kochba sports club, an affiliate of the Zionist Maccabi. I increasingly felt that I was Jewish, not German, although earlier I had seen no conflict between the two. An indication of this change were my reactions to the international football games that I listened to with Jewish friends. They would cheer for the team Germany was playing against; it took me a while, but I finally joined in. As time went by, I felt the need to attend the Jewish Talmud Torah, in order to be with Jewish fellow students. This prompted me to transfer from the Knauerstrasse school.

At this point, when I was ten years old, serious conflicts developed between my parents and myself. They considered me a stubborn and difficult child, and to an extent I undoubtedly was, since so much of my outlook differed from theirs. I became increasingly observant to the point of no longer eating meat, since neo-kosher was not acceptable to me. But this was not the core of the problem. In retrospect, I realize how sad the lives of my parents were. My father must have had a very unhappy childhood. His mother was seriously ill for years with a disease that was diagnosed very late as Hodgkin's Disease, and she died when he was fourteen. His father had a very small bank—he shared one messenger boy with another bank in the same building—that failed in 1913, and he died shortly afterward. There is speculation that he committed suicide that I find less likely than in the case of Max Minden, because of his intense orthodoxy. He is also buried next to his wife in the cemetery of the separate orthodox community in Frankfurt. Strictly Orthodox congregations would not permit a suicide to be buried within the cemetery.

Relatives apparently played an important part in the upbringing of my father and his sister. The atmosphere in this orthodox setting must have been stifling and oppressive. My father was apprenticed to the metal firm of Beer Sondheim in Frankfurt in the hope of becoming a successful businessman. This was the central ideal of his life, the commitment to respectability and what went along with it, including being the head of a respectable family. Throughout his life he was very inhibited, always afraid that he might give the outside world the impression that he did not conform to the norms of the society.

As an adult I am, however, proud of how he conducted himself during the First World War, which I was not when I was a child. Then I did not like that he tried to dodge military service. In some ways he reminds me of the *Good Soldier, Švejk*, the satirical novel by the Czech author Jaroslav Hašek about the First World War. My father was one of a small minority who in 1914 was not caught up in the war enthusiasm and was determined to participate in the war effort as little as possible. He was a Francophile and an Anglophile and did not see the purpose of the war. I am certain, however, that he did not vent his views. Although he served in the army during most of the war, he succeeded at one point in being discharged after he successfully simulated sickness. And after he was inducted he again was able to get himself assigned to a desk job in occupied Bucharest. In the closing days of the war he was actually rushed to the front on the Danube where he saw no action. Nevertheless he was recognized as a *Frontkämpfer* (someone who had fought at the front) and in 1935, along with all other *Frontkämpfer*, including Jewish ones, he was awarded a medal, which as the Jewish recipients hoped would be a protection, but in fact meant nothing. Whether his role in the war reflected ethical commitments or a desire to save his skin—it probably did both—he hated war and although he saw himself as a German he was no nationalist. In the Weimar Republic he steadily voted for the German Democratic Party, which represented the democratic political center, and voted for it as many Jews did, even after the party lost most of its voters to the nationalistic right. Unlike Wilma's parents in Czechoslovakia, my father would never have voted for the Social Democratic Party which was at the time still very much of a working class party. Later in the United States, he admired Franklin Delano Roosevelt and voted Democratic, but also acquired many of the racial prejudices of his environment. Again he never wanted to be conspicuous.

His career began satisfactorily after the war. Neither family nor friends tied him to Frankfurt. For two years he worked in the office of a Jewish-owned chemical firm, Ludwig Netter and Sons, in Ludwigshafen in the French-occupied zone of the Rhineland, not far from Frankfurt. In 1921 he accepted the opportunity to move to Hamburg to manage their office and to be close to his sister. In 1925 he established his own business. Shortly afterward he married my mother. At the age of 31 it was time for him as a respectable businessman to get married. Ernst Minden, the most successful of my mother's siblings, then at the beginning of a successful career with the Max Warburg banking firm, first at their Hamburg office and then in charge of their British operations after the Nazis came in 1933, who in fact became the head of the Minden family, introduced my mother, Lizzie, then twenty-one, to my father. After a few weeks they became engaged and were married three months later in December 1925. Almost a year to the day after the wedding, I was born.

My father's metal brokerage business went well until the depression. With the decline in the value of stocks, he suddenly lost a major part of his investments. I was shocked when in 1962 I met with the lawyer in Hamburg handling his restitution for the loss of his profession under the Nazis, and saw his tax returns for the early 1930s, since I had hoped that he would be able to retire with the help of this money. He could not have supported his family on his income in those years and most probably was dependent, as he was again later in the first years in the United States, on Ernst Minden's support. For restitution it was necessary for him to demonstrate that his income had declined under the Nazis, but it actually went up in the early years of the Nazi regime as the metal market prospered. He finally did get a pension which together with his American social security helped him to make ends meet.

My father never really got on his feet economically in the United States. He had managed to transfer about two thousand dollars illegally to the United States, but that money was quickly used up. In the United States first job was as a very poorly paid bookkeeper for a small Jewish metal firm in Richmond from his arrival there in 1939 until they let him go in 1944. He was then able to earn more as a traveling salesman for a German-Jewish firm, covering the entire South with heavy sample cases filled with sports and office supplies. He never had a car and traveled everywhere by bus, often being away from home for three months. Perhaps he did not mind this entirely. His marriage to my mother was not an easy one. He continued his travels until at the age of 78 in 1973 when he was forced to give them up due to heart problems. After my mother died in 1968, we urged him to stop traveling and to move to Buffalo where we were living, but he declined to come until six months before his death in 1974. In sum, his was a sad life full of disappointments.

My mother was highly neurotic. She had worked briefly in an office until her marriage and in her marriage felt overburdened with her two children and the household. She was constantly sick and through her illnesses attracted attention. Much of it was hypochondria or psychosomatic. She was extremely prudish and in many ways infantile. Everything related to elimination was considered dirty and referred to by childish terms. Sex, of course, was particularly obscene. When I was small she used to express her love for us children, but this ended relatively soon in my case when she reproached me for not showing her sufficient love and attention. She constantly talked about her father Max whom she revered for his magnanimity and charity, but whom she hardly knew since she was ten when he died. What made life difficult for me was less that she was authoritarian, but that she was arbitrary in what she expected of me. I was constantly accused of being disobedient, although it was often not clear how I had disobeyed. My mother tried to inculcate feelings of guilt in me. The fact that I refused to apologize when I did not feel guilty intensified our problems. To emphasize how she was neglected, she made several suicide attempts, which I believe were intended to be unsuccessful, but to attract attention. This behavior continued until the end of her life, long after my sister and I had left the house.

My relationship with my father was less strained. He was less authoritarian or arbitrary but was expected to punish me and did. I respected his intelligence and we often took walks, in Hamburg and later in Richmond, and talked about various topics, including politics, that interested him greatly. But both of my parents forbade me to do things that were normal for children my age. For example I was strictly forbidden to accept an invitation to join the boys' choir at the central Bornplatz synagogue. I was very happy that I had been selected, and would also have gotten pocket money, which I received only irregularly from my parents. I also was forbidden to join one of the youth groups to which many of my Jewish friends belonged. I secretly joined the youth group of Misrachi, the religious Zionist movement. I attended their meetings, and also one with the Chief Rabbi of Hamburg, Josef Carlebach, which very much impressed me. Religion and Zionism did not necessarily belong together, but I at this point was fervently religious and fervently Zionist. Once when the group went on a hike I slipped out and found them. They, of course, were surprised I had not joined them at the beginning of the hike and I had not paid my dues. I was ashamed to tell the truth.

About that time a serious altercation took place between myself and my father. We both screamed at each other—I don't remember about what. My father hit me and I took my shoe and smashed the glass of our apartment door. Soon the police came. The officers were actually very civil, but took the opportunity to search our library for illegal books. I became increasingly upset and depressed and for several days skipped school and instead walked all morning. None of my mother's relatives had any sympathy for me—they all considered me to be an impossible, ungrateful, and disobedient child. I had only one person with whom I could talk about my situation. The one person who listened to me and counseled me was my uncle Siegfried, my aunt Martha's husband. I not only felt at home at the Friday evening observances at their house, but spent a lot of time with him on Sabbath mornings, accompanying him to services and afterward visiting his relatives. Yet despite everything I loved my parents, and not merely because I was told to do so, but because I was seriously concerned about their well-being and for a long time took the illnesses of my mother very seriously. Nor would I say that I was an unhappy child. Already at this early age I had many interests, political, religious, intellectual, and literary ones—I was an avid reader in my parents' library—and had a very full life. On the other hand, my world and that of my parents moved increasingly apart. We did not understand each other.

A few days after my eleventh birthday in December 1937 my parents sent me to the Israelite Orphanage and Reformatory in Esslingen near Stuttgart in southwestern Germany, far away from Hamburg. I was told that I was being sent on a vacation. I was not taken there by my father, but by an acquaintance of his.

Although I was shocked when I arrived at the school, within two weeks I felt at home and actually relieved. The school, despite its forbidding name, was actually a very progressive experiment in education of which my parents were probably not fully aware. There were actually few orphans and few difficult children among the approximately sixty boys and thirty girls at the school. Many of them came from small villages and towns in the region where as Jews they were no longer able to attend the local schools. The parents of others were preparing for emigration or were waiting to have their children follow them.

The school had actually been founded in 1831 as a Jewish orphanage. Under the directorship of Theodor Rothschild who came to the school as a young man in his twenties in 1899 and continued to head it until it was closed by the Nazis in 1939—he subsequently perished in Theresienstadt—the school took a new orientation. Rothschild was deeply influenced by reform pedagogy and the model of the *Landschulen* (country schools). The latter, which were not Jewish in origin, came out of the Romantic back-to-the-countryside movement of the early twentieth century. Children were to be trained for agricultural and artisanal work, which was still much simpler and traditional, requiring less education than it would today. This orientation fitted well into a Zionist outlook that believed that Jews had for too long been living in cities, engaged in commerce and intellectual pursuits. Palestine, or Eretz Israel, was envisioned as a communal agricultural society. I am not certain that Rothschild or his teachers were Zionists; none of them went to Palestine, but at least Rothschild shared the view that Jews should learn what he considered practical occupations. With emigration becoming increasingly imminent for many German Jews, the message was spread that "practical" training was necessary. One of the young Jewish refugees in Richmond was prevented from accepting a scholarship to the University of Richmond because his parents considered a college education needless. This, of course, turned out to be a serious mistake, not only in countries like the United States where academically trained persons proved to be more successful than less educated immigrants, but also in Palestine/Israel, which became increasingly urban and industrial, ultimately with an important high technology sector.

The school in Esslingen did not prepare students either for the *Abitur*, the diploma for university entrance, nor for the Realschule diploma. It offered only an eighth-grade elementary education. However, the school also put into practice many of the ideas of reform pedagogy. I was not aware of this at the time, but found out about it only recently from archival sources and from my conversations with my teacher Albert Jonas in the 1990s. According to reform pedagogy, which went back to the Enlightenment and to Johann Heinrich Pestalozzi (1746–1827), children should not be disciplined, but encouraged to develop freely. Despite the fact that Esslingen also included problem children, the cane used at the Knauerstrasse school and the slaps in the face or on the fingers at the Talmud Thora were totally absent. When I was there, the school had three young teachers, Albrecht Jonas, at the time only twenty-two years old, Ralf Samuel and Rosie Schul, at the time not much older. Schul was the Jewish pingpong champion of Germany. Jonas and Samuel kept in close contact with the boy students, Schul with the girls. Again there was a good deal of the atmosphere of the youth movement. We went on frequent hiking excursions, sang Jewish pioneer and German folk songs, and engaged in sports. Every student was given a responsibility in the small experimental farm behind the school. I was assigned to the chicken coop. The building within which the school was housed was a magnificent, large structure built in 1913, on a hill above Esslingen behind the castle. The facilities within the school were Spartan, several large dormitory rooms with ten to twelve children in each. But this did not bother me. The meals included no meat, because of the ban on the ritual killing of animals. The teachers ate with the students, but Rothschild sat at a separate table with his wife and received better fare. In fact, in contrast to the teachers he stayed relatively apart from the children as a person of authority. On the other hand—and I learned this only recently from Jonas—Rothschild met with the teachers one evening a week to discuss pedagogical and psychological literature relevant to an open atmosphere at the school. One thing that upset me was when he asked me to assist in the kosher killing of a chicken—it shocked me not only because I did not want to participate in the killing of an animal, even a chicken, but also because it fragrantly violated the law at the time, even if it was a Nazi law. Nevertheless I felt very much at home in the school. I also liked the religious atmosphere that I did not feel was oppressive, the morning and evening prayers in the chapel, and the grace after meals. When there was talk that Rothschild was trying to move the school to America, I very much hoped that I would be permitted to come along rather than return home.

Late in August or early September 1938 I was called home in preparation for emigration. During the entire period I was in Esslingen, my parents wrote but never visited me, and never brought me home during vacations. My parents were now waiting for a visa to the United States. They had first made serious efforts to leave Germany in March 1936, after Hitler had remilitarized the Rhineland in violation of the Treaty of Versailles and neither France nor Great Britain intervened. Until then they still thought that the Nazi regime would not last. But there was no country to go to. Some of my mother's brothers and two of her unmarried sisters could still claim British citizenship since they were born in Britain. The men could take their wives and children along, but the women, such as my mother, could not take their husbands. I, of course, would have liked to go to Palestine, but this was not my parents' cup of tea, nor would it have been likely that we would have received the certificate from the British that was required to settle there. My parents' first choice would have been the United States, but they knew no one who could have given us the needed affidavit. In March of 1938 my father went for two weeks to the United States on a trip organized by a German Jewish weekly to find a sponsor. While he was on the high seas the Nazis marched into Austria. Once in New York he called all the persons with names in the Manhattan phone book that occur in our family, and was invited by a Harry Mela to visit him at his home in suburban Pelham Manor. Mela, it turned out, was a very distant relative. My father's grandfather Mela and Harry Mela's grandfather had been brothers. Mela's grandfather had come to New York in 1852. He himself was a prosperous attorney on Wall Street, was religiously assimilated, and for a long time did not tell his children that they were of Jewish descent. However, he was willing to assist refugees from Nazi Germany and offered to sponsor our family.

My father returned to Germany and my parents made preparations for leaving, liquidating our possessions and packing the most necessary items. We were still waiting for our interview at the American Consulate. At the end of September it looked as if there would be war with France and Great Britain if Hitler made good his threat to seize the Sudeten areas from Czechoslovakia. My uncle Ernst used his connections to have the U.S. consulate in Hamburg advance our interview to September 29, incidentally the date when Chamberlain and Daladier gave in to Hitler's demands. A week later, on October 5, Yom Kippur, we received the visas. We left Germany two days later. At the border we had a final unpleasant experience. We were taken off the train, our luggage was searched, and the head of my sister's doll torn off to see whether money was hidden in it. Finally we were permitted to board the train.

Our first stop was the Hague where we spent the weekend with my aunt Martha and my uncle Siegfried. They had emigrated there in the spring of 1938, joining their son Ernst who in 1933 at the age of nineteen had fled from Germany to the Netherlands after having been briefly arrested by the Nazis due to his membership in a left-wing student organization. The youngest of their three children, their daughter Lina Ruth, affectionately called Maus, my favorite cousin, then eighteen, was already in the Netherlands and was preparing to emigrate to Palestine. Her brother Herbert, now using his Hebraicized name Gershon, came to the reunion from Palestine. He had migrated to a kibbutz in Palestine in 1935 at the age of seventeen. The Levy's Gentile maid, who had worked for them since 1913 and felt as if she was a member of the family, had come from Hamburg.

This was the last time that we saw the whole family. Barely a year and a half later, the Nazis occupied the Netherlands. Ernst perished in Auschwitz. Maus luckily left Holland a few days before the Nazi invasion of the Netherlands, but then was tragically killed in Jerusalem in 1948 in the War of Independence. Gershon fought in the Jewish Legion of the British Eighth Army and later in the Haganah in the struggle for independence, and had a successful career working as an agricultural expert in developing countries, first for Israel and then for the United Nations Food and Agricultural Organization. We lost contact with aunt Martha and uncle Siegfried some months after the occupation and heard from them again only in August 1944 after-it seems almost miraculous—they were exchanged as prisoners in Belsen Bergen for Germans interned by the British in Palestine. Although in very poor physical condition on their release, they recovered in hospitals in Palestine. I was stunned when I learned that the two, who to me naively had always seemed like the ideal couple, divorced shortly after arriving in Palestine. Martha then married a friend from her youth.

From The Hague we proceeded to my uncle Ernst in England where we saw various members of my mother's family and my grandmother and then went on to America. On October 20 we arrived in New York on the French liner *Champlain*. The Melas took my sister, Lina Ruth, then eight years old, to stay with them in our early days in America. My parents and I were quartered in two rooms with a German Jewish family in Washington Heights, a neighborhood at the northern tip of Manhattan already populated by many recent refugees from Central Europe, so that it was humorously called The Fourth Reich or Frankfurt on the Hudson. That Monday the Melas registered my sister at the school not as Lina Ruth Igersheimer, but as Lena Iggers. They told my parents that Igersheimer was too complicated a name and that they wanted to Americanize it. My parents accepted this and began to use the name Iggers. I was very upset and suspected that the real reason for the name change was to hide its Jewish character. The Melas' son, Donald, told me many years later that this was indeed the case, and that his father wanted to protect us against the anti-Semitism still rampant in the United States at the time. All through high school I still used the name Igersheimer, until my parents asked the principal to issue my diploma under the name of Iggers. I then was admitted to the University of Richmond with the name Iggers and gave in.

My parents told the committee that aided us—probably HIAS, the Hebrew Immigrant Aid Society—that for religious reasons I refused to go to a public school and would only go to a Jewish one. As a matter of fact I had no objection to attending a public school, but did not want to have to go to school on a Sabbath. That would not have been a problem since the New York public schools had no classes on Saturdays. However, my parents obviously and perhaps understandably did not want to be burdened by me in their difficult early days in America. They persuaded me to go with them to inspect an orthodox boarding school in Lakewood, New Jersey. I had no intention of staying, but when I looked around they were gone. The student body in Lakewood was very different from Esslingen, as the children came from affluent families. I felt isolated among the children, but befriended a German-speaking boy who had recently arrived from Lithuania. He lent me volumes from his Karl May collection, the most beloved German author of adventure stories, which I read avidly. I also struck up a friendship with the cook, the first black person I had met. Because of my insufficient English, I was put back into the fourth grade—in Hamburg I had been in the sixth—and received extensive individual attention. My English improved quickly and I was taught a lot about American democracy. My parents visited me once, on my birthday, and brought me a Monopoly game, and in late January took me back to New York. On January 30 we moved to Richmond, Virginia.

We knew no one in Richmond. The committee that aided us wanted to resettle the refugees who were arriving in New York City where there were few opportunities for work elsewhere in the United States. They suggested three cities to my parents, Minneapolis, Gary, and Richmond. Richmond turned out not to be a bad choice. My father immediately found a position, although a poorly paying one, and my parents quickly made contacts with other refugees. Thus they, particularly my mother, who actually was quite sociable and whose English was much better than my father's, soon felt relatively at home. She started a boardinghouse for the refugee newcomers that soon failed, however, because of her sicknesses. For us children the transition was easy, although for me it was something of a culture shock.

From the world outlook of the youth movement which had influenced my thinking so profoundly in Germany, the consumer society that shaped much of American culture seemed alien.

The day before we left for Richmond, Harry Mela and his wife came to see us. He explained to us the system of racial segregation that we would encounter in Richmond, the former capital of the Confederacy. I was shocked by what I found there, which seemed different from what I had been taught in Lakewood about American democracy. We had left Germany barely a month before the insidious *Kristallnacht* of November 9 and 10, 1938, which marked the beginning of the Holocaust. Yet the Jim Crow practices in Richmond reminded me very much of the earlier stages of discrimination and apartheid, which I had experienced in Germany. I at once identified with the blacks, but there was nothing at this point that I could do. I did not make myself very popular with some of my teachers in Richmond when I pointed out the incongruence between the democracy we were taught and the discriminatory, racist practices. I also soon protested against the glorification of Robert E. Lee, hailed as a Christian gentleman and Southern patriot, whose picture hung in every classroom—like Hitler's in every German class room. After I had learned something about American history, I felt that Lee was a traitor to his country who fought to preserve slavery.

There were many things that I liked about Richmond, for example its extensive neighborhoods of small one-family houses with many trees, which contrasted with what seemed to me the sullen miles of gray apartment houses in Hamburg. I always liked to walk in Hamburg. With a 10 Pfennig child's elevated ticket I had explored the many different areas of the city and also found much beauty there, the many river outlets and canals and parks. But in Richmond people seemed much more relaxed and friendly. I liked the porches in front of the houses where people sat in good weather and chatted with passersby. Much of this has disappeared in the age of television.

I also found this relaxed atmosphere in the schools I attended in Richmond, at first in the Albert H. Hill Junior High School, then in the Thomas Jefferson High School. There were fewer discipline problems than in the German schools I had attended except Esslingen, and less enforced discipline. One did not have to be afraid of the teachers—I liked my teacher Herr Pohle from the public elementary school Knauerstrasse, but he was very much of a disciplinarian as were my teachers at the Talmud Torah school. On the other hand, much less was expected from the students academically and many of the teachers were less well prepared and informed. On the basis of my German schooling I was far ahead of the students in my Richmond classes and very soon was placed two years ahead into the eighth grade. However I soon also gained respect for my Richmond schools, particularly on the high school level. The science courses were not purely abstract with the teacher making demonstrations in front of the class as in Germany; we all individually did laboratory experiments. The history and literature instruction I found to be clearly superior to that in Germany and I was impressed by several of my teachers. They expected much less memorizing and encouraged questions.

This was particularly true of my American history courses, where the political developments were placed in social, economic, and intellectual contexts.

However, I soon found friends who shared my interests, none of whom incidentally were Jewish. I was still observant and attended Sabbath services regularly at the Conservative Temple Beth El, and had a close relationship with two of the successive rabbis.

Since I was now two years ahead in school, my classmates were too two years older than I. For the rest of my student career, through my doctoral studies, I was always surrounded by students who were older than I was, in undergraduate school two to three years, in graduate school like Wilma, an average of six years. This had obvious advantages and disadvantages. It provided me with a stimulating intellectual environment, on the other hand I was emotionally less mature than my peers.

In junior high school one of my fellow students, Charles Wainman, invited me to participate in a game we played in his basement, where he, together with another student, Hugo Leaming, reconstructed the political life of a small city. They wrote constitutions and laws, published newspapers, and simulated political parties competing for the control of the city. I was delighted to be invited to join. Charles was politically relatively conservative; Hugo considered himself a Communist. I first met Hugo at Charles's house the evening of the day when the former Soviet Union attacked Finland. Hugo defended the attack on the part of a worker's state that had to defend itself against its capitalist challengers. I, for my part, saw the former Soviet Union as a dictatorship and Finland as a democracy and saw Stalin's pact with Hitler as responsible for the outbreak of the Second World War. I considered myself a democratic socialist. Hugo met frequently with Alice Burke, the head of the marginal Communist Party in Virginia. What brought the fourteen-year old Hugo to the Communist Party was the party's opposition to racial discrimination. Actually, the party's position was more complex. Influenced by Stalin's nationality policies, the Communist Party in the United States under the direction of Moscow proposed the creation of a black American autonomous state. But Hugo, I am sure, did not think so far. There was always a certain tension between me and Hugo; we were never real friends but respected each other. He was highly intelligent, one of the most brilliant students in junior and senior high school and later as an undergraduate. Having him as a partner in the game was a real asset.

We gradually lost interest in the game. In the last year of high school a fourth person entered our circle, Dale Chapman. He became my closest friend in my university days and we are still in touch with one another. He also was a good friend of Hugo. Charles gradually faded into the background and I lost contact with him after we left the University of Richmond. But in the summer of 1940, after the shock of the Nazi victories in Europe, Charles, Hugo, and I became involved in the Union Now movement, the forerunner of the World Federalists. Clarence Streit in his book, *Union Now*,[1] had proposed a federation of the world's democracies after the war and already in 1940 after the Nazi defeat of France, a

---
[1] Clarence K. Streit, *Union Now* (New York, 1939).

federation of Great Britain and the Free French. Streit did not include the former Soviet Union in his proposed federation, and the fact that Hugo enthusiastically endorsed Streit's proposal, shows how inconsistent his political views were. We wrote to Streit to express our support and were promptly dubbed by him the Three Unioneers. With his advice, we began to organize a Union Now chapter at our high school that soon had several hundred members who with the support of our history teacher held regular discussion sessions.

In 1942 I read for the first time about the mass murder of Jews by the Nazis in the German-Jewish weekly *Aufbau,* published in New York. At first I did not believe the reports and thought they were war propaganda. Soon, as an increasing number of the refugees in Richmond received messages from the Red Cross that their relatives had died, I realized that the reports were true, although I still could not imagine the scope of the genocide. I was disturbed how little, except for an occasional article in the *New York Times,* the American media reported about the Holocaust during the war. Instead they concentrated on the atrocities of the Japanese, largely ignoring those of the Germans on the eastern front. I was troubled by the racism in the frequent caricatures that depicted the "Japs", as they were called, as sub-human and apes, and the systematic exclusion of students of Japanese origin from most American colleges and universities. The University of Chicago was one of the few that admitted Japanese-Americans.

As I approached adolescence, my relationship with my parents improved. There was little closeness, but we accepted each other. They let me go my way with little interference, although my father was unhappy about my involvement in the Union Now movement and later in the interracial Richmond Intercollegiate Council. We Jews, he argued, must not attract attention by engaging in controversy. But they had no objection to my friends. After I left Richmond, we corresponded regularly and I frequently visited them in Richmond, later together with Wilma and our children. My sister Lena's relationship with my parents, particularly with my mother, was very different. She was the obedient child and helpmate. When she was in college, she rebelled and after leaving Richmond for Chicago at the age of eighteen, practically broke with my mother but not with my father, whom she respected. I had to persuade her to attend my mother's funeral in order not to hurt my father.

The years during which she was dominated by my mother and treated like a small child left indelible marks on Lena. In many ways she never grew up. She surrounded herself with numerous pets with which she could engage in baby talk. She was a warm-hearted person who as a high school teacher in an ethnic, largely Latino neighborhood in Los Angeles, helped students who were in trouble. We kept in regular contact over the years with occasional visits and frequent telephone calls. She was particularly close to Wilma. She married a refugee from an assimilated German Jewish family which had been converted to Protestantism for several generations. Ultimately the marriage failed. Although their three sons had been brought up in a religiously indifferent home, two of them later joined ultra-Orthodox communities in England.

In the fall of 1942, my friends Dale, Charles, and I all enrolled in Richmond College, the men's branch of the University of Richmond. Hugo had already begun a year earlier. I was able to enroll at the University of Richmond at the age of fifteen not only because I was two years ahead but also because the schools in Virginia at that time had only eleven, not twelve grades. The college was affiliated with the Southern Baptist Association, a conservative, fundamentalist church committed to racial separation. All four of us went there because we could not have afforded another university. We could live at home and the tuition was remarkably low—two hundred fifty dollars a year; today it is about a hundred times as high. I received a loan for my tuition from the Jewish Sisterhood. The school had been founded in the 1830s and in 1914 had moved to a beautiful location at the western outskirts of Richmond. I still consider it one of the most beautiful college campuses in the United States. In the middle of the campus are neo-Gothic buildings and a lake surrounded by woods, dividing Richmond College for men from Westhampton College for women. Richmond College had approximately five hundred students at the time, most of them from Virginia. Many commuted daily by streetcar from the city; others came from the Virginia countryside. Today the great majority of the students come from outside Virginia and many from outside the United States. The close affiliation with the Southern Baptist Association was terminated many years ago. Many of the Richmond College students were preparing for the ministry. Attendance at the chapel services was compulsory. Co-eds from Westhampton College, the women's college of the University of Richmond, tended to come from more prosperous families. There were quite a number from the New York area, including some Jewish students. The academic standards were generally regarded as somewhat more rigorous on the Westhampton side. At the beginning of the 1943 spring semester most of the men had been drafted, leaving only a small minority of about a hundred, including Hugo and me. As a result I had almost all of my classes with the women students at Westhampton College. At that point I was very interested in the comparative study of languages and literatures. In high school I had taken French and Spanish, and on my own dabbled in Italian and Latin, and of course Hebrew, and taught myself Esperanto. I even made a very unsuccessful attempt at Chinese. I also read extensively in classical German literature. My great ambition at the time was to construct an international language that would be easier and more logical in its grammar and vocabulary than Esperanto.

At the University of Richmond I thus concentrated on modern languages with a dual major in French and Spanish, but I also took a number of philosophy courses. In retrospect I believe that I received a very good liberal arts education. I thought that the French courses in particular were excellent, including not only a survey of literature from the classical age of the seventeenth century to the modern period, but also an examination of the broader intellectual and political framework in which this literature originated. One of the two weak points was the required physics course taught by Dr. Loving, who was close to retirement. He reflected on his rural background in Fluvanna County, but gave no indication that he was acquainted with the great changes that had taken place in physics since he had started teaching four decades earlier. The other was a human biology course required of all men students in which the professor vented his racial prejudices, emphasizing, obscenely I thought, the extreme size of the genitals of "Nigroes" and their excessive sexual drive. The philosophy courses were also very good. There we learned about the great transformation in science that had taken place since the beginning of the century. There were two philosophy professors, Dr. Holtzclaw, at Richmond College, highly intelligent but politically on the far right, a fundamentalist Christian and defender of Southern traditions including the racial status quo, and a much younger woman at Westhampton College, Dr. Lucas, a recent Ph.D., who was much more open and liberal. Notwithstanding his conservatism, Holtzclaw was willing to entertain discussions in his classes, mostly with the more liberal pre-ministerial students, who sharply disagreed with him. One particularly sensitive topic was birth control, of which most of the students approved, while Holzclaw maintained that sex, even in marriage, was justified only for the purpose of reproduction. In Lucas' course on the philosophy of religion we were introduced to the discussions in modern Protestantism from Karl Barth to Reinhold Niebuhr and the crisis of the optimistic outlook of the older liberal theology. The course which I enjoyed most was Dr. Samuel Chiles Mitchell's "Europe Since 1815," the only history course I took at the University of Richmond. Mitchell, born on a Mississippi plantation in the last days of the Civil War, had been recalled from retirement to replace the history teacher who had been called into military service. Mitchell was an ardent advocate of racial equality. Since its foundation in 1916, he had been an active member of the Southern Regional Council, an organization dedicated to a New South, and, more surprisingly, he was an outspoken socialist. It is amazing that he was able to have had a distinguished career, including for many years the presidency of the Medical College of Virginia. He opened up a totally new world to students who came from rural Virginia and would correct them when they spoke of Nigroes instead of Negroes. I often visited him in his home at the edge of the campus where he urged me to switch from modern languages to sociology, which he considered politically more relevant. He himself had received one of the first doctorates in the 1890s from the newly founded University of Chicago.

The fact that Mitchell could be a respected member of the University of Richmond faculty reflected that the university was by no means as narrow as its affiliation with the Southern Baptist Association suggested. As to the male, pre-ministerial student body, most of them were fundamentalist and racist. Many of them belonged to the fraternities that incidentally excluded Jews. The administration tolerated this policy. Jewish male students belonged to a separate fraternity, which never approached me about becoming a member—obviously I was not their type—but I also would not have joined it. Part of the student culture at Richmond College was freshman initiation. Freshmen had to wear special caps and kow-tow to older students. I found this humiliating, and persuaded a number of my fellow freshmen to join me in opposing it. One morning several husky sophomores entered Loving's lecture—he must have been informed before and consented—and took me by force to the gymnasium where I was paddled on my behind. The president of the sophomore class then chided me for not yet having accepted American customs. Incidentally, the following year several sophomores, who had been my fellow freshmen the year before, took me to the gym to bestow on me the honor to administer the first blow on the behind of a helpless freshman, and were surprised when I refused.

But there was also another side to the Richmond College student body. An articulate minority of pre-ministerial students were outspokenly progressive on the racial issue and on theological matters. Many of them came from the city and we had lively discussions on the long streetcar ride to the campus every morning. Some of the non-fraternity students were organized into three literary societies, the most liberal of which was the one named for S.C. Mitchell and had about twenty-five members. We met regularly to discuss current issues, the reorganization of a post-war society and the abolition of segregation. Several of us met with the editor of the *Richmond Times Dispatch,* Virginius Dabney, who at that time was relatively liberal—later in the 1950s he joined the segregationist resistance against the Supreme Court decisions—and urged him to support editorially the end of seating segregation on buses and street cars as a first step to reforming the apartheid system.

In the fall of 1943 the YMCA initiated meetings of white and black students in Richmond in which I soon became active. Until then white and black students had lived in two separate worlds, with Whites knowing Blacks only in subordinated service positions. We formed the Richmond Intercollegiate Council which met in the city at the campus of the white Medical College of Virginia, the Richmond Professional Institute—a branch of William & Mary College—and the black Virginia Union University. We could not meet on the University of Richmond campus. Issues of current concern were discussed. The turnout was impressive, two hundred to three hundred students at a time. Soon students from the nearby black Virginia State College in Petersburg joined. A small number of black and white faculty members served as advisers. The council enabled students of both races to meet socially, something new to both of them. I worked very closely with a charismatic student from Virginia Union University, Russell Jones, who later had a very impressive career in the YMCA on a national level. At the end of the school year in 1944 we held a social which included dancing. I was too naïve to understand how explosive this was, but there were no repercussions. The council also enabled male and female students to work together. The other colleges were co-ed. On the Richmond campus all of the student organizations were male on the Richmond College side, including the literary societies, and female on the Westhampton College side. Of course, on a personal level contacts existed. My friends were all male. I very much wanted to have a female friend, but was too shy to approach any women students, all of whom were several years older than I. Finally I came to know Nancy, who majored in German, and whom I assisted with her work. She accompanied me several times to the meetings of the Richmond Intercollegiate Council.

In May 1944, the end of my second year at the University of Richmond, I had completed all the requirements for the B.A. except for two courses that I was permitted to take in the summer session at the University of Chicago. I had been taking more than the normal fifteen hours (five courses) each semester, as many as twenty-seven hours one semester, and going to summer school in the summer of 1943. I was eager to complete my B.A. before being called into the army and under wartime conditions was permitted to take this overload. I thus left for Chicago in the second week of June 1944 at the age of seventeen to begin my graduate studies.

Chapter 3

OUR GRADUATE STUDIES IN CHICAGO AND NEW YORK (1943–1949)

WILMA

In winter of 1941–1942, I applied for scholarships for graduate school. Of the two I was offered, I decided to accept the one from the University of Chicago. Chicago interested me as a city with a large Czech population. Besides, as the University of Chicago had been founded as a Baptist institution, my friends at McMaster were convinced that I would be in good hands.

I was not. Chicago was a nightmare from beginning to end, from 1943 until 1952. But first, in May 1942, I went to Ottawa to work in the postal censorship where I read the letters of German prisoners of war and their friends and relatives. We especially had to watch out for complaints about conditions in the camps, about information that might be of interest to the enemy, and about the morale of the German population. My co-workers were new Canadian B.As, Canadians of German background, Polish émigrés, and English women who had come from England with some experience in that kind of work. Thinking back now, I mainly remember funny passages in the letters. I enjoyed the work, and with monthly pay checks of $114, I felt rich. During the seven months in Ottawa, I saved enough money to live on during the subsequent nine months in Chicago.

Unlike Canadians, I had to wait for a long time for a U.S. student visa, but early in January 1943 I went to Chicago. Before I was allowed to register I had to have a medical examination, during which a tumor was discovered on my palate. The doctors decided to operate immediately, and while still under local anaesthesia I wrote to my parents, who were totally beside themselves with worry. Back in my room, I began to feel a terrible pain, which lasted for almost a week. With a compress on my cheek and almost unable to speak, I attended my lectures at the university. Nobody was interested in my condition, not even the fellow student who lived in the same building. Because of the war, the department of Germanic Languages and Literatures had only few students, all of whom had come at the beginning of the fall quarter and therefore knew each other. (Instead of semesters the university had four quarters annually of three months each.)

I had come from McMaster University believing that one should always be friendly and helpful, but in the German department at Chicago this assumption turned out to be mistaken. One of my first courses there was Middle High German, and I found it very interesting that the Egerländer dialect which I had known from childhood retained many remnants of Middle High German that had disappeared in High German. I hence proclaimed in the graduate students' common room that I would be glad to help my classmates with the work for that course. As I found out later, my offer was held against me as an example of my conceit.

Miss Gamer, the head of the department, was hostile toward me from the start. Mr. Jolles, whose fields were the German classical period and the history of German literary criticism, was not much better. In all of his courses, he drew a chart on the blackboard, tracing the history of literature, philosophy, and art to a common denominator, the pair of opposites systole and diastole. Because this framework did not impress me sufficiently, he was insulted and declared that I was above all Czech and Jewish—whether at all human was not clear. Mr. von Gronicka, with whom I studied the German novella, praised my work and even told me later, that he did not enjoy teaching the course when he taught it again after I had taken it. But he also came to understand which way the wind was blowing: When I asked him for a letter of recommendation for my file with the Dean, he said that he did not remember me well enough even to fill out a form. In the meantime I had babysat his children several times. After such an evening he asked me what had happened to his mother's silver cigarette case. He told me that it had disappeared and that apart from me nobody had been in the apartment.

I was the only student in Mr. Kunstmanns' introduction to bibliography and methods, since the other students had taken the course the previous quarter. Apart from some sexual allusions, the course was boring and uneventful. With Mr. Metcalf, who taught what was then called linguistics, I gradually took everything from Gothic to Early New High German. With him I also wrote my Master's paper about the Eger Corpus Christi play of around 1500 and about the Egerländer dialect. Miss Gamer taught medieval Latin literature. Although I had had more Latin than most of the other students and worked hard, I received the usual icy treatment. Unlike the other graduate students, I was never given the opportunity to teach language courses. Only once did Miss Gamer ask me as a "native speaker" to take part in a class for army officers to prepare them for service in Germany. When one officer asked me about differences between the United States and Canada I replied that, for example, the population in Ontario supported the war effort much more unanimously, and that a newspaper like the *Chicago Tribune* which printed articles day after day against Roosevelt and hardly any against Hitler, would be unthinkable in Canada. My comment caused a big fuss. Miss

Gamer accused me of having insulted the officers, and said that because of my tactlessness I could no longer participate in such classes.

Much later, in 1947 and 1948 I taught part time at Gary College in Gary, Indiana, which later became part of Indiana University, and at Navy Pier, the nucleus of what became later the Chicago branch of the University of Illinois.

I had friends in various other disciplines, but no close ones in the German department, except Marie Dunnington, an older student whom I saw more frequently. I helped her with her studies and she gave me some of her used clothes, something I really appreciated. When her husband, who was serving in the navy, came on furlough, he visited me, was very friendly and wanted to hand me his car keys, saying that I should use them to visit him and Marie on the weekend in their cottage. I declined because I did not have a license, but then asked him if he could recommend a hotel for a Canadian friend who was going to visit me. He mentioned a certain hotel and stressed that he could recommend it because it did not accept any Jews. As always in such situations I could not think of anything to say. Later I wrote a letter to Marie. She knew that I was Jewish, but evidently had not thought of telling her husband. I never heard from her again.

After I had completed all the courses required for my Ph.D., I returned to Ottawa to the censorship office and remained there for a year, until VJ day, August 14, 1945, the day of the victory over Japan. I roomed with a family named Porter. Mrs. Porter, with whom I got along very well, soon told me that her husband would not have rented the room to me if he had known that I was Jewish. I stayed, convinced that I would be able to change Mr. Porter's attitude. On VJ day we went to some neighbors to celebrate, and there my landlord, who had been drinking, said that it was too bad that Hitler had not killed all Jews.

When I returned to Chicago, Professor Arnold Bergstraesser had joined the department. I soon saw that he was of a different caliber than the other professors. Although he had at first been isolated, students from other departments came to his lectures and seminars on literary history, history, and philosophy. After classes they went with him wherever there was a free room, to continue the discussion with him. He was an excellent teacher, and I had the impression that he was particularly interested in what I had to say. I soon knew that I would write my dissertation with him; I only had to find a subject that he would approve.

I was curious about the writer Karl Kraus, because the intellectuals among the friends and relatives of my parents had always spoken about him with great respect. Bergstraesser's reaction: "You don't know anything about him, I don't know anything about him, let us begin", convinced me to go ahead, although the "Krausians" whom I interviewed all reacted skeptically to my plan. They were convinced that one must have "experienced" Kraus personally in order to understand him, and that one also must be familiar with his linguistic milieu. A practical objection was that once the few refugees who remembered him were dead, there probably would be no interest in Kraus.

I never tired of reading the 922 issues of Kraus' "Die Fackel", even though I certainly did not agree with all of his opinions. What I considered most positive about him was his rejection of war, and the most negative was his strong anti-Semitism.

Kraus had an unusually good ear for linguistic nuances, both regional and ethnic, and a good sense of humor, at least as long as it was not aimed at him. These talents are especially obvious in his great drama, "Die letzten Tage der Menschheit" (The Last Days of Mankind). His lyric poetry is extremely conventional, and only interesting as an expression of his longing for a world that was the exact opposite of his daily life that was filled with feverish activity.

It would be hard to find in literary history an attitude toward women that would be more objectionable, despite his love, which was almost an obsession, first for Annie Kalmar, and then for Sidonie Nádherný von Borutín. From thousands of pages of correspondence addressed to Sidonie, it does not become clear what it was about her that he loved. His enthusiasm for the milieu in which she lived, her castle and park in Bohemia, was as extreme as all of his feelings. He used prostitutes regularly, and fitted them neatly into his theoretical musings about women.

Kraus's reputation after his death has been very different from what even the Krausians prophesied. There has been a Kraus renaissance since the fifties in Austria, Germany and, where one would have least expected it, in the United States, England, and France.

Two new professors, Liepe and Schulz, were appointed as members of my dissertation committee, and Gamer was a member ex officio. Since I had had hardly any contact with the department for some time, and the two people were new, I was actually quite optimistic—mistakenly, as it turned out. Bergstraesser adopted the attitude of his colleagues toward me, and the two new people did likewise. Once I had a conversation with Bergstraesser in the office of Mrs. Schmitt, the secretary of the department. I had just answered his question about Kraus's attitude toward the Communist revolutionary Rosa Luxemburg. Suddenly he became furious; I had never seen this man, who seemed so civilized, behave in this way. He reproached me for being "nothing but red". He wanted to throw his briefcase at me, but only hit the window. The next day he apologized to Mrs Schmitt and told her that such attacks of his were caused by a war injury. She told me this fifteen years later.

From then on I only had few opportunities to speak to Bergstraesser, especially once I had moved to Akron, Ohio where Georg and I were teaching at the University after we married in December, 1948. At one point, Bergstraesser promised to return several chapters to me within a week, and when I finally called him I was told by a tenant that the Bergstraesser family had gone to Germany and would be there for several months.

Soon after his return I considered the dissertation completed. Gamer decided that each of the professors on my dissertation committee should in turn suggest changes and then pass it on to the next member of the committee. The process took a long time, as none of them was in a hurry. I received the most nonsensical suggestions that made the dissertation neither better nor worse. When it finally was accepted, Georg advised me to make photocopies of the twenty-one pages of suggestions, because he thought the professors would later claim that they had neither demanded changes nor approved the dissertation. I did not think that they would go so far, but made the copies anyway. Exactly what Georg had predicted happened, and from that time on, I saved every scrap of paper that seemed relevant. When I brought the typed thesis to Bergstraesser—almost five hundred pages in length, he did not look at it but only said, "Cut by one third."

By the time I had done the cutting, we were living in Little Rock and expecting our first child. The defense was set for the afternoon of October 4, 1951, and I went to Chicago on the first. Early in the morning of October 4, I went into labor and had to go to Chicago Lying-in Hospital. The examination was canceled and our first son Jeremy was born shortly after 6:00 p.m.

From the hospital I called Gamer and told her that the head of the clinic approved of my taking the examination after the ten days' compulsory stay after childbirth. She decided, however, that I could only take it six months later, since in my case it would not be the usual defense of a thesis, but a thorough examination of the literary history, culture, and politics in Germany and Austria in the nineteenth and twentieth centuries.

I then wrote a long letter to Dean Wick of the Graduate School and enclosed all relevant documentation pertaining to the dissertation, including copies of the criticisms and suggestions which, the committee insisted, they had not made. The dean promised not only to send an observer to the examination, but also to be present himself. Apart from the icy glances of my professors, the examination was uneventful. When all the others had left, Gamer said to me: "You know that you only passed by the skin of your teeth" and "Now you have a child; why do you want a Ph.D.?"

Why did I put up with all that? Since I was released from the Canadian National War Services only as long as I had a scholarship, for which, despite everything, I continued to receive extensions, probably because the department had very few students during the war and did not want to lose another. Moreover, without appropriate undergraduate work, I would not have been eligible for a scholarship in another department, and the horror stories I heard about the Department of Romance Languages and Literatures, where I might have had a chance, were different, but hardly more appealing. I also never gave up hope of a happy ending.

I think that by all standards by which the quality of departments is measured, the German Department at Chicago was a sad case. Not only did the faculty members, with the exception of Bergstraesser, not publish anything of note, but none of its graduates became known as scholars.

I probably would not have met Georg if we had not both been in the German department, which he wisely left after receiving his M.A. Getting to know him made all my struggles worthwhile. I think that nobody who knew both of us would have thought of us a priori as a couple. The fact that I was almost six years older than Georg would have seemed to be a problem, but never was. We were very different people and still are. We think differently: Georg says that my writing grows like a bush. I read a great variety of things in my spare time. Georg hardly has any spare time. He is religious, while I am emphatically not. I am very attached to my rural Bohemian background, in which Masaryk's Republic looms large, but even larger looms my extended family, with my father in the middle. To Georg, political organizations and a Jewish congregation are important; I was not exposed to any of that in my youth. In Georg I found somebody who goes out of his way for other people, and I can always count on him.

We met in Gamer's class in 1944, shortly before I had to return to Canada. The first time we actually spoke to each other was in the fall of 1946, after I had returned from a teaching position at the University of New Brunswick in Fredericton, Canada. We both were waiting for Bergstraesser, who was late as usual, outside his office. From then on we met increasingly often in the Hutchinson Commons, the main cafeteria on campus, where Georg worked bussing dishes. Through a lucky coincidence, I was able to live in Fensham Hall, the small dormitory for female theological students, which was connected with the now famous Robie House next door, built by Frank Lloyd Wright. Georg and I met there almost every night to study, and when the weather became warm, we often swam in the lake late at night. We felt comfortable with each other, and Georg's confidence in me was invaluable when I was preparing for my comprehensive examinations. Georg and I had not talked about marriage, but by the time my father came to visit in early October, 1947, I took a life together for granted.

GEORG

I was intent on going to the University of Chicago, because I was impressed by what I had learned about the reforms that were initiated by its president Robert Hutchins. I felt that the American colleges and universities, with their required courses and required class attendance, did not give students sufficient freedom. The University of Chicago under Hutchins resembled more closely the German university system, as I naïvely imagined it, where students had the freedom to pursue their studies in preparation for a final examination, and where the emphasis was on preparation for research. Hutchins abolished the traditional four year liberal arts college leading to a B.A., and introduced a two year course of studies based on a hundred great books of the Western tradition. Gifted younger students could be admitted even without a high school diploma. The graduate research oriented program began in the third year. I was immediately admitted to the graduate program. I had to face the question how to finance my studies. The Jewish Sisterhood in Richmond, which had previously lent me money for tuition at the University of Richmond, again gave me a loan for my tuition, which at than time amounted to one hundred dollars a quarter, and I also received a scholarship from International House on the Chicago campus for my room. Shortly after my arrival in Chicago, I received a full tuition scholarship for the academic year from the university, which apparently was impressed by my undergraduate record and by the fact that I had completed my undergraduate studies by the age of seventeen. Almost immediately after my arrival, I found a job as busboy in the Hutchinson Commons which provided for my meals.

Matters turned out to be much more difficult than I had anticipated when I had planed my program of studies. I was still committed to my project of constructing an artificial international language, and I had hoped to be accepted into the linguistics department. An interview with the chair of that department made it clear to me that linguistics was very different from what I had envisaged, not a comparative historical approach to world languages, but a highly empirical, quantitative approach to the structure of language, a scientific rather than a humanistic discipline. My attempt to enter the French department was equally unsuccessful. I had been the best student in French in Richmond, but was told by the chair that my French was not good enough for doctoral studies. The German department accepted me. The chair of the department, Gamer, was anything but friendly. She let me know that she considered me immature and would not have supported the decision of the University to give me a scholarship if she had been consulted. However, the department needed students.

Chicago had turned out to be very different from what I had expected. I seriously considered returning to Richmond and working on a master's degree there in languages or comparative literature. But I decided to stay.

The courses in the German department seemed to me uninspired, dry and lacking the intellectual stimulation that I had found in most of my courses in Richmond. In the summer I took a course with Gamer on the history of teaching German in which I received a C, although I was convinced that I and another student who impressed me with her responses, Wilma Abeles, were the two best students in this small seminar. I thought so because we were the most articulate participants, and Gamer may have resented this. I had a similar experience later in the academic year when I received a C from Kunstmann in a course on early modern German literature in which I again was more articulate than the other students. I thought that this was not a serious course, with the professor salting his lectures with frequently off-color anecdotes in front of a very small class in which I was the only male. I also took a course in Middle High German with Metcalf.

In retrospect, it is difficult to understand how these professors, none of whom had scholarly credentials beyond their doctoral dissertations, received tenured appointments at a major research university. None were active scholars. Kunstmann had come to Chicago without a doctorate, Gamer had published two medieval Latin texts, one with a co-editor, both before she came to Chicago—In fact, some years after Hutchins left as president, the German department lost the right to offer doctoral degrees, which was restored only later with a new, highly qualified faculty.

During the summer of 1944, however, I took two courses in the College of Education. I had always had a bias against education courses which I thought were of lesser intellectual quality. But I still lacked two courses for Richmond credit to complete my B.A., and they had to be in education to satisfy the requirements for the Virginia state teacher's certificate. These two courses turned out to be excellent. One was in educational psychology. I wrote an essay on teaching modern languages in which I suggested that one should thoroughly master one language in each language group, Romance, Germanic, Slavic, and Semitic, as a basis for learning the other languages in the family, for example learning French as a basis for learning Spanish, Portuguese, and Italian. The professor was so impressed that he urged me to pursue my doctorate in education and offered me financial support, which I turned down. The other course was with Professor Alison Davis, a black educational sociologist—who has since posthumously been honored with a U.S. postage stamp—on the sociology of American cities, including discriminatory patterns in housing and education.

I returned to Chicago that fall with very mixed feelings. A new member had joined the German department, Arnold Bergstraesser, not a Germanist but a political scientist, a student of Alfred Weber and a former professor in Heidelberg, who had left Nazi Germany in 1937. Bergstraesser came under a cloud. He had twice been interned for brief periods in the United States for alleged Nazi sympathies. Many students outside the German department boycotted him; however, I did not believe these allegations. I had several seminars with him in which I was the only or almost the only student, either in his office or in his apartment. Under Bergstraesser's guidance I did extensive readings in classical German philosophy and literature and also took a fascinating course on the Weimar Republic. Bergstraesser had known many of the leading figures. I felt that we understood each other. He assured me that he had always been a good democrat, like my father a supporter of the German Democratic Party, and that he left Germany for political reasons.

My favorite German poet was Heinrich Heine, and Bergstraesser supported my proposal to write my M.A. paper on Heine and Karl Marx in Paris. Heine was witty, radical, and a critic of German conditions. In 1831 he left Germany for Paris as a political refugee, and in 1844 befriended Karl Marx and his young family who had just arrived there. Marx assisted Heine when Heine wrote his satiric poem "Deutschland, ein Wintermärchen" (Germany, a Winter Tale) after his trip to Germany during the brief period in 1844 when he could travel in Germany free from a warrant for his arrest.

I never made it to 1844 and Marx. I became so involved in Heine's contacts with the utopian socialist Saint-Simonians shortly after his arrival in Paris that I wrote an essay entitled "Heinrich Heine and the Saint-Simonians." Heine was fascinated by the Saint-Simonians who were rebels against bourgeois society, and explored new paths in the critique of the status quo, of laissez-faire capitalism, and quite importantly of the relations between the sexes. In the course of my work with Bergstraesser I came to the realization that my world language project was unrealistic and that my real interest was in the history of ideas. On Bergstraesser's advice I sat in on Richard McKeon's course on Aristotle and on my own initiative sat in on Louis Wirth's lectures on modern sociological theory where I first became acquainted with the ideas of Max Weber.

Apart from my unhappy relations with the German department, this turned out to be a good year. At International House I found myself in a multinational and multiethnic circle of persons with whom I could exchange ideas. My best friend was Walter Levy, a young Jewish refugee from Königsberg, more recently from Arkansas, with whom I am still in touch. At the Hutchinson Commons I served breakfast to the soldiers in the Army Special Training Program who were studying Chinese and Japanese. Among them were a handful of refugees from Germany including Stefan Brecht, the son of the famous German playwright Bert Brecht, and Franz Schurmann, who later became a leading sinologist, publicist, and outspoken critic of American policy in East and South East Asia. Both were Marxists at the time. They proposed that we form a Hegel Club, reminiscent of the Hegel Club to which first the young Marx, and then the young Friedrich Engels, belonged in Berlin in the late 1830s. Brecht and Schurmann argued that Marx could not be understood without a thorough knowledge of Hegel. We met regularly on Sunday afternoons, joined by Steven Jarislowsky who had more conservative views and ultimately became a leading Canadian financier, and a young German-Jewish woman, whose name I have forgotten. All of the discussions were in German. We set out to read Georg Wilhelm Friedrich Hegel's *Science of Logic* without understanding anything. We invited several faculty members, who actually came, including Bergstraesser.

In the course of the year, I gradually ceased to be observant, while still considering myself to be a religious Jew. I had been deeply impressed by an essay by Simon Dubnow, the author of a ten-volume *History of the Jewish People*,[1] portions of which I had read avidly as a teenager, in which he portrayed a dualism of traditions which ran throughout Jewish history. One tradition, which went back to the Talmud and portions of the Pentateuch, defined Judaism in terms of ritual and ethnicity, and the other found its expressions in the writings of the Biblical prophets that viewed Judaism in ethical and universal terms. I identified myself with the latter. Being Jewish in the sense of the prophetic tradition for me did not mean an absolute break with Jewish customs and rituals; instead I began to observe them as they seemed meaningful to me. I did not, and still do not consider myself a secular Jew, although I no longer identify myself with Orthodoxy. I continued to observe the Jewish holidays, including fasting on Yom Kippur. I took to heart the reading from Isaiah for the morning of Yom Kippur that the purpose of the day is not the fast, but to free the oppressed and to relieve the poor. Wilma and I during the years have always invited Jewish and non-Jewish friends to our home to observe the Passover seder, which celebrates the liberation of the Jews from Egyptian slavery. I am too much of a workaholic to refrain from work on the Sabbath—although I feel that I should—but we say the blessing over the wine and the bread on Friday nights in our family circle. During my first few months in Chicago I ate vegetarian because I could not easily obtain kosher meat,

---

[1] Simon Dubnow, *Weltgeschichte des jüdischen Volkes von den Anfängen bis zur Gegenwart,* 10 vols. (Berlin, 1925–30).

but gradually before the end of the year I began to eat nonkosher meat, to write and to use public transportation on the Sabbath.

I received my M.A. at the end of the summer of 1945. I had no intention to stay in the German department, and it was not keen to have me in the doctoral program. The department did not support my application for a scholarship for the following year, although I had the strong support of Bergstraesser. Nor did I expect to be in Chicago because I expected to be drafted into the military. I had had a physical earlier, but the university had obtained a deferment for me so that I could finish my M.A. Shortly after I completed the degree, I was issued a notice to report for induction in Richmond in early October. That date, however, happened to be Yom Kippur. I asked for a new date which I was granted for the following week, and this time I failed the physical: my blood pressure was elevated and I was sent home. Had the war not been over, the physical might have been stricter. I had returned the evening before from Newark, where I had visited Nancy. We had occasionally exchanged letters which contained no expressions of love. Nancy's mother had invited me to spend several days with them in their home in Newark. We did get to know each other better, but the relationship was still fully platonic.

By this time the academic year had already begun. Instead of returning to Chicago, I decided to go to New York. Nancy was one reason, but the main reason was that I wanted to attend the Graduate Faculty of Political and Social Sciences at the New School for Social Research. The New School had been established in 1919 for adult education in downtown New York with classes mostly in the evening, so that working people could attend. It was founded by three outstanding left leaning intellectuals, the sociologist Alvin Johnson, the social philosopher Thorstein Veblen, known for his brilliant satire of bourgeois society and culture, *The Theory of the Leisure Class,* and Charles Beard, the author of *The Economic Interpretation of the American Constitution,* who, although he had supported the war against German militarism, had resigned his chair at Columbia University in 1917 in protest against dismissals of faculty who opposed the war. The New School provided positions not only to social scientists but also to artists and writers who had been victims of purges during the war as well as of the Red Scare that followed. In 1933 the Graduate School of Social and Political Sciences was founded at the New School to offer a haven to scholars who had been expelled from universities in Nazi Germany and Fascist Italy. After 1936, refugees from Franco Spain came and in 1941 a French branch, the *Ecole Libre des Hautes Etudes,* was established in New York. Popularly the school was known as the University in Exile. The New School appealed to me as an embodiment of what was best in European scholarship.

When I arrived in New York—hitchhiking with only $20 in my pocket—I immediately went to the Employment Office of the Jewish Federation of Philanthropies. They found me a six-week temporary job at the New York Public Library, where I replaced a Ph. D. candidate at the reference desk of the Jewish Division. I then went to the New School, where the dean, Horace Kallen, permitted me to enroll free of tuition charges.

The year in New York was the most valuable of my career as a student. This time I was not studying for a degree but followed my intellectual interests. Most important for my later scholarly career were the courses on the history of social theory and of sociology which I took with Albert Salomon, a student of Max Weber and editor of the German Social Democratic cultural journal, *Die Gesellschaft*. Salomon encouraged me to translate the *Doctrine of Saint-Simon*, the public lectures of the Saint-Simonian circle in Paris in the years 1828–1829, which I began to do the following summer. During the year I was able to discuss my concerns extensively with the phenomenologist Felix Kaufmann, the religious socialist economist Eduard Heimann, the labor economist Frieda Wunderlich, and the sociologist Carl Mayer, in brief a valuable sample of the representatives of democratic intellectual opinion. I unfortunately did not meet Hannah Arendt, nor know yet of her existence.

The émigrés were only one part of the Graduate Faculty, and there was also an important American contingent. I was most impressed by Horace Kallen, who since the beginning of the century had been a liberal Jew with a social conscience. Kallen was a close associate of John Dewey and a friend of Sydney Hook who had turned from an admirer of Marx to a critic of the authoritarian aspects of Marxism. With Kallen I took two seminars which reflected his view of American values, and which impressed me greatly. In one we read and discussed Saul Padover's edition of the writings of Thomas Jefferson. The second dealt with William James' pragmatism. I also took advantage of courses and lectures outside the New School. When I had my mornings free after my job at the New York Public Library ended, I regularly went to Union Theological Seminary to listen to the American critic of the Protestant social gospel, Reinhold Niebuhr, and to the German exponent of a dialectical theology, Paul Tillich, who was one of the first non-Jewish professors dismissed by the Nazis in the spring of 1933. I was particularly attracted by Tillich's religious socialism which came very close to my own views. Tillich was very approachable and I had a long conversation with him in his office. One evening a week I went to Columbia University to sit in on a seminar conducted by Paul Tillich, Susanne Langer, and John Randall on the role of symbols in contemporary philosophy, based in part on the writings of Ernst Cassirer, the German refugee philosopher, who had died a few months earlier.

My best friend was a young Viennese doctoral candidate at Columbia, Henry Loeblowitz Lennard, who was very much influenced by psychoanalytical theory. I myself was critical of psychoanalysis, particularly its orthodox forms, but I learned a lot from our ongoing conversations. Together we attended the lectures of Erich Fromm, an unorthodox émigré psychoanalyst, now largely forgotten, who was committed to what he considered a "sane society" dedicated to democratic and humanistic goals. Lennard also introduced me to his circle of fellow sociology students who were deeply involved in questions of the methodology of the social sciences which I had not followed closely before. With several of these students I attended the lectures of Abram Kardiner at Columbia, the co-author of

The Mark of Oppression,[2] a psychoanalytical study of the personality damage that racial discrimination inflicted on Black males, and this opened a new perspective to me. Through Lennard I met Herbert Strauss, many years later the director of the Center for Antisemitism Studies in Berlin, who in 1945 had just begun interviews with Holocaust Survivors.

The stay in New York was a wonderful experience. I took advantage of the cultural offerings in so far as they were free or nearly so—museums, particularly the Museum of Modern Art, plays by the Equity Actors League, Sunday afternoon concerts of Medieval music at Fort Tryon Park, a beautiful park and museum at the Northern edge of Manhattan. I still loved walking and from Fort Tryon Park I walked over George Washington Bridge to the New Jersey side and along the Palisades high above the shores of the Hudson.

After my temporary appointment at the library ended, the Federation employment office found me a position as an office boy at the Jewish Agency for Palestine, the predecessor of the State of Israel. My main assignment consisted of bringing press releases to various news agencies. I appreciated the opportunity to have at least an insight into the operations of the Agency, but I did not like the atmosphere there. I was a great admirer of Einstein's Zionism which sought a binational state. This was the very reason why the persons in the office passionately rejected him. Unlike in the Library, I was treated with considerable condescension, which I resented. I also could not live on the pittance they paid me. I had the impression that they spent money freely, while they declined to give me even a slight increase. I thus was forced to look elsewhere and with the help of the Federation's employment agency found a job in a factory in the Garment Center where for four hours every afternoon I packed dresses. The Garment Center in mid-Manhattan was predominantly Jewish, the workers were mostly second generation immigrants from Eastern Europe, still very ethnic and with little advanced education. The owners were also largely first or second generation Eastern European Jewish immigrants. The work was dull, but the atmosphere was relaxed and my foreman was very friendly, even ready to check out for me if I had to leave a few minutes early to make my class. And I was able to squeeze by on the money I earned.

While I was in New York my friendship with Nancy came to a sudden end. I visited her generally about once a week at her mother's house in Newark, and we spent the evening talking. Only twice did she come to Manhattan to see me. Suddenly after several months she told me that she did not want to see me any more, that we should have no further contact, and that I should find myself a girl friend closer to my age. I was stunned and told her to no avail that I did not understand why, if we could not have a loving relationship, we could not be good friends. I went into a deep depression which prevented me for several months from concentrating on my studies. The summer, still depressed, I spent at home in Rich-

---

[2] Abram Kardiner and Lionel Ovesey, *The Mark of Oppression. A Psychosocial Study of the American Negro* (New York, 1951).

mond and spent my time translating the *Doctrine of Saint-Simon*. In September I returned to Chicago to work on my Ph. D.

I decided to pursue my doctoral studies in the general area of intellectual history in an interdisciplinary program. There were two such programs at the University of Chicago, the prestigious Committee on Social Thought inspired by Hutchins and the less well known Committee on the History of Culture. I understood intellectual history not merely as the history of ideas in isolation from politics, society, and culture, but as a reflection of them. I had become fascinated by the Saint-Simonians in the setting of their time. Heinrich Heine had seen them as progressive and liberal thinkers, but I viewed them much less positively, as a strange mixture of advocacy of economic development and authoritarian politics. The core of their philosophy was the view of Henri de Saint-Simon's student Auguste Comte that the modern world lacked the unity of doctrine which Medieval society had possessed, and that a doctrine was needed that would recreate the "organic" character of Medieval society. A new order was to be created in which the inequalities which marked both the medieval and modern societies would yield to a social order that would do away with inequality and guarantee equal opportunities for all. Foreshadowing later critics, they viewed their present as a "critical" epoch in which older certainties gave way to pluralism and uncertainties. In reading the *Doctrine de Saint-Simon* I was struck by how deeply they had been influenced by French Catholic critics of the French Revolution and the Enlightenment such as Joseph de Maistre and Louis-Gabriel de Bonald. Unlike the utopian socialists Charles Fourier and Pierre-Joseph Proudhon, who sought to foster small communal societies with a maximum of individualism, the St. Simonians aimed for a total reorganization of society reminiscent of Plato's *Republic*. All aspects of life would be controlled from the top, not by philosophers in Plato's sense, nor by scientists as Comte would have it, but by priests who could impose doctrinal order and unanimity on an "organic" society.

Still deeply committed to the rational outlook of the Enlightenment, I was disturbed by what I saw as a totalitarian vision. In my dissertation I wanted to study the ways the Saint-Simonian critique of modern civilization reflected more broadly shared attitudes that contributed to anti-democratic political currents later. Soon after my return to Chicago I met with Prof. Yves Simon, a Belgian émigré, of the Committee on Social Thought to discuss my program. Simon, a professed Catholic, had little sympathy for my plan of studies. For him the Committee focused on the great thinkers of the West, foremost Aristotle and Thomas of Aquinas, not on a diffuse study of political mentalities as I had in mind. In retrospect it was a good thing that I was not accepted into the Committee on Social Thought, as it would have seriously restricted my freedom of inquiry.

I was, however, accepted by the Committee on the History of Culture, which permitted me to pursue the interests I had outlined. I was able to concentrate on one period in history, and I proposed to study European civilization in the period from the French Revolution to the aftermath of the 1848 revolutions in Europe. The five fields in which I was to be examined were French political and social history, German or Central European history, and philosophy, religion, and literature with a focus on France and Germany. I assembled a doctoral committee with the historian Louis Gottschalk as chair, and Arnold Bergstraesser and the theologian James Luther Adams.

I took courses or seminars with all three that fall, with Gottschalk on the French Enlightenment and the following quarter on the French Revolution, with Adams on the social doctrines of the Protestant churches with an emphasis on Ernst Troeltsch, and a course with Bergstraesser—I do not recall the topic. Shortly after the beginning of the quarter Matthijs Jolles, with whom I had never had any courses, appeared on behalf of the German Department, to oppose my admission to the doctoral program. Nevertheless the committee consisting of Gottschalk, Adams, and Bergstraesser, who all thought highly of me, decided to support my application with the concession to the German department that I be put on probation for one quarter. At the end of the period I had received A's in all three courses, the probation was removed, and the dean extended a waiver of tuition to me for the rest of my doctoral studies.

I now could pursue my studies as I had planned. Adams became a life long friend to me and Wilma. I worked very closely with him and learned a good deal about theological currents in nineteenth- and twentieth-century theology from him. Adams was a professor of religious social ethics at the Unitarian Meadville Theological Seminary at the University of Chicago, who soon after I finished went to the Harvard Divinity School. I admired the way in which he combined serious scholarship with a commitment to civil liberties and social justice. I later dedicated my *The German Conception of History*[3] to him and not to Louis Gottschalk, who was benign and supportive but had little time for me and tried to persuade me to stop my social and political involvements which he considered counterproductive to my academic career. I enjoyed my studies. Other courses which made an impression on me were a seminar on social Catholicism and social Protestantism in the nineteenth century, which dealt with Catholic conservative thinkers whom I had encountered in my study of the Saint-Simonians and also Nikolai Grundvig, the Danish theologian whose social and democratic understanding of Protestantism differed markedly from the conservatism and state orientation of the Evangelical Lutheran churches in Germany.

I found two small seminars by Hans Rothfels very useful, one on the Reforms in Prussia during the Stein period in the years immediately after the Prussian defeat by the French in 1806, the other on the German National Assembly in Frankfurt in 1848. For the first time I was forced to study documents carefully, which I had not been required to do in my previous training. However, I had a very unpleasant exchange with him. The often critical questions I had raised in my courses had irritated Gamer and Kunstmann, and also Rothfels, but were received positively by Gottschalk and Adams. Rothfels made no secret of his right-

---

[3] Georg G. Iggers, *The German Conception of History. The National Tradition of Historical Thought from Herder to the Present* (Middletown, 1968).

wing and nationalistic Prusso-German views and I challenged him. Although I never expressed this openly, I could not understand why he with these views had left Germany. He called me in his office and told me, although he had given me A's in both seminars, that with my views I had no understanding of history and should not pursue a doctorate. In the spring of 1948 I took my qualifying examinations for the Ph. D. and began my dissertation.

On my return to Chicago I began to work again as a busboy at the Hutchinson Commons. We busboys all were graduate students and generally all worked one meal. I bussed at breakfast and received a meal ticket and a small salary. I was able barely to make ends meet. I lived in the least expensive dormitory room in the graduate students' residence which I shared with nine other students. My parents for a while sent me one dollar a week. A friend handed down his discarded army uniforms to me. When I needed dental work I was in real trouble. Most of the employees at the Hutchins Commons were poor older men and women, many of them immigrants, and some Blacks, all of them poorly paid. We graduate students decided to unionize these employees and succeeded, but subsequently we were fired. However, the union found me a better paying job operating the elevator in the library.

Shortly after I returned to Chicago in the fall of 1946 I became better acquainted with Wilma. She began to have breakfast at the Commons and I joined her after I finished my work. I had a tremendous respect for her; after all she had just returned from teaching at the University of New Brunswick in Canada. We met to go walking once a week, and occasionally had a meal together. As her qualifying exam drew close, she told me that she would have less time for me, but actually we began to see more of each other. Wilma had the key to the Robie House, the Frank Lloyd Wright House next to the women's residence of the theological seminary, where she lived. We now spent every evening together studying for our examinations and often at about ten in the evening walking through Jackson Park, something which no one would dare today, to Lake Michigan to go swimming. At this point I was very much in love with her but was afraid that if I declared my love she would rebuff me, as I was almost six years younger than she. After her exams she went to Canada for several weeks to be with her parents. When she returned I finally mustered the courage to tell her that I was in love with her and she assured me that it was mutual. From then on we were together and very soon knew that we wanted to get married.

My second stay in Chicago was thus generally pleasant and a fruitful. Wilma's was more complicated. It is difficult to establish that she or I had been victims of anti-Semitism. Among the few students in the German department there were several young Jewish women who did not represent a challenge. Except for Arnold Bergstraesser, who was a political scientist and not a Germanist, the faculty, including Mattijs Jolles, were not particularly outstanding or productive scholars. The composition of the department and the fact that a medievalist with virtually no scholarly credentials was chair had something to do with the general political and ideological orientation of the Hutchins administration. I had viewed Hutchins as a liberal reformer, but today we associate the University of Chicago with neo-conservatism, although this label does not apply to a majority of the faculty. Yet recent scholarship has revealed to what extent the foundations of neo-conservatism at the university were laid by Hutchins. His politics were complex. As a committed pacifist he was vigorously opposed to U.S. entry into the war in 1941, and this led him into strange company. He supported the America First Committee in which vociferous anti-Semites such as Father Coughlin and Charles Lindbergh, who had a great deal of sympathy for the Nazis, played an important role. However, Socialists such as Norman Thomas, who clearly rejected anti-Semitism and opposed the Nazis, also supported the America First Committee. Milton Mayer, Hutchins' close associate, a Quaker and pacifist of Jewish background. published a bizarre article, "The Case Against the Jew," in the *Saturday Evening Post* in March 1942, in which he recited the crude anti-Semitic stereotypes applied to the Jews in America and warned that the Jews would be held responsible for having driven the U. S. into the war. Hutchins brought a number of conservative émigré scholars to Chicago. Leo Strauss, who was appointed in 1949, developed a critique of modern democracy. The literary historian Erich von Kahler, who once had been close to the Stefan George Circle, came in 1945. Hans Morgenthau, with whom I took a fascinating seminar on international organization in which he debated with students who were confident about the future of the just established United Nations, argued for a foreign policy based on *Realpolitik;* this position twenty years later made him an outspoken opponent of the Vietnam War. F. A. Hayek, who had just written the *Road to Serfdom,* which opposed economic planning, pointed in a direction that was pursued later by the Chicago school of economics of which Milton Friedman, a student of Hayek, but no immigrant, became the leading figure. The refugee intellectuals brought to Chicago by Hutchins thus represent a different orientation from those of the New School, although in the case of Leo Strauss who was at the New School before he came to Chicago there was an overlap.

Two of the scholars, Bergstraesser and Rothfels, had had close links to the Nazis. The allegations against Bergstraesser, which I did not want to believe, turned out to be true. It was true that, as he had told me, he had been active in the German Democratic Party, but this was the case only for a very brief period in the early 1920s before he turned to the nationalist right. In a very shameful manner he participated in the campaign in Heidelberg initiated by the Nazi student organization to remove the mathematician Emil Gumbel from the university. They held against Gumbel that he was a Jew, a pacifist active in the German League for Human Rights, and an advocate of reconciliation with France who felt that the First World War was criminal. Bergstraesser presided at the hearings against Gumbel which resulted in Gumbel being stripped of his *venia legendi,* the right to teach at the university. Bergstraesser worked closely with the Nazis after 1933, as a spokesman for the New Germany in France and as one of the chief organizers of the 500th anniversary of the University of Heidelberg. Due to internal conflicts it was suddenly revealed that he had a Jewish grandmother, and he was forced to emigrate.

The case of Hans Rothfels was similar. Born in 1891 into a Jewish family, he converted to Evangelical Lutheranism as a young man. As a professor in Königsberg he became an ardent spokesman for the expansion of German domination over the non-German ethnic groups in Eastern Europe, and implicitly for ethnic cleansing. He became the mentor of a young group of historians including Werner Conze and Theodor Schieder, who became the two most influential historians in West Germany after 1945. During the Nazi period they had pursued a racial interpretation of European history and provided plans for ethnic cleansing. Rothfels was removed from his chair in 1934 as a Jew, but considerable efforts were made by leading Nazis, including Joachim von Ribbentrop, who personally interceded on his behalf with Hitler. Two attempts by Rothfels to be recognized as an honorary Aryan failed. He emigrated in the last minute in August 1939. Hutchins must have been aware of Bergstraesser's and Rothfels's past without being particularly disturbed by it. Both returned to Germany very soon after the war to occupy positions as founders of important institutes in political science and history respectively. They moved away from the earlier ultra-nationalist, antidemocratic positions to a more moderate conservative orientation, in harmony with the early Federal Republic. Rothfels could not affect my student career negatively and I never had any problems with Bergstraesser who presented himself to me as a good democrat. But Wilma may have suffered from his political biases when he wanted to force her to make revisions in her dissertation on Karl Kraus based on his ideological outlook.

Chapter 4

THE STRUGGLE AGAINST RACIAL SEGREGATION: LITTLE ROCK AND NEW ORLEANS (1950–1960)

WILMA

At the end of January 1949 I joined Georg in Akron, Ohio, where both of us had accepted teaching positions at the University of Akron, and the following semester I accepted an additional part time position at John Carroll University, a Jesuit university in Cleveland. I was the first woman and the first non-Christian who taught there. During my first classes people often looked curiously through the little window in the door. The novelty of my position is suggested by a conversation I had with a fellow train passenger on my way to Cleveland. When he told me that he had two sons at John Carroll, and I said I taught there, he replied angrily that there were no women teaching at John Carroll, and turned to his newspaper.

During this period we were both working on our dissertations and took hardly any time off. When I was looking for a typist for my dissertation, I became acquainted with Henrietta Hronek, a woman of Czech descent who became a good friend. She was an ardent Catholic, a follower of Dorothy Day, the founder of the Catholic Worker Movement and of the newspaper of the same name. The members of the movement maintained hostels for the homeless and soup kitchens. They lived simply, and preferred to be given an old refrigerator from people of modest means, than to receive a check from wealthy people. Henrietta worked as a matron at the women's prison in Cleveland. When she invited us for Thanksgiving, she had another guest, a woman who had been in prison for prostitution. The priest who hired me seemed impressed by my friendship with Henrietta. I became a faithful reader of the *Catholic Worker*.

While we were in Akron, my parents, together with Uncle Hugo and Aunt Martha, bought Oak Park Farm. It was near Brantford, Ontario, on the Grand

River, and was exactly as large as Neuhof/Nový Dvůr. For my father that meant that he "had again made it." Prior to this time, he had spent much time on his seed business, Greenlands Permanent Pasture. He would visit farms, analyze the soil and then recommend mixtures of seeds and offer advice on how to enhance the pastures and increase the milk production of the specific breed of cattle involved. He helped develop highly productive pastures in both Canada and the United States, and it became a very successful enterprise.

A short time after the two families moved to Oak Park Farm on May 1, 1949, fate struck three times in a row. Ten days after the move my father, who had always been so proud of his good health and his physical strength, suffered a massive heart attack. He recovered, but was absolutely not willing to change his active way of life. The second tragedy occurred in the summer of 1949, while Georg and I were spending a few weeks at the farm. During these weeks Georg and I worked on the second floor of the large, hundred year old house that without exaggeration could be called a mansion. The interior had been decorated by an architect, a member of a circle who had become friends, especially of my mother. While we were working we suddenly heard disturbing voices and learned that my cousin Karli, Uncle Hugo and Aunt Martha's son, the only male descendant (and potential heir of the farm) had fallen into a combine harvester while loading fodder into the silo, and had died a horrible death.

Mother was next. She had never been one to complain, and thus we should have paid more attention when, in the late 1940s, she began to complain of severe stomach pains. In March 1950 she was diagnosed with inoperable cancer of the pancreas. What followed was worse than I could have imagined. During the summer Mother had a second operation, at the Sloan-Kettering Hospital in New York City. My conviction of the cynical greed of doctors—yes, I know that there are exceptions—has its roots there. It was almost impossible to speak to the doctors. What remained most vivid in my mind was a doctor's reply when I asked him why my mother had a blister the size and color of a large egg yolk on her knee: "It isn't worth a conversation."

Although Mother had been pessimistic ever since she was first diagnosed with cancer, she was convinced at the end that she was getting better. In her words: "I have always known that when daddy decides on something, he can make it happen." She died in the Brantford hospital on November 20th, 1950.

A few months later my father married Gerta, the widowed daughter of a cousin. Both Marianne and I felt that it was right that he did not remain alone.

At the end of the summer of 1950, Georg and I moved to Little Rock, Arkansas. The move was simple; apart from clothing and books we had almost nothing. Both of us had accepted teaching positions at Philander Smith College. The modest campus of Philander Smith was located near Ninth Street, the center of the black business district. Since the college at first had no housing for us, we rented a small unfurnished apartment in a white neighborhood, and furnished it from Mr. Brown's Second Hand Furniture Store. After we woke up the next morning covered with flea bites, Mr. Brown was willing to exchange the flea-infested mattress for bookcases. We still have one of them. Within weeks, however, we were able to move to the campus, to a house at 1116 Izard Street. Our house was of a type called a shotgun house, with all the rooms in a row. One entered the living room from the porch, then the bedroom, and finally the kitchen. The bathroom obviously had been added later. Like all houses in the neighbourhood, ours was made of clapboard and stood on brick blocks, so that cats and chickens could go beneath the house to protect themselves from the heat.

I normally taught fifteen to eighteen hours a week. I took my heavy teaching schedule for granted. While we taught, students came to the house, took care of the children, and helped with the housework. After the birth of each child we moved to a larger house on the same block. The third and last one was not a shotgun house, had a large kitchen and was very homey. The kitchen was in dire need of new wallpaper, and so I went to see the president of Philander Smith, as one did with all problems. President Marquis Lafayette Harris agreed that I could pick out wallpaper, but said that it must not cost more than ten cents a roll. I had no idea what wallpaper cost, and when I went to the store, a salesman informed me, that for ten cents I could get only toilet paper. But then he remembered that he might still have some paper from before the depression. The paper which had yellowed with age, was pink and decorated with tea- and coffee cans. When Georg once was in Little Rock decades later, he saw that our house was being torn down, the last on the block. Only one wall was left with my pink paper.

In addition to my classes, I attended faculty meetings and wrote evaluations of the students' IQ tests or of their reading levels. Classes were often held early in the morning and late at night, because many students worked in the daytime and because the heat was bearable early in the morning. Before we had children, I often sat in the bathtub, let cold water drip in slowly, and graded papers.

On Saturday mornings I taught French. Most of the students were teachers and pastors who came from all parts of Arkansas to accumulate credits for their B.A. We came to know one student, Mrs. Alice Preston, particularly well, and once visited her and her family in Murfreesboro in the southwest of Arkansas. We had our baby Jeremy along and wanted to put his milk bottles in the refrigerator, but the Prestons did not have one. Years later when Bill Clinton was governor of Arkansas, he appointed Mrs. Preston to his educational advisory board.

The students came, almost without exception, from poor families. I remember one student who came from Detroit, and perhaps for that reason was not as timid as most of the students. He came to our house a couple of times and said he was hungry. Now I know that I should have done more than given him a sandwich. Another student with whom I caught up on my way downtown would not walk beside me and instead kept a few steps behind me. When I asked her if she had trouble walking, she replied hesitantly that she did not think she was supposed to walk next to a white person.

German and Spanish were also part of my normal teaching load. In the summer of 1953, when our son Danny was two months old, I decided not to teach summer school. However, one morning I found a note in the mailbox asking me to teach the upper level English courses, beginning that day. They were Shakespeare, Chaucer and Children's Literature. When I told the dean that I did not think that I was qualified, he replied that "We are a small Negro college in the South and not the University of Michigan, and have to be able to teach anything." So I taught those courses..

We also had white friends in Arkansas. For me the Eliots were especially important. They were Quakers. After completing his medical studies at Harvard and interning at the Mayo Clinic, Jo Eliot had moved with his wife Fran and their three children (eventually they had five), to Little Rock. Jo, a pediatrician, was in charge of the free well-baby clinic in Little Rock and taught at the University of Arkansas medical school. Together with the only other Quaker couple in the city they developed various projects, such as painting the black YMCA on a weekend; there were of course two YMCAs. Like other "white liberals", we were members of the Wider Quaker Fellowship. Georg wanted to be a member of a Jewish community, but soon found that he had less in common with the Little Rock Jews than with the members of some other religious groups. Another couple, the McKees, also members of the Wider Quaker Fellowship, passed their Community Concert tickets on to us when they could not use them.

A short time after our arrival the Little Rock Unitarian Fellowship was founded, a first step toward the establishment of a Unitarian church. Felix Arnold, a native Arkansan, had founded it, and we joined, although we did not make a secret of our Jewishness. One of the most faithful members was John Kimball, a city building custodian and pacifist who was fired for refusing to raise the American flag. John was an enthusiastic member of the Esperanto club and worked there with Georg. The chairman of the club was Mr. Post, formerly Postnikov, an old Russian who had been an officer in the Russian balloon corps in the Russian war against Japan, had fled after the revolt in 1905, and then had been a candidate of the Socialist Party for the position of mayor of Berkeley, California. In the early twenties, he had come to Arkansas to teach at Commonwealth College, a "labor college" that was reputed to be Communist. When Mr. Post died in his eighties, Georg and John Kimball were the executors of his will. He had stated in his will that a nursery school should be founded at his house for children of both races. His will, however, was not valid, because according to Arkansas law he would have had to at least mention his children, and that he had not done. During my ride to the cemetery with one of Mr. Post's sons, the principal shareholder, as he told me, of the Dole pineapple company, I came to understand why his father had not felt the need to remember his children in his will.

During the early 1950s we had to be very economical, but did not feel that to be a problem. The fact that all three children were premature worried us more. Dan, who was born in 1953, weighed a little over three pounds at birth, and had to spend four weeks in an incubator. Because I wanted to nurse him eventually, Georg carried daily tiny amounts of milk to the hospital. After Dan came home, he however refused to nurse, because drinking from the bottle was so much easier.

There were a few other white professors at Philander. Next to us lived the Ewbanks, who were half a generation older than we. John had studied theology, taught sociology, and hoped to get his Ph.D. They seemed to us like leftovers from the time when white people went to the South as missionaries. Although they advised us on many practical matters, we never became really close. I am sure that they also considered segregation wrong, but hardly thought that they could do anything to help bring about a change. We of course addressed each other as Mr. and Mrs., or with titles and surnames. When the Ewbanks moved to Kansas where he was to serve as a Methodist minister, we moved to their roomy, comfortable house. They sold us a lot of household goods that they did not want to take along.

Behind the houses on Izard Street there were back yards, and behind them outhouses, which belonged to the shacks facing Chester Street. Unlike the other faculty children, our children played with the children on Chester. There we became acquainted with a large black family. When Georg found out that the oldest boy could not go to school because he had no decent clothes and no shoes, he took him to Goodwill Industries, and for a few dollars he got everything he needed. We became good customers of Goodwill. The children's mother was sick in bed most of the time, but their father, Mr. Zachariah, once brought us a pound of butter, which he had gotten from welfare. He said he knew that we only bought margarine.

Both of my parents died while we were in Little Rock. I had never thought about the possibility of them dying, and it hit me particularly hard. That was especially true in the case of my father, who never wanted to admit to others or to himself that he could have any physical weaknesses. After his heart attack he was not willing to listen to doctors, and he continued to live as he pleased and traveled, often in search of a doctor who would tell him that he was as good as new. He finally found one, who was mainly a gentleman farmer in Alabama.

My father visited us at Christmas in 1953, enjoyed Jeremy and Danny, and became acquainted with our black neighbors. He died suddenly on February 20th, 1954. The following night Georg kept rubbing my ice cold feet to warm them up. I do not remember the long train trip to Canada at all. From the farm Uncle Hugo drove me to Brantford to the undertaker's, so that I could see Daddy once more. Uncle Hugo said Don't kiss, and I turned around and left.

Uncle Hugo continued to run the farm for some time after my father's death in 1954. There was no reason to hold onto the farm, and it was sold.

I had taken the academic year 1955–56 off, and Georg took the following year for his sabbatical. During the summer of 1956, we moved to Fayetteville, the small town in the Ozarks that was home to the University of Arkansas, where we had contracted to teach part time for a year. Georg had missed the intellectual stimulation of a university town, and we both hoped to get tenure track positions there. We rented a house in Fayetteville from a man who had owned it for nineteen years but who had never had a key. We continued that tradition.

Within a few days, we felt part of the university community. I became a member of WAG (World Affairs Group), a group of women, actually all faculty wives, who met regularly, discussed political problems, and worked together on projects. One project involved ending the segregation at the small children's wading pool. The lack of a black middle class in Fayetteville made our task more difficult. The Blacks in Fayetteville lived in a poor neighborhood called "Tincup". Our next project was to persuade the university administration to let the only black woman graduate student live in the women's dormitory, rather than in a formerly private home, which had just been damaged by an unexplained fire. I do not know how much the WAG actually accomplished, but, at any rate, these problems were solved a short time later.

In Fayetteville Jeremy went to a Catholic kindergarten, and Danny attended a co-op nursery school where the parents shared all the work. Georg took our family's turns alongside all the mothers, while I taught. He was the only father to do so. Our youngest son Jonathan, who was not quite a year old when we came to Fayetteville, was a quiet child. He spent part of his time watching from his playpen as a house was being built across the street.

By then we had our first car, and so we took trips to the beautiful areas of that sparsely populated state: Mount Magazine, Devils Den State Park, and Roaring River State Park across the state line in Missouri.

In September of 1956, we moved to New Orleans, but during our time there we spent a few more summers in cooler Fayetteville. We never again encountered as much informal cordiality as in Fayetteville. During one of the first summers there we met Lyell and Marki Thompson and their five children. When an acquaintance took me to meet them, Marki was barefoot, standing on a chair, rearranging something over their fireplace. With her always cheerful voice she asked if we would like some coffee. It was friendship at first sight. She was studying to become a grade school teacher, and became a very enthusiastic one. Lyell was a professor of agronomy, who, although a Southerner, was very much involved in the struggle for racial equality. Their parents were farmers in Oklahoma. Marki once took me along to their farm in Perry, Oklahoma, where I met her aunt, who spoke only Czech, and Marki showed me the Czech cemetery that dated from the nineteenth century.

In New Orleans, Georg and I taught at Dillard, a black university. There was no campus housing available at Dillard, so we rented an apartment at the Parkchester apartment complex nearby. It consisted of brick buildings, each of which had eight apartments. Most of the people who lived in the complex were relative newcomers from Southern states who felt insecure economically and socially. They knew that we taught at Dillard, and someone kept scribbling the letter "N", in front of our name on the mailbox. It was also at Parkchester that, for the first and only time during our stay in the South, we were threatened with violence. The violence was especially nasty because some of it was directed against our children. A doctoral student in history from Tulane University lived with his family in the same building as we. He had arrived recently from Memphis. One day, after a black colleague and his wife had visited us, we received a call from the manager of Parkchester. He told us that two couples, including the doctoral student, had complained about our black visitors and had asked him to give us notice. The manager defended our right to invite whomever we wanted—he was a Quaker, but advised us not to accompany our guests to their cars and to pull our blinds when we had black guests.

That evening when the children were in the playground behind the building, we heard some screaming and saw the student's wife push four-year-old Danny off the swing and chase him away. Then the man came, insulted Georg, and challenged him to a fistfight. We suddenly were surrounded by neighbors, who watched silently except for one man who called us names. The next day we told the president of Dillard about the incident. He made sure that within a few days we could move to Gentilly Gardens, which was owned by the university and where mostly Dillard faculty lived. At that point several of the Parkchester neighbors, who had ignored us up to that time, became particularly friendly and let us know that they were sorry about what had happened.

On the Dillard campus, where we were the only white family, we were treated very cordially. The first morning after our move, the football trainer came over, picked up the children, and showed them the sports facilities. Living on the parklike campus was pleasant, but we did not have a close circle of friends as we had in Arkansas. We were very busy at both ends of the city, at Dillard and at Tulane, where we both taught part-time. Georg was also involved in the NAACP. Our best friend was Sam Gandy, the campus minister at Dillard. Georg knew him from Richmond, where as a professor at the black Virginia State College Gandy had been faculty adviser of an interracial student organization. Trained in philosophy and theology, Sam was able to build bridges not only between blacks and whites, but also between Christians and Jews. He was active with the NAACP, which not many faculty members were, either black or white, as well as with the Council for Christians and Jews, and in the peace group we organized. He remained a good friend until his death in 1988.

GEORG

In September 1948 I began my first teaching job as a German instructor at the University of Akron. In my small German literature class I was at the age of twenty-one by far younger than any of my students who all were veterans. In addition to the German courses, except for the one in literature, all were in beginning and intermediate German, I volunteered as an overload to teach a discussion section of the Humanities course, which essentially was a survey of Western civilization focusing on selections from the great classical writings. Wilma was still in Chicago, but we saw each other on several weekends. After our wedding in late December, she joined me in Akron in January after the end of the semester at the University of Illinois at Navy Pier where she was teaching at the time.

The two years in Akron were uneventful. We had almost no contact with the community. We had two sets of friends, Johnny and Marianna Schmidt, both from the University of Chicago in sociology and social work respectively, and Harry Fleak, a political scientist and his wife Audrey, a specialist in Elizabethan English literature with whom we maintained loose contact over the years. The Schmidts later divorced, but we remained in touch with each of them until their deaths many years later. Akron was the rubber tire capital of the United States, and the university with a large rubber chemistry program served the needs of the local industry. The liberal arts played a relatively minor role in the course offerings. I had only one person with whom I could exchange ideas, Ray Nelson who had just come to Akron with a Ph. D. in philosophy from the University of Chicago. Wilma also taught sections of the Humanities course in addition to teaching at John Carroll University in nearby Cleveland which she already mentioned. Just as we had spent our evenings in Chicago studying, we now devoted our free time to our dissertations, Wilma on Karl Kraus and I on the political philosophy of the Saint-Simonians.

One matter of concern was Wilma's immigration status. Her student visa had expired and she feared deportation to Canada. The quota for Czechoslovak immigrants was filled for several years, and it would be some time before she would be eligible for admission to the United States. It was therefore urgent that I receive my U.S. citizenship, so that she could immigrate as my wife. But my naturalization was complicated, due to the witch-hunt mentality of the Cold War that began under the Truman administration even before Senator Joe McCarthy appeared on the scene.

Both my parents had their naturalization hearings in the fall of 1943, and my mother received her citizenship a few weeks later. My father was asked by the hearing officer to provide proof that he had been honorably discharged from the German army after World War I, which seemed a strange request in 1943, when the United States was at war with Germany. It had never occurred to my father when he left Germany that he would need his discharge papers in the United States. He was required to produce a statement under oath, and finally received his U.S. citizenship over a year later.

In the meantime I had turned eighteen. Under the regulations at the time children were automatically naturalized if they were under eighteen. But I could not apply for citizenship until I was of age at twenty-one. I immediately applied for citizenship in Chicago on my twenty-first birthday in December 1947, and a few weeks later I was summoned to a hearing. The other applicants were mostly older persons who had been in the country for many years. All were asked whether they had ever been arrested—two had been—and then asked simple questions about American history and government. I was the only one who was not asked whether he had ever been arrested. Instead the hearing officer engaged me in a discussion of Montesquieu and the division of powers, and then began to quiz me on my political affiliations. I stated that I was a member of Labor Rights, a student organization on the University of Chicago campus that was formed in the summer of 1944 in support of the Montgomery Ward strike. (Incidentally the one organization that came out in opposition to Labor Rights was the campus Communist group, which opposed all strikes during the war.)

One of the two witnesses who spoke in my support noted that Labor Rights was a moderately left of center student organization, but definitely was not Communist. The hearing officer then informed me that no organization left of center could be anti-Communist. Then he asked whether I was or had ever been a member of the Communist Party, and I said I had not. He then asked whether I was a member of the American Students for Democracy, the Communist student organization, which I denied. He then asked whether I had ever attended any meetings of the American Students for Democracy, which again I could honestly deny. He then said that I should not make self serving statements. I protested that I had testified under oath, and that he had no right to question my veracity. That was the end of the interrogation. About a month later I read in the newspaper that the others had received their citizenship. I inquired several times about the status of my application and was told each time that my case was still under investigation.

Wilma's status in this country became increasingly precarious. After we were married in December 1948, I turned to Senator Paul Douglas for assistance. Douglas, a professor of economics at the University of Chicago, in the summer of 1948 had agreed to be on my dissertation committee, but then withdrew after he very unexpectedly was elected to the U. S. Senate in November 1948, when Harry S. Truman defeated Thomas Dewey for President. I trusted Douglas as a liberal and a New Dealer, but was not aware of his passionate anti-Communism. He referred me to his representative in the Chicago office, an old unionist, who secured an extension of Wilma's visa but apparently did nothing about my stalled citizenship application. In the meantime we had moved to Akron, and my files had been transferred to Cleveland. I received the same answer whenever I called the naturalization office, namely that my case was still under investigation.

Douglas' representative asked me to come to Chicago to meet with a member of the Public Workers of America. Unbeknownst to me, the Public Workers of America, for which I had recruited workers at the Hutchinson Commons at the University of Chicago, was suspected of including Communists or Communist sympathizers on the national level. I was questioned at length by the union member, and I managed to convince him that I had no Communist affiliations. Things then began to move forward. I was told by the Cleveland office of the Immigration and Naturalization Service (INS), that I would have to be interviewed by their official in Akron. When I finally did meet him, he told me that he could not conduct the interview because his secretary, who was supposed to take the minutes, was not available, and would not be available for some time. He turned down my offer to hire a stenographer. When I appealed to the Cleveland office, I was told that I could be interviewed by the INS in Chicago. There, I was again questioned about my political views and affiliations and was asked to make a list of all organizations to which I had ever belonged. All this seemed very humiliating, but given Wilma's immigration status I had no choice. A few weeks later I was again called to Chicago, and in November 1949 sworn in as a citizen. A short time later Wilma was admitted as an immigrant.

Our positions at the University of Akron terminated at the end of the 1950 academic year. The employment situation at universities and colleges had changed in the two years since I was first hired in Akron. Many of the veterans had now completed their studies, and there was a glut of new Ph.D.'s on the job market. Moreover, neither Wilma nor I had yet completed our doctorates. I was therefore very glad when I received an offer from Philander Smith College in Little Rock, Arkansas, relieved that I had a job but also eager to teach at (what at the time was referred to as) a Negro college in the South. Almost immediately after we arrived at the college, Wilma also was offered a position.

The reception at the college was friendly. Higher education in Arkansas was still segregated. The Law School at the University of Arkansas in Fayetteville had just admitted its first black student, and the medical school was about to do the same. Public facilities were still segregated.

Philander Smith was founded in 1877 for black students by the white Methodist Church, initially with a vocational focus, but as time went on, there was an increasing emphasis on the liberal arts. Until 1948 the school had not been accredited. Its faculty was all African American with one exception, John Ewbank, a Methodist minister, who had come to the College in 1932 with his wife while still working on a Ph.D. in sociology that he never completed. The college until 1948 consisted of several dilapidated buildings covering two blocks between Izard and State Streets and Eleventh and Twelfth Streets. The campus was one block from Ninth Street, the main black business street, and half a mile from the center of Little Rock. In 1948 the college acquired the campus of the adjacent white Little Rock Junior College. The proximity of the two colleges reflected how interwoven white and black neighborhoods were in the South, in contrast to Northern cities where there was sharper residential segregation. Little Rock Junior College moved to the suburbs, an indication of the changes in residential patterns that ultimately brought about greater separation between white and black neighborhoods.

Until 1948 the college had only one person with a doctorate, namely the president, Marquis Lafayette Harris, a charismatic Black, still relatively young, with a Ph.D. in philosophy from Boston University, and a Methodist minister. Harris succeeded in recruiting an interracial faculty who held doctorates or who, like us, were about to complete their doctoral studies. The student body at the time numbered about six hundred and was all black. Many came from rural Arkansas, a fair number from Little Rock, most of them the first in their family to go to college; a majority came from economically disadvantaged homes. Some were young people from Northern cities such as Detroit and Chicago, who wanted to attend a Black institution. There also were women school teachers, often middle aged, who traveled on Saturdays over long distances from impoverished school districts to complete their B.A.s. There were also students from the British West Indies and occasionally from Africa, some of them quite gifted, who attended on athletic scholarships.

In terms of educational preparation the student body was worse than mixed. Many had attended poor segregated school systems, and tested on a seventh or eighth grade level in reading and writing skills. On the other hand, there were also a few excellent students who could not attend the segregated white schools in the state and could not afford out-of-state schools. One of our students was Joycelyn Elders, who went on to the University of Arkansas medical school. She became a pediatrician, was the first Black professor at the University of Arkansas, and under President Clinton was appointed Surgeon General of the United States.

We came to Little Rock without any clear idea as to how we could contribute to the struggle against segregation. Very soon, however, we had an opportunity to become active. During my first semester at Philander Smith, I taught a course on the world since 1919. The Korean War had just broken out a few months earlier and I wanted to find background literature for my students. The poorly equipped college library had little that was relevant. Little Rock, like most larger American cities, had a good public library, but it was not accessible to blacks. There was a small branch library for blacks, that was open only a few hours a week, and a small children's library. Theoretically, black readers could order any books from the main library, but there was no catalogue of the holdings of the main library at the branch. Moreover, a librarian at the main library told me that books that are in demand there are generally not forwarded to the black branch.

I decided to write a letter to the editor of the *Arkansas Gazette,* the more liberal of the two Little Rock newspapers, outlining the situation and urging the main library to open its doors to all readers regardless of race, and the letter was published. I did not expect my letter to have any results. But we know now from the minutes of the board of the library that the board took my letter very seriously. They called in President Harris for consultation. Harris then told me that I could send my students to the main library. They went and were served without problems. In fact, the board, which consisted of five members of the Little Rock establishment, had voted unanimously against the opposition of some of the staff to open the library not only to my students, but to all readers. The board also decided against making a public announcement, but word soon spread.

A short time later I was visited by a small delegation of the Little Rock branch of the National Association for the Advancement of Colored People (NAACP). The NAACP from its founding in 1909 had always included white members, but there were very few white members in the South, where they faced the possibility of adverse consequences. The delegation asked whether I would be willing to join the executive committee of the branch and chair its education committee. The branch consisted of earnest and committed members, mostly postal employees or persons who were self-employed and thus were not susceptible to economic pressure. One of the most active members was the Reverend J. L. Crenchaw, who had a small tailor shop. There were also a handful of black lawyers, doctors, dentists, ministers, and funeral directors who were members, but there was no one who could, or was ready to do the research required for the work of the branch.

Since its founding the NAACP had avoided direct confrontation and instead relied on bringing legal action in the courts to challenge segregation laws. It had a great deal of success in the years after 1945 in gaining admission for black students to law schools and medical schools in the South, and in opposing segregation in public interstate transportation and discriminatory housing covenants.

I was the first and until then only white member of the local executive committee. Wilma also joined the NAACP. As chair of the education committee I began to contact organizations and individuals who might support our efforts to end school segregation. Within the black community there was the Urban League, a black social service organization that also included whites. Moreover, the library board's decision reflected changing attitudes on racial separation. In 1951 public facilities were still fully segregated, but an increasing number of persons realized that this had to change, although they did not all agree on how quickly and how fully these changes should take place. Thus when I approached the presidents of the three major department stores in Little Rock about desegregating the drinking fountains, they all complied. I considered this a minor victory, but it was taken very seriously in the black community for its symbolic significance.

There was a small chapter of the Southern Regional Council in Little Rock, consisting of Whites and Blacks committed to change. Among its members were Forrest Rozell, president of the Arkansas Education Association, and Emma Scott, its general secretary. Rozell and Scott were members of the suburban white Pulaski Height Christian Church, whose minister, the Reverend Lewis Deer, fully supported my work in the NAACP as did his successor the Reverend Bert Cartwright. In about 1953 the chapter of the Southern Regional Council was transformed into the Arkansas Council on Human Relations, with a paid secretary and an office. I was instrumental in selecting the secretary, Nat Griswold, a Methodist minister who during the Second World War had worked with Japanese Americans in an internment camp in Arkansas. The Arkansas Council also recruited members outside of Little Rock, including many faculty members at the University of Arkansas in Fayetteville.

During my association with the Little Rock chapter of the NAACP, I worked closely with Daisy Bates, the young president of the Arkansas State Conference of Branches of the NAACP, a dynamic activist and the wife of L. C. Bates, the editor of the outspoken *Arkansas State Press*. As the conflict over school desegregation became more bitter in the course of the 1950s, she became the most hated black person for the radical racist right. As attitudes have changed in more recent years, she has come to be recognized as a heroine, particularly for her role in the desegregation of Little Rock Central High School. She and her husband were made honorary citizens of Little Rock, a school was named after her, and when she died at the age of eighty-three in 1999, she lay in state in the Arkansas State Capitol. More recently, an important thoroughfare was named after her.

One of my first projects as chair of the education committee of the NAACP was a study of educational inequalities in the small town of West Helena, Arkansas, along the Mississippi across from Helena, Tennessee. We still had to operate under the 1896 U.S. Supreme Court decision in *Plessy vs. Ferguson*, which had established the doctrine of "separate but equal." Our task was to document that the separate facilities were unequal everywhere. In West Helena I was met by a local black attorney, and together we visited all the black schools and interviewed the teachers. I then went alone to the white superintendent and introduced myself as a doctoral candidate in education at the University of Chicago. He willingly answered all my questions about facilities and curricula. Wilma then went to the Department of Education in Little Rock, also introduced herself as a graduate student in education at the University of Chicago, and obtained all the statistical information we needed, including the salary scales that showed striking inequalities, with Blacks earning about half as much as white teachers. We then filed a suit that resulted in a court order that mandated major improvements.

I then began investigations of further school districts. The most important was, of course, Little Rock. In the spring of 1952 I prepared a study of inequalities between the city's two public high schools, white Little Rock Senior High School—soon afterward renamed Little Rock Central High School—and black Dunbar High School. Little Rock Senior High School had a capacity of 3,000, and in 1950–51 had only 1,438 pupils. Dunbar had been built for 1,600 pupils, but was seriously overcrowded because the 1,525 senior high school students shared the building with the junior high school and with the junior college. Because of a lack of classrooms for study halls, three to four hundred students were required to be in the auditorium during their study periods. Three classes met generally in the cafeteria, where the band also practiced and interfered with instruction. Because of the lack of space, classes at Dunbar ran for only 42 minutes, whereas classes in the white high school, Little Rock High ran for 55 minutes. The library was so small at Dunbar that teachers were advised to issue only two or three permits an hour for the use of the library, while students at Little Rock Senior High School could use theirs freely. In addition to Little Rock Senior High School, there was a special technical high school for whites. Moreover, there was a marked discrepancy in student load, per capita per student expenditure and teachers' salaries. The "Peabody Report" rated Little Rock Senior High School as well as the Technical High School as "good," as to size and condition, and rated Dunbar High School as "poor."

Finally, the schools had very different curricula. In addition to the courses offered at the Technical High School, Little Rock Senior High School had extensive college preparatory, commercial and vocational courses that were not offered at Dunbar. Dunbar offered only the most rudimentary courses, virtually none in the liberal arts or in business—not even a course in bookkeeping—and almost no preparation for technical occupations. Thus Dunbar offered no courses in mechanical training, auto or aviation mechanics, machine shop, or radio. There were seventy-six courses offered at the two white high schools that were not offered at Dunbar. The report called upon the Little Rock School Board to make a beginning toward overcoming inequalities by admitting a select group of Dunbar students to courses at Little Rock Senior High School that were not available to them at Dunbar. The two schools, moreover, were in easy walking distance.

The report was released to the Little Rock press in the name of the Little Rock Council on Schools, an interracial organization I had initiated, which had the support of the Little Rock branch of the NAACP, the Urban League and the Southern Regional Council as well as of a number of distinguished white public figures such as Rev. Deer. We asked for and were granted, a meeting with the Little Rock School Board, which would not have been possible at the time in most Southern cities. We asked the board to begin a process of gradual desegregation by admitting a small number of Dunbar students to courses at Little Rock Senior High School as the report had suggested. The reception at the board was cordial. Our inside information was that at least three of the six members of the board favored the plan, although the superintendent opposed it. The understanding was that the meeting was to be held strictly confidential until the board had arrived at a decision. For some reason, unbeknownst to me, Thaddeus Williams, a young black attorney and president of the Little Rock NAACP chapter, who had been at the meeting, revealed that the meeting had taken place, with the result that the board broke off negotiations with us. He soon afterward resigned, although I do not know whether his resignation had anything to do with his breach of confidentiality, and he left town.

We considered bringing a suit against the Little Rock School Board based on the findings of inequalities in the report, but were dissuaded from doing so by the national office of the NAACP, which was awaiting a decision of the U.S. Supreme Court in the case of *Brown vs. the Topeka Board of Education*, challenging the separate but equal doctrine as unconstitutional.

Rev. Crenchaw, the tailor I have mentioned, whom I respected very highly, succeeded Williams as president of the Little Rock NAACP chapter. Before choosing Crenchaw, members of the branch urged me to accept the presidency, but I made it clear that I could not possibly accept. The segregationists attacked the black civil rights movement, claiming that it was controlled by white "outside agitators," and I was vulnerable to attack not only as an outsider but as a foreigner. I tried to remain anonymous in the general community. Because of my German accent, I avoided appearing on radio and TV (the latter only started in Little Rock in 1953). My name appeared occasionally in the press, but as George, not Georg, and as "instructor at Philander Smith College." I was relatively well known among blacks and in white liberal circles, but the radical segregationists, who had little contact with the black community, probably assumed that I was black. After I turned down the offer to become president of the chapter, a special post was created for me, which was less visible to the white public, as chair of the executive committee.

There was another development which reflected the color blindness of the branch. A black minister from Detroit had boarded a city bus and sat down in front. When the driver ordered him to move to the back, he tried to leave the bus from the front. The driver slammed the front door, told him that he had to leave through the rear door, and when he refused and sat down again in front, the driver summoned the police and had him arrested. The city, afraid of a suit challenging its segregation practices, dropped the charges against the minister. We then decided to bring a civil suit for damages against the city and the bus company.

We needed white witnesses who could testify that whites in contrast to blacks could freely leave the bus from the rear as well as from the front. Wilma, who has no detectable accent, was in the hospital giving birth to our son Daniel and thus was not available. The branch wanted me to testify. I was reluctant, however, because of my accent and explained that the attorney for the city and the bus company would surely ask me: "Where were you born?" In fact, after I had answered the NAACP attorney's questions as to whether I had ever left the bus through the rear door without any problems, the attorney for the defense had only one question, not where I was born, but where I went to school. To his surprise, I could honestly reply "Richmond, Virginia." This was a jury trial and although we had clearly demonstrated that bus segregation was discriminatory, we lost, as expected. Two years later, however, when a federal court ruled that the separation of the races on intrastate common carriers was unconstitutional, Little Rock immediately complied. In many other Southern cities, including New Orleans, several years of litigation were required for the implementation of the decision.

At approximately that time, I was pledged as the first and only white brother into the Little Rock chapter of the Phi Beta Sigma fraternity. Our dean at Philander Smith, William Pipes, who was active in the fraternity on the national as well as on the local level, had sought for over a year to have me join. I had always been very critical of the social exclusiveness of fraternities, but was gradually convinced by Pipes that this fraternity was different and in fact that the local chapter supported the work of the NAACP. Once pledged, I spoke for the fraternity on civil rights issues in Atlanta, Memphis, St. Louis and in smaller towns in Arkansas. In December 1955 I was the keynote speaker at the fraternity's national conclave in Louisville, where I urged the fraternity to come out in support of Carl Braden, who was serving time in a federal prison on a subversion charge. He and his wife Ann, both white, had been very active in the Southern Conference Educational Fund efforts in the South against racial segregation. After we left Arkansas for New Orleans in 1957, I briefly attended the fraternity meetings there, but unlike the situation in Little Rock I felt very much as an outsider and found that the New Orleans chapter corresponded closely to my earlier conception of what fraternities were all about. I subsequently became inactive until the fraternity rediscovered me a few years ago and convinced me to again become active in the fraternity.

In 1953, unbeknownst to us, Wilma and I were subjected by the FBI to a full scale investigation about possible Communist affiliations. We learned about this only in the early 1970s when we succeeded in obtaining parts of our files under the then-recently enacted Freedom of Information Act. To my surprise I learned that there had been seven reports on my activities in 1941 when I was fourteen years old. I suspect that they had to do with my role in the Union Now chapter at Thomas Jefferson High School, although it is conceivable, but less likely, that teachers complained about my critical stance on segregation. I asked for these files but was informed that they had been destroyed. I received the same reply when I asked for possible files relating to my naturalization. We did receive two files from 1953 originating in the Little Rock office, and were totally astonished when we saw them. It was apparent that the FBI knew nothing about our roles in the NAACP. The first document stated: "Information has been received by the Little Rock office that propaganda material was mailed from Czechoslovakia, and addressed to Mrs. Wilma A. Iggers, 1113 Izard Street, Little Rock, Arkansas. The material consisted of a book entitled 'History of the Communist Party of the Soviet Union—Bolsheviks'." The next paragraph stated: "A confidential informant of the Little Rock office advised that George Iggers has been mentioned on various occasions by"—The rest of the sentence is blacked out. The two of us were then identified as teachers at Philander Smith College.

What had happened is that in 1948 two of Wilma's classmates in Czechoslovakia had bought a beautiful folkloristic coffee set from the town where they had gone to school, as a wedding gift for us, but they were unable to get an export permit from the Communist authorities. They kept trying to obtain a permit, always without success. Finally, after several years, they hit on an idea. They wrote us that they would put an English copy of Joseph Stalin's *Short History of the Communist Party of the Soviet Union* in the box. Shortly afterward they wrote us that it had worked and that they had been able to send the gift. But the box did not arrive. After waiting several months we inquired at the post office and after a while were called to come. We were told the box was at U.S. Customs in St. Louis and could not be delivered to us, because it contained subversive literature. If we agreed to have the literature removed, we could have the box. We had no interest in the book, but nevertheless insisted on our right to have it. It had never occurred to Wilma's friends in Czechoslovakia or to us that there would be a problem on the American side. We asked the American Civil Liberties Union (ACLU) for assistance—in fact, I was the state representative of the ACLU at the time—but the ACLU, which was very fearful in the McCarthy period, wrote us that under a law passed by Congress in 1949, the post office was entitled to remove the book. Several weeks later the box with the coffee set was delivered to us without the book. A second document indicated some months later that neither the Little Rock nor the Chicago office of the FBI were able to establish that we had any connection to the Communist Party.

The unanimous U. S. Supreme Court decision in *Brown vs. Board of Education,* overturning *Plessy vs. Ferguson,* came on May 17, 1954. I heard of it on the radio at noon at home and was surprised that my students in the class I taught were not more excited. We almost immediately asked for and were granted a meeting with the School Board. The new superintendent assured us that Little Rock would abide by the Supreme Court decision and presented us with a plan for gradual desegregation. Two high schools were currently under construction, Horace Mann on the east side, intended for blacks, and Hall on the west side for whites. Under the new plan, once construction was completed in 1956, both schools, as well as Little Rock Central High School, would no longer have a racial designation. In the fall of 1957, the junior high schools would be desegregated and between 1958 and 1960 the elementary school would be desegregated in three stages. We considered this plan acceptable.

In the spring of 1955 the Supreme Court issued an implementation decision. It set no schedule for the desegregation of the schools, but merely stipulated that this be implemented with "all deliberate speed." In the year since the May 17, 1954 decision there had been little active opposition to the decree. The school board had announced that it would comply, as did the relatively conservative governor of Arkansas, Francis Cherry. However, there were some early signs of opposition. Governors in Arkansas could serve up to two consecutive two-year terms, and normally a win in the Democratic primary—the only one that counted at that time—assured a second term. It was a surprise when Orval Faubus forced Cherry into a runoff and then defeated him. Resistance to desegregation had built throughout the South after the "deliberate speed" decision, and after the so-called White Citizens Councils called for massive resistance and even resort to violence. The Little Rock school board reacted to this changed climate and in the summer of 1955 announced that the new Horace Mann High School, when opened in 1956, would have an all-black faculty, while the teachers at Little Rock Central High School and the new Hall High School would be all white.

In the fall of 1955 Lee Lorch, a well regarded mathematician, joined the Philander Smith faculty. The majority of the white and of the Black faculty remained aloof to the civil rights conflict. Among the white Philander Smith faculty, Wilma and I were the only active white NAACP members prior to Lee's arrival. He had lost his position at City College of New York in 1950 after he and his wife Grace invited a black family to occupy their apartment in Stuyvesant Town, a huge housing project in New York City, owned by the Metropolitan Life Insurance Company, that enjoyed massive financial support from New York City but excluded blacks. (Subsequently the New York City council and then the New York state legislature enacted laws outlawing discrimination in housing. In 1990 the City University of New York apologized for the wrong it had done to Lee forty years earlier, by awarding him an honorary doctorate.) After a one-year appointment at Pennsylvania State University which was not renewed, he obtained a professorship at Fisk University, one of the elite historic African-American universities, in Nashville, Tennessee.

At the beginning of the new school year in 1954, following the Supreme Court decision in *Brown vs. Board of Education,* the Lorches attempted to enroll their daughter Alice in a nearby black school. Shortly thereafter Lee was subpoenaed by the House Un-American Activities Committee. The president of Fisk University warned him that if he refused to cooperate with the committee, he would be fired. Lee refused to admit whether he had ever been a member of the Communist Party, and he also refused to invoke the Fifth Amendment as the committee urged him to do. He was subsequently indicted for contempt of Congress but later acquitted. While he was still under indictment, President Harris appointed him as a full professor at Philander Smith. Harris was a tyrant as far as faculty and students were concerned, but he also had principles. He was willing to stick his neck out politically. He did not have to be afraid of local white pressure because little financial aid came from these sources. He was a member of the Southern Conference Educational Fund in New Orleans, even though it had been repeatedly denounced as a Communist front. He thus had the courage to appoint Lee. A second positive side was his respect for serious scholars on the faculty. After all he had earned a doctorate in philosophy. Unlike most of my colleagues, I was not afraid of his authoritarian and often arbitrary manner. Despite the precarious financial position of the college, he almost always gave me travel money to academic conferences that I considered important for my work. Similarly he was proud to have Lee on the faculty.

Despite our differences on broader political questions—Lee and his wife Grace were relatively close to Communist positions and for instance were little shaken by the Soviet suppression of the Hungarian uprising and by Khrushchev's speech at the 20th Congress of the Soviet Communist Party about Stalin's crimes, shortly after he came to Little Rock. Nevertheless, we agreed almost fully on what should be done in Little Rock. Along with Daisy Bates, president of the Arkansas State Conference of Branches of the NAACP, we worked closely together in the NAACP during this critical period. He was particularly skilled in composing public statements for the local NAACP in reply to illiterate attacks by the White Citizen Councils. The national office of the NAACP, still afraid of being attacked for Communist sympathies, brought pressure on us to exclude Lee from the executive committee, but we did not give in.

The situation about the Little Rock schools became increasingly tense in the fall of 1955 and in the winter of 1956. The School Board announced in the fall that Horace Mann would open at the beginning of the spring term in early February 1956 as an all-black school, Hall school as an all white school, and Little Rock Central High would continue as a white school. This, of course, was totally contrary to the promise the Board had given to us in 1954.

The new so-called Blossom Plan, named after the new superintendent, meant in fact that Black students living west of Little Rock Central High School would have to make a long trip each school day from their homes to the far East Side. We decided on the following strategy: We would ask students who had to pass Central High to seek admission to Central High, and if they were turned down we would take legal action. The task now was to find parents and children who were willing to participate. We formed four teams of two persons each—Wilma, myself, Lee, and Daisy Bates were each members of teams together with black NAACP members who would visit homes in the areas affected. The response was overwhelming. A surprising majority of the families we visited were willing to participate. We had to dissuade several because their jobs were vulnerable.

The plan was for parents and children to meet the morning of the first day of the new school semester at designated places and proceed together to the school. The evening before, we had a final planning meeting at our house. The meeting included Daisy Bates, Lee, Wilma, and myself and several of our executive committee members. President Harris, who knew what we were doing, had become frightened and called to ask that no Philander Smith faculty participate. We decided to go ahead nevertheless and there was no recrimination afterward. We expected approximately twenty-eight children. Word had spread and about eighty came. As we expected, their applications to attend Central High were turned down, and we accordingly decided to bring suit.

However, we had problems finding a lawyer. The local black lawyers either did not want to take on the case or demanded exorbitant fees. Then Wiley Branton, a young African American lawyer from nearby Pine Bluff, offered to take the case for free provided we would find the approximately three hundred dollars he needed for court costs to file the suit. Three hundred dollars was a lot of money for us at the time; we did not have it nor did the treasury of the local NAACP branch. We then did something that had to remain strictly confidential. We wrote to Wilma's relatives in Canada to ask for assistance. We soon had the money, and the suit was filed. Now financial contributions began to flow in from members of the local black community and from sympathetic whites, and the national office of the NAACP took over the case.

Here my direct involvement in the Little Rock case ends. Wilma and I both were entitled to sabbaticals. The amount of money that Philander Smith was prepared to pay, however, was too little for us to live on. Dean Guerdon Nichols at the University of Arkansas in Fayetteville with whom we discussed our situation offered us each part-time appointments, Wilma in German and me in Western Civilization, to supplement our sabbatical salaries from Philander Smith. President Harris had no objection to this arrangement. We repaid the sabbatical money since we did not return to Philander Smith College.

Nichols was a remarkable dean. The University of Arkansas had been a very provincial school before 1945. Nichols took the opportunity to hire promising young émigrés who had escaped from the Nazis, and this strengthened the liberal arts and the social as well as the natural sciences. We had had some contacts with the university since shortly after we arrived at Philander Smith. There were various people there who were active in the Arkansas Council on Human Relations, and Fayetteville had been the first school district in Arkansas in the fall of 1954 to comply with the Supreme Court decision and to desegregate its schools. In the summer of 1956 we left Little Rock for Fayetteville.

This also meant that I had to give up my role as director of the Little Rock Film Society. In the spring of 1953 after the only theater in Little Rock that had shown foreign and art movies closed, I began, together with Johan Eliot, our Quaker friend, to show such movies at the Sam Peck Hotel near the Philander Smith campus. It reflects changing attitudes that the owner of the hotel not only permitted us to show the films there, but also charged us no rent for the use of the hall. I encouraged my students to attend and many of them did, as did many whites. This was the first time in Little Rock that films were shown to an interracial audience. The film society was reviewed positively in the press, and after my departure was taken over by the municipal fine arts museum and remained interracial.

We felt very much at home in Fayetteville. We enjoyed the liberal atmosphere and soon found friends in various departments. One unpleasant problem arose at the beginning. The chair of the history department, Clifton Westermeyer, refused to let me have an office in the department. The reason he gave was that he had not been consulted by Dean Nichols, but it was apparent that he did not approve of my politics. Fortunately, he left fairly soon and my relations with the other members of the department were generally congenial. The small philosophy department was very glad to have me and to give me office space.

During the year in Fayetteville I kept in close contact with the Little Rock branch of the NAACP. The federal courts finally ruled in our case, not quite as we had hoped, with a broad ruling mandating the desegregation of the Little Rock schools, but in a much more limited way, ordering the admission of nine black students to Little Rock Central High School at the beginning of the school year in September 1957. Although the White Citizens Councils threatened violence and the Attorney General of Georgia traveled to Little Rock to urge noncompliance, we expected everything to go smoothly. I flew to Little Rock once more two weeks before the opening of school for a planning meeting. We drove to Little Rock over the Labor Day weekend to say goodbye to friends on our way to New Orleans, where we had accepted positions at Dillard University. No one expected trouble. The headline of the *Arkansas Gazette* on Labor Day was "Little Rock Quiet on Eve of Opening of Integrated Schools." Our last stop was at the Bates'. Their house was barricaded. Bullets had been shot through windows and we met in their basement with our children, who did not understand why we could not meet upstairs. That evening, Labor Day, the day before the schools were to open in Little Rock on Tuesday, September 3, we arrived in New Orleans. We were totally surprised and shocked when we heard on the radio the next morning that Governor Faubus had called out the National Guard to bar the nine students from entering the school.

What happened hit us very deeply. Eight of the students had arrived at the school together; they were unable to reach the ninth student, Elizabeth Eckford, who had no telephone and went by herself. When she arrived outside the school she was surrounded by a threatening mob. Grace Lorch, Lee's wife, who had come to observe, went into the crowd to rescue Elizabeth Eckford, and took her to the nearest bus stop, where she was now surrounded by a host of reporters. Grace then brought Elizabeth home. The next day the story appeared in newspapers throughout the country. Not long afterward Grace was subpoenaed to appear before Senator James Eastland's Internal Security Subcommittee of the Senate Judiciary Committee in nearby Memphis, without being given time to obtain counsel. The subpoena was clearly intended to smear her in the press as a Communist. Now the home of the Lorches became the target of acts of violence. Their daughter Alice, then fourteen years old, was repeatedly insulted and threatened. They nevertheless remained in Little Rock until the end of the academic year and then went to Wesleyan University where Lee had a one-year visiting appointment. At the end of that year, with Lee blacklisted in the United States, they emigrated to Canada, first to the University of Alberta in Edmonton and then to York University in Toronto. Lee had a distinguished career in Canada and became a fellow of the prestigious Royal Canadian Academy of Science.

Governor Faubus' action surprised us, as he had a relatively liberal reputation. He had been in the cabinet of Sid McMath, the governor of Arkansas from 1948 to 1952 who had represented New Deal outlook. During the runoff election for governor in 1954, Cherry, the incumbent governor, accused Faubus of Communist leanings. Cherry charged that Faubus had attended Commonwealth College in Mena, Arkansas, a school where the students paid no fees, had free housing and food, and earned their keep through work, primarily on the agricultural lands of the school. Cherry claimed that the college was Communist sponsored, that Faubus had been elected president of the student body, and that he had given the May Day speech in the related Highlander Folk School in Tennessee. In a TV appearance Faubus admitted that he had attended Commonwealth College, but only for two weeks until he realized the nature of the school. He claimed that he had gone there not knowing anything about the school, because they had offered him a college education which he, coming from a poor family, could not have afforded elsewhere. In the summer of 1964 when I taught a graduate research seminar at the University of Arkansas, I had my students examine the Commonwealth College papers that had just been deposited there. All the charges Cherry made were true except one: the college at the time had no affiliation with the Communist Party, but rather with Norman Thomas' Socialist Party.

It is not surprising that Faubus attended Commonwealth College. He came from Madison County, a predominantly white district with many subsistence farmers. Madison County was also one of six counties in Arkansas that had remained loyal to the Union during the Civil War. Faubus' father was an ardent supporter of the Socialist Party. In his living room hung a photo of Eugene Debs who had preceded Norman Thomas as head of the Socialist Party. It is thus not surprising that the elder Faubus should have sent his son to Commonwealth College. In 1957 Faubus was in his second two-year term as governor. His defiance of the federal government on the matter of desegregation enabled him to mobilize masses of whites of the lower classes, particular in the delta region of east Arkansas, and thereby seize political power from the moderate establishment that favored gradual reform. For several years radical segregationists dominated Arkansas politics, making it possible for Faubus to serve six terms as governor, something only Bill Clinton achieved after him.

The Arkansas legislature, now controlled by radical segregationists, took the opportunity to mete out vengeance against the liberal intellectuals at the state university. So-called Article 10, passed in 1958, required all state employees to list under oath all organizations to which they had belonged. The act was directed less against Communists than against members of the NAACP. Arkansas had been relatively free of the witch-hunts of the McCarthy period, and both U.S. senators from Arkansas, William Fulbright and John McClellan, had opposed McCarthy. Article 10 led to the dismissal of half of the six member philosophy department who refused to sign the required oath, one of them our good friend John McKenney who had worked closely with the Quakers. Another was Fritz Friedmann, a refugee from Nazi Germany and an active Quaker. After hesitating for a year, Friedmann accepted a professorship at the University of Munich where he developed one of the first centers for American Studies in Germany. The liberal *Arkansas Gazette* commented bitterly that someone who had escaped Nazi persecution now had to return to Germany as a result of persecution in Arkansas. The *Arkansas Gazette* with its editor Harry Ashmore had been under considerable attack and threat of boycott because of its pleas for moderation before and during the Little Rock crisis, and was honored with the 1958 Pulitzer Prize for its courageous reporting on the Little Rock school integration crisis. Dean Nichols at the University of Arkansas received a special award from the American Association of University Professors for his unfortunately unsuccessful efforts to protect his faculty against the onslaught of Article 10.

We very much enjoyed the year in Fayetteville. We liked the liberal atmosphere. Fayetteville, at that time was very small with only 18,000 inhabitants (today it has over 60,000 and over 150,000 in the metropolitan area), was a very pleasant community located in a beautiful area in the Ozark mountains, in the northwest corner of the state. The University at the time had only 5,000 students (today it has over 15,000, small enough to know the people in various departments with outlooks similar to ours.) In the mornings I often had coffee in the Student Union at a table where members of the liberal faculty met. Years later, long after we had left, Bill and Hillary Clinton began their careers as teachers in the law school at the university, and regularly joined this circle. We never had an opportunity to meet them, but several of our Fayetteville friends, particularly the Thompsons whom Wilma has mentioned, became friendly with them. During the year in Fayetteville I finally had time for research and writing and completed the revisions of my dissertation on the Saint-Simonians for publication.

Fayetteville had become a second home for us, even after we left. From 1957 until 1964 we spent every summer there except for the two years we were in Europe. My relations with the history department became increasingly cordial after Westermeyer left. I taught as a visiting professor there in the summer of 1964. I had always hoped to teach at a state university in the South where I would have better opportunities for research and teaching in my field, and still be able to be active in civil rights. I had contacts with several Southern universities, including the Universities of Georgia and Florida, but the very reason why I wanted to go there was a reason why they hesitated to hire me. We would have loved to have gone to the University of Arkansas, and Dean Nichols would have backed my appointment. Finally, in the fall of 1966 after we were already settled in Buffalo, I received a phone call from the chair of the history department in Fayetteville offering me a chair. But it was too late; we did not wish to move the children again. At about the same time the University of Florida in Gainesville invited me for three lectures and then offered me a full professorship, which I also declined.

At the end of the academic year in 1957 we were supposed to return to Philander Smith. However, we wanted a lighter teaching load and better research facilities than we had had during the six years we were there. The solution that I would have preferred was a joint appointment at Philander Smith and at the University of Arkansas. As one of the persons in the philosophy department was planning to go on half time, Dean Nichols saw the possibility of a half time appointment for me in the philosophy department. President Harris was willing to cooperate. The plan, however, fell through when the person who was to go on halftime changed his mind.

It was already late summer in 1957 when I began to look for openings elsewhere. Two traditionally African-American colleges, Dillard University in New Orleans and Talladega College in Talladega, Alabama, invited me for interviews. A few days before I left Fayetteville for the interview at Dillard University, I received a letter from Mississippi Southern University in Hattiesburg to the effect that the University of Chicago had informed them that I was looking for a position, and inviting me for an interview. I immediately replied, thanking them for their interest, but explained that my association with the NAACP made an appointment at a state institution in Mississippi impossible. I mentioned in my letter that the following week I would be going by train from New Orleans to Talladega and thus passing through Hattiesburg. I would phone them from New Orleans to ask them whether they indeed still wanted me to stop. I did call them after my interview at Dillard, and to my surprise was told that they wanted me to stop in Hattiesburg. I was met at the station by the department chair and by the dean, who had both done their doctorates in history at the University of North Carolina with Howard K. Beale, very much a liberal on Southern questions and incidentally a member of the Dillard board of trustees. Both assured me that they would very much like to see me appointed, and although I told them that under the political circumstances at the time in Mississippi I did not think that this was possible they asked me for permission to submit my name to the president. A week later I received a very nice letter from the chair informing me that the reason the president did not approve the appointment was because of the unfortunate political circumstances at the time, but that he would have very much wanted me to come.

I had a very pleasant interview at Talladega College, which had a stronger academic program than Philander Smith and a better faculty, that included several German Jewish refugees. The president of Talladega wanted to offer me and Wilma a position. But Talladega seemed even more isolated than Philander Smith, and I turned down the offer, although Wilma would have preferred the small rural college.

When I arrived in New Orleans for my interview at Dillard, John Snell, a young historian from Tulane University, who already had made a name for himself in the field of twentieth-century German history, visited me at the hotel to urge me to accept the offer from Dillard. Snell, who was quite influential in the Tulane liberal arts faculty and a short time later was named dean of the graduate school, assured me that if I came to Dillard, I could regularly teach a graduate course or an advanced undergraduate course at Tulane. Moreover, Professor Albrecht, the chair of the German department, made Wilma a similar offer. At Tulane we also would have access to a good library.

The president of Dillard offered both of us positions. The course load there was fifteen hours a week; we would not be obligated to teach summer school. Unlike

Philander Smith, where I had taught history, languages and political science, at Dillard I would only teach history, including the introductory American history course. I was very interested in teaching this course, because it would give me the opportunity to acquaint the students, who had only been exposed to the official Southern version of history, with alternative, problem oriented interpretations.

Dillard differed from Philander Smith in various ways. Supported by the liberal Congregationalist as well as by the white Methodist Church, it had higher social and academic ambitions. The students came predominantly from the black middle class in New Orleans. They were academically better prepared, and the credentials of the black faculty were on the average more impressive than at Philander Smith. The school was located on a beautiful campus with white, Grecian style buildings in a large, park-like area.

Meanwhile, the unrest in Little Rock continued. People in New Orleans told us that we should be glad that we were not there. New Orleans thought of itself as cosmopolitan and liberal in contrast to provincial, racist Little Rock. We saw it differently. In Little Rock the white establishment, counting on the support of a significant part of the white middle class, had been prepared to take the first steps toward desegregation. Many of the white lower class objected to desegregation, because they feared that large numbers of black students would be accepted in their schools. In the school board elections in Little Rock, voting participation by the white lower class had until then been low. Many of the people who demonstrated at Little Rock Central High School to oppose integration did not come from the city, but rather from the rural areas in the southeast section of the state and from neighboring states.

As far as relationships between blacks and whites were concerned, New Orleans seemed to us much more backward than Little Rock. New Orleans and Louisiana generally were still very much part of the Deep South in their racial attitudes, while in the course of badly needed economic modernization, Little Rock and the western parts of Arkansas were prepared to gradually remove racial barriers.

Soon after my arrival in New Orleans I was named chair of the education committee of the local branch of the NAACP. The situation there proved to be considerably more difficult than in Little Rock. In New Orleans a discussion with the school board was unthinkable. The school board had to be forced, through a long process of legal actions, to finally admit five black girls into the first grade at two elementary schools in November of 1960. One of the girls was soon expelled because she turned out to have been born out of wedlock. The state of Louisiana banned the NAACP, an action which, however, was soon declared unconstitutional. While the case was still pending, the state of Louisiana persecuted the NAACP with arrests and house searches. The arrests included two white lawyers who had given legal assistance to the NAACP. The state legislature created a Committee for Un-American Activities, which harassed pro-integration activists. My name, I was told, also appears in the committee's files. The local branch of the NAACP at that time continued to work illegally under the name "The New Orleans Improvement League."

My first major project as chair of the education committee in New Orleans concerned the admission of blacks into the public Benjamin Franklin High School. It had been founded recently by the school board as a school for gifted students. An IQ of 130 and excellent grades were required. We thought that that was a good place to begin desegregating the schools. The school board turned our first request down, claiming that there are no blacks with an IQ of 130. This simply was not true. Together with a young black postal worker, Llewelyn Soniat, who was president of the youth chapter of the NAACP, I began to search for such students. We were supported by the predominantly white Louisiana chapter of the ACLU (American Civil Liberties Union) and its distinguished lawyer George Dreyfous. His sister, a respected school psychologist, offered to test the children. The interest among black parents and children was great. A considerable number of children passed the test and applied for admission to Benjamin Franklin School. As expected, they were turned down. The local NAACP and the state chapter of the ACLU were about to file the suit, when a telegram came from Thurgood Marshall, the chief lawyer for the national NAACP, advising against the law suit for strategic reasons, because the central NAACP did not want a partial integration that was limited to just one locality.

We attended various synagogues without joining one or wanting to join. Our sons Jeremy and Daniel went once or twice a week to the New Orleans Community Hebrew School, which was maintained by congregations of all orientations, Orthodox, Conservative and Reform, and where Jeremy received good basic training in Hebrew and Jewish religion. Dan was younger and unfortunately profited from it a good deal less. Off and on we also attended a Unitarian service. The church, which was founded in the 1820s, was one of the oldest in New Orleans. Against the opposition of a conservative minority, the minister insisted that blacks be able to become full-fledged members.

I attended the weekly luncheons of the Frontiers of America, where leading black personalities met to discuss the situation in New Orleans. One of them was Ernest Morial, the lawyer who later became the first black mayor of New Orleans. I was the only white person in this circle. The luncheons took place in the black Dooky Chase restaurant, even though, according to the laws of Louisiana, as a white person I was forbidden to enter the restaurant. Sometimes I brought along German journalists who were very impressed by the discussions.

One of the first evenings in New Orleans I accompanied Wilma and the children to Tulane University. I left her the car and took the streetcar back. We changed on Canal Street and sat down in the last row of seats, where there was room for all of us. In Little Rock, segregation on public carriers had been abolished, and I had forgotten that this was not yet the case in New Orleans. With the children—Jonathan was not yet two—and without witnesses I had not intended to test the law. But when the driver stopped the streetcar and asked me to go to the front, I told him that this violated federal law and remained seated. The streetcar remained standing in the middle of the traffic until two matronly police women came and led me away. They did not arrest me, but left us standing in the street and only asked me if I would not feel better with my own people.

Since the schools were still segregated by race, our children were bused to the closest white school several miles away. An empty bus picked up Jeremy and Dan, who was only in the first grade, in the morning and returned at noon with Dan only, and then drove some distance to a white neighbourhood, where other children gradually filled the bus. At noon the bus arrived at Dillard University with Dan, who as a first grader had only half a day of school, as the only passenger, and in midafternoon again, this time with Jeremy as the only passenger. One of the main arguments of the segregationists against desegregation was that it involved the massive bussing of children away from their neighborhoods. But in fact, a very large number of schoolchildren were bussed in New Orleans to keep the schools segregated.

The connection with Tulane was of great benefit to us. Not only did we have a good library at our disposal, but we also had contact with colleagues in the social sciences and the humanities. My relationship with the history department, however, was problematic. Tulane considered itself very much of a Southern institution, the Harvard of the South, as they liked to call themselves. The sociologists, political scientists, and philosophers with whom I had contact all had liberal attitudes on the race question, or at least moderate ones. This was also true of some of my colleagues in the history department, which was deeply split. The department's largest single program was in Southern history with a particular emphasis on the ante-bellum period. The historians of the South, including the chairman Hogan, were all defenders of the old ways and emphatically racist. On the other hand Snell, who was a moderate, had considerable influence with the administration. The year I came to Dillard, Robert Reinders, who had worked on the history of free blacks in New Orleans in the decades immediately preceding the Civil War, was brought to Tulane from black Xavier University in New Orleans. He directed an M.A. thesis by Hugh Murray, a New Orleans native, on the Scottsboro boys, the seven blacks who had been wrongfully sentenced to death in the 1930s for allegedly having gang-raped two white women. Murray made himself unpopular among the historians at Tulane because of his involvement in the sit-ins in 1960. Incidentally, he came frequently to my classes at Dillard. Reinders also came under pressure for his views on race and decided after spending a year as a Fulbright teacher in England not to return to Tulane but to stay in England.

As Snell had promised, I taught a course at Tulane every semester while I was in New Orleans. However, when the department sought to fill an appointment in modern European history, I was not even considered.

I enjoyed teaching the American history survey at Dillard. I had never taken a course in American history and learned a lot while preparing for the classes. I supplemented the textbook readings for each period of American history with Rayford Logan's useful small collections of documents on American black history. I also used the Heath series of Problems in American History with its presentation of differing interpretations of selected topics in American history. A major focus of my classes was the Reconstruction. The students only knew the official account they had been taught in the Louisiana high schools, according to which Reconstruction was a tragic period when Northerners used Blacks, who were unable to govern, to impose their will on a helpless South. We read John Randall's chapter on the South Carolina legislature in his *Civil War and Reconstruction,* in which he expounds this thesis, and W. E. B. DuBois' *Black Reconstruction* describing the positive achievements of Blacks in the South Carolina legislature, who succeeded in finally bringing that state into the nineteenth century. I also taught a course "The World Since 1918," both at Dillard and at Tulane. Tulane at the time was still lily-white. I succeeded in bringing my Dillard and Tulane students together once a semester at Dillard for a session when I taught the course. Several of the Tulane historians were unhappy about this, but almost all of my Tulane students came.

Chapter 5

RETURN TO EUROPE (1960–1962)

GEORG

For the summer of 1960 I received a stipend from the American Philosophical Society to work on the Enfantin archive in the Bibliothèque de l'Arsenal, which contains the most important Saint Simonian sources. I had decided to spend the summer in Paris alone, because it would have been too costly for all of us. But when I received an additional stipend from the Guggenheim Foundation for a whole year, we were able go to France together. The Guggenheim was intended for a stay in Germany from September on. Rents in Paris were too expensive, but fortunately we found a little house in Le Mée, a small village on the Seine near Melun, with good train connections. From there I regularly visited libraries in Paris.

Although we always wanted the same professional chances for both of us, Wilma in Le Mée was busier with children and household than ever before or after. I worked on two projects simultaneously. One was my work on the Saint-Simonians, which I wanted to finish. The other, for which I had received the Guggenheim fellowship, was a study of the decline of the idea of progress in the nineteenth century. This larger study was related to my interest in the Saint-Simonians. I was interested in the connection between the idea of progress and cultural pessimism. In preparation for that I had in 1958 published an article in the *Journal of Modern History* about Oswald Spengler, Arnold Toynbee, and the nineteenth century Russian cultural philosopher Nikolai Danilewski, about the comparative intercultural direction of these thinkers who all lacked an empirical foundation. I had spent the summer of 1958 with a small stipend at the University of Michigan and read theoretical discussions about historiography. At that time I also began to write abstracts of articles in the *Annales* for the newly founded journal *Historical*

Abstracts. I was very much impressed by Geoffrey Barraclough's *History in a Changing World* (1956). I also read historiographical and social science literature—Ernst Troeltsch, Max Weber, Friedrich Meinecke and Wilhelm Dilthey. I was struck by how differently Leopold von Ranke was understood in Germany and America in the nineteenth century. In Germany, his rootedness in the tradition of German idealism was emphasized. In America, on the other hand, he was celebrated as the father of scientific historiography and in 1885, one year before his death, was elected the first honorary member of the newly founded American Historical Association. In America, he was considered a positivist, who had freed historiography from philosophy and had, by his rigorous critique of sources, given it its scientific character. This resulted in my article about the different views of Ranke in Germany and America, which appeared in 1962 in the new journal, *History and Theory*.

By chance I met my friend from Chicago, John Day, who was living in Paris. John introduced me to several interesting historians and philosophers. We went to lectures of Fernand Braudel at the Collège de France. Braudel was already well-known because of his great book about the Mediterranean, in which he was less concerned with events and persons than with structures and processes that extended over longer periods of time. Like his teachers Marc Bloch and Lucien Febvre, Braudel was interested in a historiography that deals with the manifold aspects of life. What was also unique about his historiography was that he no longer presented history as a running master narrative, but was very conscious of the breaks and discontinuities in history. After Febvre's death Braudel was the leading scholarly personality around the *Annales*, which had been founded in 1929 by Bloch and Febvre as a social and cultural historical alternative to the traditional historiography dealing with states, the military, and diplomacy. Under Braudel's leadership the so-called Sixth Section of the *Ecole Pratique des Hautes Etudes* was founded, where not only scholars in the social sciences and humanities and historians, but also economists, sociologists, demographers, ethnologists, psychologists, psychoanalysts, and historians of literature and of art worked together to lay the foundations for a science of man.

In 1960 Braudel was not yet as well-known as he was later, and at his lectures at the Collège de France rarely more than a dozen listeners were present. He would sometimes invite John Day and me after his lectures to a café, and so I discussed my projects with him. I also met repeatedly with Robert Mandrou, at that time Braudel's closest co-worker, who in his writings about early capitalism had shown the close connection between economic history and mentalities. John and I also attended lectures by Lucien Goldmann, a student of Georg Lukácz from Hungary, which introduced me to an open, Marxist cultural criticism, similar to that of the Frankfurt School.

In the fall of 1960 I went to England for a week, in order to discuss my central projects. In Cambridge I visited Herbert Butterfield, whose two books *The Whig Interpretation of History*, which criticizes the optimism and the smugness of classical English historiography, and *Man on His Past*, which placed the development of modern historical science in the tradition of the Göttingen historians of the eighteenth century, were of critical importance for my work. But most of all, I was interested in Sir Isaiah Berlin and Karl Popper. Like them, I saw myself as a liberal, for whom the protection of individual liberty against arbitrary states was of primary importance. From that perspective I could largely identify with Berlin's small book, *Two Concepts of Liberty,* which was published about that time. On the other hand I was a liberal more in the American than in the European sense and believed, unlike Popper, that the state should play an active role in order to guarantee social justice, and that it could do that without infringing on citizens' rights. Like Popper and Berlin I was aware of the dangers inherent in speculative philosophies of history like those of Hegel and Marx, but I did not give up my faith in the possibility of an empirical social or historical science that would work with limited hypotheses and theories.

Although at that time I was a totally unknown historian at a totally unknown Black college, Butterfield, Berlin and Popper received me very cordially and were willing to discuss my in many ways half-baked projects with me. Popper spent with me an entire afternoon in his office at the London School of Economics, Berlin a whole evening at All Souls College and then accompanied me to the station at midnight. As I found out only recently, Popper wrote a very positive report about our discussion to Friedrich Hayek, whose rejection of a social welfare state I certainly did not share. Popper probably misunderstood me. My closer contact with Geoffrey Barraclough, Toynbee's successor at the Royal Institute of International Affairs in London, lasted for many years.

There were three more historians with whom I discussed my project. In Utrecht I visited Pieter Geyl, a sharp critic of Toynbee, and Gerhard Ritter, the nestor of the German historical profession during the first two decades after the Second World War in Freiburg. Ritter, whom I had met at a lecture he gave in New Orleans, was an archconservative who had been a member of the Kreisau circle of resistance against Hitler around Carl Goerdeler. I did not agree with Ritter's central thesis that the roots of National Socialism were not to be found in specifically German traditions or in a lack of democracy, but in an excess of democracy. Ritter saw National Socialism as a product of the general European development that had its roots in the French Revolution. Like Rothfels he believed that the only real resistance had come from conservative, nationalistic circles, which for the most part had consisted of officers and aristocrats, most of whom had been believing Christians, who only with a heavy heart had participated in the plot against Hitler. In his view, the communists of the "Rote Kapelle" were traitors who deserved to be shot summarily.

In spite of our differences, we were able to have a frank discussion. Ritter had said in the *Historische Zeitschrift* that historians should reevaluate their narrow concentration on the history of events and pay more attention to social aspects. At that time I was not yet aware of his article in which he accused the *Annales* of "historical materialism" because they ascribed to social and economic factors a great, although not exclusive, role. This article marked his return to the methodological premises of traditional German historiography. His bitter controversy with the historian Fritz Fischer about the responsibility of Germany for the First World War had not yet taken place. Ritter's reaction in a letter to me in 1963 to an article I had sent him and in which I had expressed my regret of German academic history's neglect of social history, was friendly but critical. After all, Marx and Weber were also Germans, he wrote.

I absolutely wanted to meet Othmar Anderle, who at that time was almost unknown and now is totally forgotten. He had published an essay, "Theoretical History. Observations about the Crisis in the Foundations of Historical Science," in the *Historische Zeitschrift*. There he referred to Barraclough and to the Dutch historian Jan Romein who had emphasized that a highly specialized historiography by historians for historians no longer met the mid-twentieth century demands. Empirical research was not to be separated from theoretical questions. "Historical science must be capable of expressing itself in an understandable form that corresponds to the scientific standards of our time." And: "Here theoretical history is given the task to push forward as far as the principle of verification allows." I had already written Anderle from New Orleans, and he invited me to visit him in Salzburg, where he was about to found an institute for theoretical history. I had considered spending my Guggenheim year if possible at that institute, but at that time it only consisted of Anderle and had neither a building nor a library. He invited me to a conference that he planned for fall 1961 in Salzburg, which Toynbee and the American sociologist and philosopher of history, Pitirim Sorokin, had agreed to attend.

Early in May 1961 we started out for Göttingen. We had been in Germany once before. In the summer of 1952 we had flown to Germany with ten month old Jeremy, and had taken along a supply of baby food and disposable diapers for the whole six weeks. From the airport in Shannon we had gone by bus through green, backward, but very friendly Ireland to England where we visited relatives.

Our first stop on the continent in 1952 was Hamburg. We succeeded in tracking down and visiting my grade schoolteacher Fritz Pohle from Knauerstrasse. He remembered me well. He had made a big impression on me as a teacher influenced by the youth movement. Now he seemed petit bourgeois. The conversation, also with his wife, was friendly but empty. Of course in 1952 the time had not yet come to ask questions about the Nazi period, so we probably did not ask the right questions.

The day of our arrival in Hamburg we found out that the next afternoon a monument for the civilian victims of the bombing attacks on Hamburg was to be dedicated. We were anxious to know what we would hear there, and were pleasantly surprised. We went by streetcar through Barmbeck, which was still largely in ruins. Facades of six- and seven story houses protruded grotesquely over the devastation. Much more had been destroyed in that formerly working class neighborhood than in bourgeois Eppendorf. The British attempt to break the morale of the population through bombing of civilian districts had been just as counterproductive as in London in 1940. The main speaker at the Ohlsdorf cemetery was Max Brauer, the mayor of Hamburg, who had been mayor of Altona until 1933 and, after being released from prison, had spent the Nazi years in exile. He emphasized that the bombing of Hamburg had been preceded by the destruction of Warsaw, Rotterdam, and Coventry by the German Luftwaffe, and spoke of the expulsion and murder of the Hamburg Jews. In 1943, when the bombs fell on Hamburg, most of the inhabitants had been powerless, but many of them shared in the guilt of the Nazi regime by their support of the Nazis in 1933. We had not expected such frank language. Later we spoke with several people who agreed with Brauer.

The next morning I visited a history class in a *Gymnasium* in the St. Georg district of Hamburg. The teacher, with whom I had a fairly long discussion, had been a student of the liberal Catholic historian Franz Schnabel, who had been forbidden to write and teach during the Nazi period. He made a very good impression on me. On the other hand, the owner of the bed and breakfast place where we stayed asked me if I would have been prepared to fight against Germany. She refused to accept the fact that Germany had been wrong.

In Hamburg we had a horrible experience. Ulla, the daughter of a sister of my mother's lived there. Her mother had been married to a man of whom my parents had told that he had joined the Nazi party. My aunt broke off all contact with her Jewish family and managed to survive the war. My English relatives had suggested that we contact Ulla, since she was, after all, not responsible for her parents. When we visited her, she, in contrast to most of the Germans we met, spoke about "how we Germans suffered." In her living room she had a picture of a young man in Wehrmacht uniform. Although we were going to leave very early the next day, she insisted on having breakfast with us at six o'clock in the morning in our pension and accompanying us to the train station. We carried our baggage; Ulla carried Jeremy. We thought nothing of Ulla hurrying in the wrong direction in the station and called her back. However, when we arrived at the counter, Ulla had disappeared with Jeremy. After Wilma had looked for her in the toilet and had her name called out, I went to the police. The policemen were neither friendly nor helpful and told us to check in Ulla's apartment. Finally she appeared with Jeremy and claimed that she had stood behind a pillar the whole time. By then our train had left. We were speechless and asked ourselves why we had gone to Germany. We can only speculate about what Ulla's reasons had been.

Our next stay was in Schluchsee in the Black Forest at a conference of Esperantists. It took place in a large house that was used for international meetings that formerly had belonged to a Jewish family and then to Martin Bormann, Hitler's adjutant. We could choose between two cradles: a plain one or one with an ornate rim of swastikas. We chose the simple one. From Freiburg, which was still in ruins, we went to Regensburg, where we met Wilma's father and a number of friends and acquaintances from Bischofteinitz /Horsovský Týn. She had the impression that difficult topics were largely avoided. The main emphasis was on the joy of meeting again, and not on the terrible things in the past.

Although people were generally friendly during our visit in 1952, we realized that only a few years earlier our lives would have been in danger. An event that proved to us that not everything was well was the trial of Phillip Auerbach, the chair of the Jewish community in Munich, who was convicted by former Nazi judges for allegedly passing on money illegally to displaced persons. Auerbach committed suicide in jail. Many years later he was exonerated by a different German court.

We arrived in Göttingen in early May of 1961, on the very day when the trial of Adolf Eichmann began in Jerusalem. We came not without apprehension, since we were a Jewish family with three young children. Nevertheless we were not really worried, and I even looked forward to returning to Germany with which I had so many cultural and intellectual ties. In many ways my views about the involvement of Germans in the Nazi regime of terror and in their attitudes after the war were naïve. On the basis of my childhood experiences I believed that most Germans had not been Nazis, but had been forced to conform in view of the terror, and that they did not approve of the crimes perpetrated by the regime insofar as they knew about them. We were received very cordially in Göttingen and met people who for us represented a better Germany.

The year 1961 was a turning point in the way the German past was treated. During the Adenauer period, the German public largely refrained from speaking about the Holocaust. The government of Konrad Adenauer, however, enacted compensation for the Jewish victims of the Nazi regime and paid reparations to Israel, but included persons in the cabinet who had occupied official positions under the Nazis, such as Hans Globke, who had played a central role in the formulation of the Nuremberg racial laws of 1935, which stripped Jews of almost all civil rights, and Theodor Oberländer, who was involved in ethnic cleansing in the East and suspected of direct participation in massacres of Jews in Poland. Oberländer's ministry of Displaced Persons, Refugees, and War Victims in the Adenauer government sponsored the large-scale documentation of the expulsion of Germans from Eastern Europe in the aftermath of the war, which stressed the fact that Germans had also been victims. One of the editors of this study was Hans Rothfels, who paid little attention to what had happened to the Jews. Adenauer obviously wanted to integrate former Nazis into the democratic Federal Republic and to come to terms with its former enemies, the Western democracies, and thus to prevent a repetition of what had happened in the Weimar Republic to which many Germans, possibly a majority, had been bitterly opposed. With the threat of the Soviet Union, cooperating with the Western democracies now seemed to be an unavoidable choice. However, in the 1950s, the conservative political parties, and to an extent the Adenauer government, spoke about how Germany had suffered from the Western bombings of its cities and from the brutality of the Red Army, not about the crimes committed by the Germans. We were only dimly aware of this when we came to Göttingen in 1961.

A noticeable shift of outlook was taking place, as a younger generation appeared on the scene. We had the impression that those who bore the greatest responsibility for what happened felt little guilt, while those who had opposed the Nazis as well as the new generation who had been too young to share responsibility felt most guilty.

Every evening during prime time, the television news reported on the Eichmann trial in Jerusalem. Of course, some, even many Germans, put the blame for what happened on the Nazi leadership and believed that most Germans were innocent. The news reports were accompanied by an excellent thirteen part series, "A Nation on Trial" *(Eine Nation steht vor Gericht),* which tried to show that the Nazi regime had deep roots in German history. From then on and until now German public television has consistently reminded the German public of the criminal nature of the Nazi regime and of the persecution of the Jews. At about this time in 1961 Fischer's *Germany's Aims in the First World War* (German: *Deutschlands Griff nach der Weltmacht*), assigned to Germany a major responsibility for the outbreak of the First World War. Until then most Germans had conceded that Germany had launched the Second World War, but believed that all the European powers had been equally responsible for the failure of the alliance system in 1914. Fischer argued that Germany's aim in the First World War for the domination of Europe and beyond foreshadowed the expansionist policies of Germany in the Second World War and had roots in Germany's incomplete democratization which permitted industry, older social elites, and the military to influence German policies. Fischer's book was highly controversial at first, but was soon taken seriously by a younger generation of historians who no longer saw Otto von Bismarck's unification of Prussia under the Hohenzollern monarchy as a high point in German history, but as an unfortunate move that led to the German catastrophes of the first half of the twentieth century. Thus the years following our arrival in Göttingen saw the beginning of a process of rethinking in Germany.

In Göttingen, we tried to establish contacts with the university. I had read three paperbacks that had come out in the Kleine Vandenhoeck Reihe dealing with historical theory: Reinhard Wittram's *Das Interesse an der Geschichte* (The Interest in History), Hermann Heimpel's *Kapitulation vor der Geschichte* (Capitulating in Front of History), and Alfred Heuss's *Der Verlust der Geschichte.* (The Loss of History). I had visited Wittram in September 1960, when I was in Göttingen looking for an apartment, and attended his seminars at his invitation. In his Vandenhoeck publication as well as in an essay, "Das Faktum und der Mensch," in the *Historische Zeitschrift* in 1958, he had questioned various principles of traditional historiography, among them Johann Gustav Droysen's idea of the existence of "moral forces" in history. In agreement with Paul Tillich, one of the first non-Jewish professors dismissed by the Nazis in 1933, he wrote that "the state is no person," and that the nameless, the anonymous, must no longer be neglected, and therefore a social and structural history was needed. Those were also my views, but I wondered to what extent they were evident in Wittram's own historical writing, such as his biography of Peter the Great. He was the only Göttingen historian with whom I had contact at that time and who spoke relatively openly about his past during National Socialism. He had been rector of the "Reichsuniversität Posen." His writings from that time, which dealt with the Baltic countries, were emphatically racist (völkisch). He admitted his mistakes, which he ascribed in part to his Baltic background and to his fear of the threat of Soviet communism, and stressed his Christian view of "man created by God" as the focal point of history.

I also soon met Hermann Heimpel, the first director of the Max Planck Institute for History, which had been founded in 1955. He invited me to use the institute. Although I never had any official connection with it, I have always felt welcome there during the more than forty years since then. The institute with its library and scholars who came from many sectors of the discipline and many geographic areas, became increasingly important for me. In recent years there has been a fair amount of research into Heimpel's Nazi past, but back then he was considered a good democrat. In 1956, he had been discussed seriously as a candidate for the presidency of the Federal Republic, to succeed Theodor Heuss. His wife Elisabeth attended the meetings of the Society for Christian-Jewish cooperation. She was a scholar herself, had written a dissertation during the Weimar period about the Enlightenment, and when we met, was co-editor of the outspokenly liberal journal *Die Sammlung.* (Collection). Heimpel's well-attended lectures were always rhetorical masterpieces, but continued to be very nationally oriented. It was his ambition to write a great German national history from its Germanic beginnings until the present. His historical writings had never been *völkisch,* but continued to be predominantly political and church history, in which social aspects were secondary. When Heimpel finally completed the work in 1970, it was so badly out of date that it was not published.

Although Percy Ernst Schramm had visited us in New Orleans in our apartment, we had almost no contact with him. He was friendly and saw to it that I could use the history departmental library. His lectures may have been even better attended than Heimpel's. I knew him as the historian of the Hanseatic League and as the writer of the diary of the high command of the Wehrmacht during the war, which obviously would not have been possible if he had not been on good terms with the Nazis.

In 1959 and 1960 we frequently had German visitors who wanted to learn first hand about the racial situation in New Orleans. Schramm had only been interested in one thing: New Orleans is located between the Mississippi and Lake Pontchartrain, and Schramm wanted me to accompany him to the lake. He had never understood why the English in February of 1815, when they were defeated in the Battle of New Orleans by the American troops under Andrew Jackson, had attacked the city from the Mississippi and not from Lake Pontchartrain.

We also knew Alfred Heuss, who published the *Propyläen History of the World* together with Golo Mann. Heuss would pick me up regularly on Sunday mornings to go for walks in the woods. I not only knew the little book he had published with Vandenhoeck, but also his biography of Theodor Mommsen. To me he seemed like an old liberal who sympathized with my critical view of classical German historiography. Heuss also invited us several times to his house. We had heard that during National Socialism he had never made concessions to racism or to anti-Semitism. Later our relationship became more distant. I also was a liberal, but there were many differences in our views. Heuss, who insisted on the privileges of the "Ordinarien" (full professors), turned out to be one of the emphatic opponents of the protesting students in the late sixties, and had little sympathy for the critical social history of the Bielefeld School of historical social science, with which I identified in the seventies.

From the perspective of the turn of the twenty-first century it seems strange how little was spoken about the Nazi past at that time. We knew something about people like Wittram, Heimpel and Schramm, but not exactly what role they played under National Socialism. Only when the archives in the former GDR were opened in the nineties did one learn more. One also did not ask many questions. Suddenly all were democrats and had opposed the persecution of the Jews under the Nazis. Gerhard Ritter and Hans Rothfels who remained very nationalistic, after 1945, asserted that the German historians with few exceptions had remained loyal to the principles of scholarship and had kept their distance from National Socialism, which with many had not been the case. I had not been aware of how close the majority of German historians had been to National Socialism.

Through Wittram we came to know his assistant Rudolf von Thadden and his wife Wiebke, who are still among our best friends. At that time von Thadden was not yet thirty. He and Ernst Schulin, who had just received his doctorate in Göttingen, were among the few historians we knew at that time who were seriously concerned about the German past. Von Thadden at the age of thirteen in 1945 had been forced to leave his parents' Pomeranian estate. He came from a conservative Protestant family that had suffered under the Nazis. His father was involved in the oppositional Confessional Church and had spent some time in prison, and his father's sister was executed. After 1945, his father was elected first president of the Lutheran Church Council. Von Thadden attended a lycée in Geneva, where he learned fluent French, which served him in good stead in his lifelong work promoting German-French understanding. Our friendship with both von Thaddens contributed much to our feeling at home in Germany.

On von Thadden's suggestion we took part in the conference of the Ranke Society in the fall of 1961 in Mainz. The reader may wonder why we or von Thadden went there. The Ranke Society was a very conservative outfit, founded by historians such as Adolf Rein, Günther Franz, and Erwin Hölzle, who had played an active role in Nazi historiography and had basically not changed their outlook. The background of the conference was that Helmuth Plessner had just republished his *Die verspätete Nation* (The Belated Nation), on how the cultured German middle classes succumbed to the seduction of the Nazis. In the book, which originally appeared in 1935 while he was in exile in the Netherlands, he saw the roots of National Socialism in the failure of democratization as it had taken place in other west- and north-European states. Plessner's book constituted one of the first important formulations of a German *Sonderwegsthese,* the thesis that Germany developed differently from other Western industrial societies that moved toward democracy. The Ranke Society had invited Plessner to discuss his theses about German history.

Von Thadden also took me along to a discussion group organized by Wittram, which met regularly at the university, in order to discuss questions of historical theory, in which the well known legal historian Franz Wieacker took part. One lively exchange I had with Wittram concerned the ethical justification of slavery in earlier societies. While he insisted that every age has to be judged by its own standards, and that one therefore must not condemn the institution of slavery either in Greek and Roman antiquity or in other cultures, my position was that there are unchangeable human rights that are valid at all times.

The question that occupied me was how conceptions of history affected attitudes in regard to human rights. This was the guiding motif of the book on which I was working at that time. My work about the decline of the idea of progress in the nineteenth and twentieth centuries had led to a critical analysis of historicism in German historical thinking. I had begun reading about the theoretical discussions in Germany. While German historicism from Ranke and Droysen to Meinecke rejected the idea of progress as schematic, and emphasized the uniqueness or individuality of every epoch, it was based on a powerful optimism regarding history that saw in every period "moral energies" (Von Ranke) and "moral forces" (Droysen) at work, and saw the European world of the nineteenth century as the climax of historical development.

My book was not conceived as a history of German historical science, as the title chosen by the publisher for the German translation suggests, but as a critical investigation of the basic theoretical premises of the main current of German historiography. Very much like Plessner I saw a development of political thinking in this line of tradition, which deviated from the Enlightenment idea of natural law. While Meinecke viewed this turn away from natural law positively, as the highest stage reached in the understanding of things human, and gave German intellectual tradition credit for this achievement, I saw this repudiation of Enlightenment values of rationality and human rights as a dangerous loss. The focus of my book, on which I was working in Göttingen, is the crisis of German liberalism. In the critical times of the so-called wars of liberation, 1813–15, the revolution of 1849, of the Prussian constitutional conflict of 1862–66, the establishment of the Empire in 1871 and Bismarck's turn to conservatism in 1878, the majority of the liberals again and again sacrificed their principles in favor of creating a powerful German national state. The idea that a powerful state incorporated the moral values of the nation played a central role in the thinking of the German historians. Later, my book was misunderstood as an attempt to draw a straight line from von Ranke or even from Johann Gottfried Herder to Hitler. That was not my intention. I had not yet written the section about the historians under National Socialism that I wrote for the German edition that appeared in 1971. I wanted to show that the ultra-nationalistic ideology of German historicism with its emphasis on political power outlined a road which did not predetermine the rise of the Nazis, but did make it more acceptable for many Germans.

In Göttingen I developed a daily routine. Every morning I took a bus into town with our son Jeremy, who attended the Max Planck Gymnasium. Then, I sat in a bakery and read or talked with an Indiologist who was always there until the library opened at nine o'clock. I spent most of the day in the typing room of the library or in the "Dozentenzimmer" where Wilma and I had shelves for the books on which we were working. At noon Jeremy often had lunch with me before he went home.

At that time the University library, where I found almost all the literature I needed, was more important for me than the Max Planck Institute. This gradually changed. In the spring of 1962, Dietrich Gerhard became associate director of modern history of the Max Planck Institute. I struck up a friendship with him and his wife Grete, which lasted until his death in 1985. He conducted a major comparative project concerning feudal estates in Europe before the French Revolution, for which he recruited promising younger historians. Although he came from a very different historiographical tradition than Fernand Braudel, he also wanted to move away from a narrative history of events to an analysis of social and intellectual structures during long historical periods, in Braudel's term "longue durée," "Old Europe", as he called it, which lasted from the late Middle Ages to the upheavals of the late eighteenth and early nineteenth centuries.

One of our closest friends was the philosopher Hermann Wein. He was an outsider in his department, which was mostly interested in analytic philosophy. He came to Göttingen as Nikolai Hartmann's assistant. Wein felt very humiliated because he was shunned by his colleagues and never received a full professorship. He was interested in the turn away from Cartesian rationalism in continental European philosophy since the Enlightenment. His main interest was the growing cultural pessimism in the nineteenth and twentieth centuries, which was also of crucial importance for my work. A group of up to forty students met in his seminar, where he dealt with Hegel, Marx, Friedrich Nietzsche, Jean Paul Sartre, Albert Camus and nihilism as intellectual movements. There I also presented my project for discussion.

Although Wein was rather conservative in his lifestyle and his political and social outlook, many students from the new student movement came to his seminars and formed the core of a circle that continued for years. Wein was the only philosopher in Göttingen who conducted seminars that were of increasing importance in the restless years that followed.

We developed a friendship with the Weins that included our children and that continued after he took early retirement and moved with his family to his early sixteenth-century farmhouse in his native Bavaria, where we visited them frequently, as did some of his students.

In the fall of 1962 I received an offer of an associate professorship from Roosevelt University in Chicago. It would have meant a better salary, twelve hours of teaching instead of the fifteen at Dillard, and all in modern European history.

Roosevelt University had been founded in 1945 when George Williams College, then associated with the YMCA, had refused to admit black students. The president and the majority of the students left the college in protest and founded a new college, which was named after President Franklin Delano Roosevelt who had just died. A Chicago philanthropist donated to the college the famous Auditorium Building on Michigan Avenue, that was designed by the architect Louis Henry Sullivan. It was a ten-story building that housed the whole college. For me it was important that the student body reflected the composition of the population of Chicago, and that many classes took place in the evening in order to accommodate students who had daytime jobs. I also liked Jack Roth, the chair of the history department, whom I had known when I was a student at the University of Chicago. Roth was eager to employ young, recent Ph.D.'s. Roosevelt University would have been a challenge for me, and I would be able to work with a multiethnic student body. However, I turned down the offer. We did not want to leave the South during this critical phase in the civil rights struggle, and we returned to New Orleans in the middle of August.

WILMA

Unlike Americans who lived in Paris we soon felt at home in Le Mée. We were fortunate to have the Dejaegers as neighbors. They both were teachers, Protestants, and members of the Parti Socialiste Unifié of Mendès-France, which had split from the Socialist Party during the Algerian war. Our landlady, Renée Bonnet, was secretary of the League for Human Rights for the Departement Seine et Marne. They took us along on excursions of Amitié et Nature, which, also because of their opposition to the Algerian war, had split from Amis de la Nature. We soon had a variety of friends. There was the very cultured German Jewish couple, the Herzfelds in Larchant near Nemours, the enthusiastic Krausian Madame Kohn from Vienna in Maisons-Laffitte and her husband and finally John Day, Georg's friend from his Chicago days, a wonderful human being who remained his friend until his death in 2003. Jeremy and Danny started going to an all-day summer camp almost as soon as we arrived, and learned French very quickly.

Jeremy attended the grade school in the village. At first the teacher at first did not want to admit him to fourth grade until his French was better, but he insisted and she gave in. Soon he was the best in the class. Dan attended school in Melun, where I drove him in our VW bug. Jonathan refused to go to the *ecole maternelle*, where he and fifty other children were supposed to sit quietly with hands on the desk. I finally found an English kindergarten in Fontainebleau intended for the children of the NATO troops, where he was satisfied. While he was in class I went for walks, gradually read *Le Rouge et le Noir* or French plays, in preparation for seeing them in Paris.

From September 1960 on we were supposed to be in Germany or in another German speaking country, on Georg's grant from the Guggenheim foundation. During the summer we went on various trips looking for housing. In Freiburg, Heidelberg and Munich we had no luck. There was little housing available, especially for Americans with three children. Near Innsbruck we were offered a nice, reasonable house, but when the school authorities advised us not to tell anybody that we were Jews, we decided to keep looking, though somewhat regretfully, because of the beautiful scenery and because to me people's speech sounded almost like home.

As we stood in the Innsbruck post office under the portrait of Emperor Francis Joseph and wondered what we should do, it occurred to me that we had not tried Göttingen. Despite somewhat of a prejudice against Northern Germany, I called the Foreign Students' Office there and was told that an apartment was available and we should come to look at it. When Georg went to Göttingen, it turned out that the apartment, actually in the village of Geismar, would actually not be vacant until the following May. The Guggenheim foundation agreed to the delay, and we were glad to stay longer in Le Mée, where we had come to feel quite at home. We also were pleased to shorten our stay in Germany (or so we thought) to only three months.

Our discomfort at the prospect of living in Germany soon melted away once we arrived in Göttingen. We liked our life there, despite the fact that we had to live very economically, on five thousand dollars for the year. Jeremy went to the Max Planck Gymnasium. Danny attended the grade school in the village of Geismar, and Jonathan at first went to the kindergarten and then to the "Schulkindergarten". They all made friends and learned German as quickly as they had learned French.

Before we came to Göttingen, the question had often occurred to me: How am I going to know which of the people I meet are murderers? This question seemed less an issue as time went on. For instance all the students who lived in the same house as we did had been children "back then". We soon became friends with Uli Justus, one of the students whose father had suffered from cold and starvation as an American prisoner or war and had died soon thereafter, and with Irene Hoerner, his 18 year old friend and later wife, whose father died in Stalingrad. Would they not have to hate the war and the Nazis as much as we did?

The father of one of Jeremy's classmates had refused to carry out an order on the Eastern front and had barely escaped with his life. Danny's best friend was the only boy in the school with whom he could talk French. His father, Karl-Heinz Tolle, was an organ builder who had met his wife Marcelle in France after being released from a prisoner of war camp. Many years later he showed us his diary from the war, which clearly expressed his opposition to the war and to the Nazis. In Göttingen we came to know people of many social classes, among them Frau Rehbein, the cleaning lady in the house who was proud of the social democratic tradition of her family and had secretly worked on alterations for a Jewish-owned clothing firm long after it had been forbidden. We are still in touch with her son and daughter in-law.

The Association for Christian-Jewish friendship was important for us. I remember how I first met the secretary of the organization, Heide Friedrich. One day I went to a lecture by Renate Riemann, the chairperson of the Deutsche Friedensunion (German Peace Union), which took place in a school. While I was looking for a seat, I heard that a policeman wanted to prevent a woman from entering, claiming that all seats had been taken. I protested, and Frau Friedrich was able to find a seat. Our friendship lasted until her death. She and her husband, who had died in the war, had been imprisoned in 1937 as members of a Communist splinter group.

Through the Society we also met other people who had actively opposed the Nazis or had been in exile. Some of them were active in the Social Democratic Party. One woman, the writer and politician Hannah Vogt, had spent several months in the women's concentration camp Moringen because of her communist affiliation. Later she studied political science. Before we met her we had known her book *Schuld und Verhängnis,* (English title: *The Burden of Guilt*), which Georg had used with his students. After leaving the Communist Party, she was for many years a very active member of the Göttingen city council and at one point was a serious candidate for mayor. After her death in 1993, a street was named for her.

Another prominent member of the Society was Artur Levi, who was mayor of Göttingen for twenty years. He had emigrated as a teenager alone from Munich to England, and after the war came to Göttingen in order to help with the reconstruction of democratic unions. After his studies at the University of Göttingen, he taught at the Pädagogische Hochschule (Teachers College) and represented the Social Democratic Party in the city council. In 1994 he became an active member of the reconstituted Jewish religious community. As mayor he succeeded in having a plaque mounted on the new city hall honouring the deserters from the Wehrmacht in World War ll. The plaque faces Hiroshima Platz, another of Levi's initiatives. Only when we came to know him and his wife Liesel better did we find out that things were not easy for them. He had received innumerable threatening letters and phone calls, and he and his family sometimes had to be guarded by the police. He worried about the future of Germany, he told us.

Already before the reunification I gradually had the impression that Germans spoke increasingly about their and their friends' and relatives' Nazi past, and that some did not abhor it as much as I thought they should. I think that being citizens of a once-great European power that is now subsumed in the European Community means something to them. The standing applause to Martin Walser's speech in October of 1998 about Auschwitz being a moral club held over Germany, depresses me more than the speech itself, as does the fact that in 2002 Chancellor Schröder was willing to sit on the same podium with Walser on the anniversary of the German surrender. In the former GDR national socialist beliefs that had been preserved undisturbed during the decades of communism re-emerged.

After our first stay of fifteen months in 1961–62, we returned to Göttingen again and again, for whole summers and Sabbatical years. In recent years we have been alternating, spending half the year in Buffalo and half in Göttingen.

During our first stay in Göttingen, I attended Professor Walter Killy's lectures on the German novel. They took place in the Paulinerkirche, with more than 400 students in attendance. The students' rustling newspapers was so noisy that I had trouble understanding anything, even when I sat in the front row. After the lecture the students had to file past the professor and have him stamp their study book. I am sure that this was the closest contact he had with most of the students. But I liked two little books by Killy, one about the German kitsch, and the other about the attitudes of the Germanists under National Socialism. Unfortunately studies about Nazis in other fields came out only much later. A few times I also went to lectures of the legal scholar Hans-Gunther Seraphim. I was especially interested in the issue of euthanasia and in his emphatic view that it should never be legalized, because it would never be possible to prevent its misuse.

Ignorant about how things were done in German academia, I once asked Professor Albrecht Schöne, the respected Germanist, if I could take part in his Oberseminar. I think it dealt with Faust, and having taken three graduate courses on Goethe in Chicago, I was curious about how such a seminar would be handled in Germany. As I found out later, I had made the mistake of not introducing myself at least as "Frau Professor". His answer was: At most once or twice", whereupon I decided not to go at all.

I regularly attended a colloquium with Thomas Nipperdey, a noted German historian, about political themes in the novel of the Weimar period. The course consisted of papers presented by students. I decided to present the popular novel *Der Tunnel* by Bernhard Kellermann, from which one could learn more about political attitudes than from most "high" literature. Nipperdey neither suggested a discussion about the novel, nor did he show the slightest interest in who I was. It must have been clear that I was about twice as old as the other students.

Chapter 6

TURBULENT YEARS IN BUFFALO (1962–1970)

GEORG

In mid-August, after visiting our friends in Paris and in Le Mée once more, we returned to the United States. After a brief visit with my parents in Richmond came the long train ride to New Orleans. We were exhausted when we arrived there in a heat wave, with swarms of mosquitoes from the nearby swamps infesting the city. To make matters worse, our furniture arrived damaged from storage, and neither our refrigerator nor our air conditioner worked. As our VW was still on the ocean, we were not mobile.

When we wanted to register the children in school, we were required to prove that we are white, even though Jeremy and Danny had attended school in New Orleans before we went to Europe. Since their birth certificates were in the baggage that had not yet arrived, we had to get a sworn affidavit from the black NAACP lawyer that we are indeed white. Because we lived in a black neighbourhood, the children were jostled and taunted as niggerlovers on the school bus, and the principal, to whom we complained, refused to do anything about it. Jonathan's first grade homeroom teacher made difficulties for him because he refused to swear the oath of allegiance, since he was unfamiliar with it. On this occasion the principal did intervene, and the teacher left Jonathan alone. The other two soon felt at home among their classmates. We were glad to be again in an apartment on the Dillard University campus, and felt totally accepted by our black neighbors.

We again lived in two worlds. I again was elected chairman of the education committee of the New Orleans NAACP, and again regularly attended the lunches of the "Frontier of America" group. I considered it a great compliment that I was the only white person invited to participate in a discussion with a representative of President Kennedy's Commission on Civil Rights. When the guest inquired who I was, the president of the New Orleans chapter of the Urban League responded: "Iggers is really black; he just happens to have white skin."

Wilma and I taught again at the Graduate School of Tulane University, Wilma in the fall taught a seminar about Karl Kraus and in the spring about social criticism in German literature, I taught two courses about European and world history since 1919, which I also taught at Dillard University.

Many professors at Tulane, including even John Snell, who considered themselves liberal on the race question, considered the NAACP too radical. They also totally agreed with the American foreign policy in the Cold War. The German professors whom Snell invited to lectures were mostly highly conservative, of which Snell was not quite aware, like Gerhard Ritter and Ernst Percy Schramm, or on the far right Walther Hubatsch. Snell and his colleagues were convinced that the black intelligentsia shared their views concerning American society and the role of America in the world. When the English historian Hugh Seton Watson gave a lecture at Tulane and expressed the wish to speak with blacks, I organized an informal meeting at Dillard, where in addition to Watson and Snell, Hans Schmitt, a German emigré, Daniel Thompson, a black sociologist, and Adolph Reed, a black political scientist from Southern University, the black Louisiana state university in Baton Rouge, participated. I had succeeded in organizing a joint session of Dillard and Tulane. Reed was a Marxist, Thompson rather middle of the road. For Snell and Schmitt, the critical attitude of the two blacks toward American conditions and their bitterness were a painful surprise. Thompson by no means identified with the Soviet Union, but considered American foreign policy just as racist and imperialistic as Reed did. The views of neither of them were typical of the black population, but they were clear proof of the dissatisfaction and impatience of a black minority.

Much had happened since we had left for Europe. Despite strong resistance, the school board gave in to the federal court and allowed a small number of black children to attend the formerly white schools. Benjamin Franklin High School for gifted students had opened its doors. About three hundred blacks were registered on the New Orleans campus of the formerly white Louisiana State University. At the same time the state also founded a campus of the black Southern University in New Orleans, in order to prevent "too many" blacks from attending the white Louisiana State campus. Tulane admitted a few black students. Racial segregation had been abolished on public carriers in 1958 by the federal courts. In the private sector, restaurants, hotels, movie theaters, hospitals and swimming pools were still segregated, but that did not prevent us from frequenting Dooky Chase, the restaurant where the Frontiers of America met.

While the struggle against the abolition of racial segregation was fought in the fifties almost exclusively in the courts, around 1960 a new phase of civil resistance began. Young blacks and whites sat down together at lunch counters and were promptly arrested. Many young blacks and whites had the courage to travel together in the South, where they were often brutally mistreated by the police. The mood of the black population had changed completely. For many, especially students, the tactics of avoiding direct confrontation seemed outdated. Two new radical groups emerged: SNCC, Student Non-Violent Coordinating Committee, and CORE, Committee on Racial Equality. To begin with, whites had participated in these groups, but by 1962 they were largely excluded. There also was Martin Luther King's Southern Christian Leadership Conference, which tried to build bridges between the races and to overcome racial discrimination through civil disobedience.

On behalf of the NAACP I investigated conditions in the New Orleans schools on the basis of statistics from the school administration. The inequalities were shocking. As in Little Rock several years earlier, in 1962 the black schools in New Orleans were overcrowded, while there was plenty of space in the white schools. In the black schools the children were taught for half a day, mornings or afternoons, while the white children were taught mornings and afternoons. Besides, there were not enough teachers in the black schools.

Transporting the children in school buses was another ticklish issue. Following the legal abolition of segregation, the segregationists fought bussing, even though ironically, bussing had been used extensively in order to maintain segregation.

The Southern racists knew that they would have to give in to the legal abolition of segregation sooner or later, but wanted to postpone the implementation of the decision of the courts as long as possible. For that they had the support of whites who considered themselves moderate and who rejected violent resistance. The populist-racist wing of the white voters, which was represented especially in the rural districts and had a majority in both chambers of the Louisiana legislature, launched a witchhunt against supporters of desegregation and civil rights, and the legislature declared the NAACP illegal. Following the example of the Un-American Activities Committee in the U.S. House of Representatives, the Louisiana legislature created a "Louisiana Un-American Activities Committee." LUAC was supposed to prove that there was a connection between the civil rights movement and the Communist Party, but was not able to prove it. However, LUAC held many ugly and hateful hearings, mainly with whites on the stand.

In October of 1962, there was the Cuban missile crisis. My enthusiasm for Fidel Castro had ended in spring of 1959 when he began to execute political opponents, which sympathetic Americans saw as an expression of revolutionary justice. We found out more clearly what was going on in Cuba politically when one of my students at Dillard, who had visited his family in Cuba during the Christmas vacation, returned shaken and told us that he had been questioned by the police for hours after he had met friends in a café. On the other hand, we felt that the economic sanctions that the United States had imposed on Cuba were wrong, and that the invasion in the Bay of Pigs and guerrilla attacks that were organized by the United States had practically forced Castro to turn toward the Soviet Union.

In October, everyone expected a nuclear conflict between the U.S. and the Soviet Union. We were shocked that the majority of Americans, including our black colleagues at Dillard, supported Kennedy's willingness to go to war. In New Orleans an attack on the city was considered likely. New Orleans is largely located below sea level and surrounded by dikes, so that it would be flooded if there were an attack. There were only two highways leading out of the city, so that an evacuation would have been impossible. We decided to go to Hattiesburg, Mississippi, about a hundred miles North of New Orleans, where the rabbi of the reform synagogue had offered us refuge. On the Friday evening when we were packing, we heard the news that Kennedy and Khrushchev had reached an agreement and war was averted.

A few days after the crisis ended, Wilma and I, together with Mary Allen, a professor from the women's college of Tulane, founded an organization that we called the New Orleans Council for Peaceful Alternatives. We met alternately at Dillard and at Tulane. Mary, who was close to retirement, was a pacifist and had been a member of the American Socialist party of Eugene Debs and Norman Thomas since her student days. Colleagues of hers from Tulane joined us, as well as a group of leftist students, two women from an Orthodox Jewish congregation, a number of Quakers and Philip Berrigan, a Catholic priest, who together with his brother Daniel became the driving force of the Catholic peace movement in the midsixties. However, the New Orleans Council, although it was by no means Communist, was rejected by other Catholics who had worked with us in the civil rights movement but were vehement anti-Communists and supported the Cold War. We organized several demonstrations against nuclear weapons that proceeded peacefully, although counter-demonstrators tried to provoke us. Unfortunately, few blacks participated. They felt that the peace movement did not have anything to do with the struggle for racial equality. When a few years later King took a stand against the Vietnam War, many blacks were critical of him. For many people our group was also probably too academic. Ben Smith, one of the two civil rights lawyers who worked with the Council, had been jailed in the course of his activism, talked about war crimes and the Nuremberg trials, and Stephen Ambrose, who later was a leading American military historian, spoke about nuclear war.

In the fall of 1962 Jack Roth, chairman of the history department at Roosevelt University, again offered me a position at Roosevelt University in Chicago, and a good friend, the liberal Catholic historian Edward Gargan, recommended Wilma for a position at the Jesuit Loyola University, also in Chicago, which she enjoyed the most of the positions she has had. This time I accepted the offer.

Now that the legal barriers to the abolition of segregation had been abolished, different strategies were needed in the North as well as in the South. Now it was a matter of addressing social and economic discrimination and the problem of continuing de facto separation, which was much harder to fight.

We arrived in Chicago in early September 1963. For the first time, I taught exclusively modern European history and did not have to teach introductory courses in American history. Wilma taught language and graduate literature courses at

Lewis Towers, the downtown campus of Loyola. Living once again in Hyde Park, we found the library of the University of Chicago, as well as Newberry Library, very accessible. For Newberry, Hans Baron, a student of Ernst Troeltsch and Friedrich Meinecke, had just acquired the collection of books and journals which I needed for my work on German historicism.

I established contact with the NAACP and became a member of its advisory council, but the situation in Chicago was different from Little Rock or New Orleans. Chicago was a much larger city and the NAACP had close ties to the Democratic Party. In many ways I was an outsider. Also, the situation with regard to the relationship between blacks and whites was much less transparent than in the South. The goal still was equal rights for all Americans, but its realization on the social, economic and cultural level proved to be complicated. Since I could not actively participate in the NAACP, I joined the Teachers for Integrated Schools, and became coeditor of their information service, "The Chicago School Integration News."

We again spent the summer 1964 in Fayetteville, Arkansas, where I had a guest professorship. In the fall I had a research scholarship at Newberry Library where I could devote myself fully to my manuscript on historicism. At Roosevelt my place was taken by Manfred Schlenke, a young German historian from Marburg, whom James Luther Adams had recommended. I was very much concerned about the strong anti-German resentment among our students, not only the Jewish ones, which was due at least in part to a lack of knowledge. Schlenke's stay in Chicago, which was accompanied by lively discussions about the German past and present, was a huge success.

Being on leave from Roosevelt in the fall of 1964 made it possible for me to accept an invitation to attend a conference on historical theory in Salzburg, Austria, and to combine it with a three weeks' stay in Europe. The conference was organized by Otmar Anderle. It was only after I had arrived in Salzburg that I realized fully to what extent Anderle and two of his guests, Joseph Vogt and Georg Schachermayer, had been implicated in National Socialism. Anderle's earlier enthusiasm for Oswald Spengler had been replaced by his enthusiasm for Arnold Toynbee. He also had invited guests with a different intellectual background, for example Georg Kotowski, the political scientist from the Free University of Berlin, and Michael Landmann, a Jewish philosopher influenced by Stefan George. There were two participants from Czechoslovakia, Jaroslav Novák, a natural scientist from Prague, who was a Communist, and J.L. Fischer, a philosopher from Olomouc in Moravia, a rationalist and democrat who had been in prison under the Nazis as well as under the Communists. Kotowski invited me to visit him in Berlin, but I decided to accept an invitation to Prague instead.

I first went to visit Wilma's friends in the Bohemian Forest. I stayed with František and Růža Hruška in Domažlice. For years František had been writing us letters following the party line to which I had written critical responses. I was therefore totally surprised when he complained bitterly about the regime. He evidently had written the letters expressly for the censorship. The next day I was received very cordially by Wilma's friends, Anita Knížková and Iva Kouříková. They saw conditions in Czechoslovakia critically, but were not as embittered as Hruška. With him I went to Prague a few days later. When the train arrived in Prague as it was getting dark, it made on me the impression I had expected of a Communist city, without bright lights and neon signs. The next day it looked very different, a beautiful although neglected metropolis. Novák had arranged for me to meet with the historians Bedřich Loewenstein and Mikuláš Teich at the Academy of Sciences on Hradčany. Teich, originally from Slovakia, had spent the years of Nazi occupation in England, where he had met and married his wife Alice, who was originally from Vienna. They moved to Prague as convinced Communists, where he worked as a historian of science at the Academy of Sciences and she as an economic historian at Charles University.

Loewenstein was neither a party member nor a Marxist. As the son of a Jewish father and a Gentile mother, he survived the Nazi occupation in a work camp. As a student in the mid-50s, he had to leave the university because of his non-Marxist views. Nonconformists could sometimes work at the academy where they had no contact with students. As a specialist on Germany, Loewenstein was supposed to do research on the history of Germany, which the academy planned to publish in several volumes. Bedřich, an intellectual with a classical education, and I talked much about Marxist historical theory and its importance for the writing of history. He and Mikuláš stressed that neither Marx nor Engels had ever been economic determinists. According to them, Marx's early humanist works had already contained a considerable part of the mature Marx's critique of capitalism. I soon realized that a political thaw was in progress in Czechoslovakia. I saw Mikuláš again in 1969, when I invited him and his wife to lecture in Buffalo during a stay in the United States. They wondered if they should return to Czechoslovakia under the Soviet occupation or to return to England where their children lived. They decided to return to England. Bedřich, with whom we both became friends and whom we saw every time we were in Prague, decided not to leave Prague, although I had been able to get him an offer in Buffalo. It was only in the late seventies that he accepted a position at the Free University in Berlin.

Starting in the summer of 1964, we and many of our friends were preoccupied with the war in Vietnam. We did not believe the official declaration about the incidents at the Gulf of Tonkin on the first and second of August, which led to the Senate resolution which voted 98 to 2 for giving President Johnson a free hand in Vietnam. The skepticism of Wayne Morse, one of the two senators who had voted against the resolution, was proved justified, as became clear from the hearings in the Fulbright Commission in the Senate in 1968. Johnson had ordered the bombing of North Vietnam, although the attack of a North Vietnamese torpedo boat against an American destroyer had not been confirmed. In the fall of 1964, a group was formed, consisting mainly of colleagues at the various Chicago universities with the purpose of enlightening the public. Our group organized several demonstrations against the war and placed ads in the Chicago newspapers and in the *New York Times*. Teach-ins took place at universities throughout the whole country; the goal was to discuss the Vietnam policy in its historic context.

In the South, the struggle for voting rights for blacks was coming to a head. Small groups of students, black and white, went to the Deep South to register black voters, and were often attacked by whites, in some cases even killed. In the summer of 1965, shortly before the Voting Rights Act was passed, which guaranteed the vote to blacks, I was invited to a workshop in Atlanta, where young people were being trained to register voters. Together with several other historians I was to discuss the historical background. Standing in front of the gym where the event was to take place, I saw Martin Luther King leaving his car alone and without bodyguards walking toward the gym. I considered that very foolhardy. King made an impressive speech about the indivisibility of human rights, and also pointed out the desperate situation of people outside the United States, which the civil rights movement should keep in mind, especially in view of the American intervention in Vietnam, which he criticized strongly. King was one of the first African Americans, who openly opposed that war. Some blacks supported the military, as it was one of the few institutions that at that time offered them relatively equal opportunities.

In October 1964 I had a job interview at the State University of New York at Buffalo. New York had been the only state in the Union, which until 1960 did not have a full-fledged state university. In contrast to the Midwest, the West, and the South, where prestigious state universities were founded as early as the nineteenth century, the Northeast relied on the time-honored tradition of private colleges and universities with high tuition. City College of New York, founded in 1853 and later renamed City University, was an exception. In 1960, Governor Rockefeller announced his plans to establish four university centers, each with the right to grant Ph.Ds, in which almost all fields would be represented. That was when the private University of Buffalo was taken over by the state. It was renamed State University of New York at Buffalo, but still generally referred to as UB. After the educationally lean fifties, the sixties saw an expansion of higher education throughout the country, and Buffalo, it was said, was to become "the Berkeley of the East", Berkeley being the most important center of the University of California. In 1966 Martin Meyerson, the chancellor of Berkeley, was named president of U.B.

The offer I received from U.B. was very attractive: a full professorship, a salary fifty percent higher than at Roosevelt, and a teaching load of only six hours a week. At Roosevelt the teaching load had been twelve hours, at Dillard fifteen, and at Philander Smith often even eighteen hours. I was to work primarily with doctoral students, and my teaching was to be closely related to my research. I was to concentrate primarily on European intellectual history, and also German history until a specialist in that field was found.

A short time after the offer from U.B., I received a very similar one from the newly founded branch of the University of Illinois in Chicago. We could have stayed in Chicago, but decided in favor of Buffalo after Wilma received an offer from Canisius College in Buffalo, a sister institution of Loyola.

We had to decide where we would live in Buffalo, and decided in favor of Amherst, a suburb that bordered on the university campus. For the first time we lived in an exclusively white neighborhood. We did so with a heavy heart, and mainly because of the superior quality of the Amherst schools. We bought an old frame house on a shaded street. I later conducted my seminars in the large living room.

The University of Buffalo, which had been founded in 1847, was supposed to train mainly physicians, dentists, lawyers, judges, and teachers, many of whom settled in western New York. Liberal arts were added only later. In 1962 the university had about 10,000 students, mostly Protestants and Jews, while many Catholics attended Canisius College, which had been founded in 1870. When we came to Buffalo in 1965, the university had 25,000 students, many of whom came from New York City or Long Island, about four hundred miles away, to be at a state university with low fees. At that time it was expected that the university would grow to 40,000 students.

President Meyerson wanted to transform UB into a progressive, modern, internationally recognized university. Conventional traditions of literary scholarship were discarded and new currents of a critical theory were adopted, as at Yale University and in France since the fifties. A number of important writers and critics, among them Leslie Fiedler, John Barth, Robert Creeley and Lionel Abel, were recruited. René Girard taught at UB for many years, Michel Foucault spent two semesters there as a guest professor, and Jacques Derrida came several times to lecture. The newly created Department of Comparative Literature experimented with new directions in literary theory and criticism. The American studies program was also new and served as a base for feminist, black, Puerto Rican, and Native American studies, as well as for the history of everyday life, with a special emphasis on the history of workers in the city of Buffalo.

Meyerson not only wanted to upgrade the faculty and to enlarge the student body, but also to restructure the university radically, away from the anonymous "multiversity," as he had experienced it at Berkeley and found initially at UB, which he considered responsible for the alienation of the students and for the campus unrest. UB with its 30,000 students was to be divided into about thirty separate colleges, each with about a thousand students, with its own buildings and a new campus. Undoubtedly the university, whose student body had increased threefold in a few years, needed a larger campus, but there was disagreement about where the new campus was to be built: in the inner city, where minorities would have easier access, or in the more distant suburbs, where students would be removed from the turbulence of the city. This conflict delayed the construction of the new campus by several years; ultimately the decision was made in favor of exurbia.

The first buildings on the new campus formed a gigantic ensemble of arid postmodern concrete structures called the Ellicott Complex, after Joseph Ellicott who as agent for the Holland Land Company in the early 1800s had transformed Western New York from a backwoods to a major center. Half of the students would live on campus. There would be dormitories for the students, and apartments for the faculty, a dining room and lecture halls. The colleges shared a theater, where concerts took place regularly, a bookstore and a library.

Meyerson's concept was never really implemented. His ideal was classical and elitist, and he was hoping for something like Oxford or Cambridge. Only Vico College, which was devoted to history and to the philosophy of history, corresponded with his ideas. The others went in different directions that reflected the political climate of the sixties. College A—many colleges did not have a name yet, but only an initial—moved into an empty storefront on Main Street, and sent its students downtown to become involved politically and socially in the poorer community. Other colleges stressed alternate themes that became increasingly important: the Women Studies College, Tolstoy College devoted to questions of male, including gay sexuality; Rachel Carson College devoted to questions of the environment, and the heavily Marxist Social Science College. At the left extreme there was Rosa Luxemburg College which, however, was not officially recognized. The director of the colleges was a young German, Konrad von Moltke, an historian, the son of Helmut von Moltke of the Kreisau resistance circle, who was executed by the Nazis in 1945. Both the students and the administration trusted him, and he was surprisingly successful in bringing about a dialogue between the two sides. After he received his Ph.D. in Göttingen in 1967, I recommended him for a position in our department. In Germany and in Buffalo he hoped to establish an alternative university. However, Meyerson's concept of university reform was bound to fail; the existing structures and outlooks were too firmly entrenched. Centralization won out. The colleges were dissolved in the seventies and eighties. The Ellicott Complex became a gigantic student dormitory, and departments moved into the rest of the complex. In the end anonymity was greater than it had been prior to the Meyerson era.

Throughout the United States, but particularly in a small number of universities, including UB, many of the students had become radical due to the civil rights movement and the Vietnam War. In 1962 the Students for a Democratic Society, generally known as the SDS, was founded in Port Huron, Michigan. By coincidence, this organization had the same acronym as the radical German student organization, the *Sozialistische Deutsche Studentenbund* (Socialist German Student Association), with which it had many similarities, although the American SDS was more pragmatic and less ideological than its German counterpart. A basic concern of the SDS was U.S. foreign policy, which in its view was closely intertwined with the capitalist economic order. Colonialism, imperialism, and racism were all aspects of this social system. The critique of capitalism restricted itself not to economics and politics but included culture and everyday life. The critics called for a counterculture free of the compulsion for conformity and from the pressure for achievement. The radical students turned to the Critical theory of the Frankfurt School, less to its two most important theorists Max Horkheimer and Theodor Adorno who had returned to Frankfurt from the United States after the war, than to Herbert Marcuse, who was much better known to them and who several times visited the Buffalo campus. Foucault too played an important role in their thinking and to an extent replaced Marx.

In order not to lose my contacts with the South and with the black colleges, soon after my arrival in Buffalo I explored the possibility of establishing a cooperative arrangement between UB and Philander Smith College. My initiative was received positively by both sides, in UB by the dean of the College of Arts and Sciences who set funds aside for the exchange, and in Little Rock by the president of the college. I organized a committee on the Buffalo campus with about thirty of my colleagues in different departments. A number went to Little Rock to discuss how they and UB could be of help. However, it is questionable whether very much was actually achieved in terms of improving academic standards at Philander Smith. The college was too entrenched in its ways. When Wilma and I taught there in the 1950s, the college had a small number of gifted students who because of discriminatory practices at other schools, could not study elsewhere, but who later had impressive careers. One of them was Joycelyn Elders, whom Wilma and I had taught, who under President Clinton became Surgeon General of the United States. By the late 1960s many of the state schools which previously had barred black students, had opened their gates and elite colleges and universities began to award scholarships to gifted black students. Many of the black students from the Little Rock area now went to the previously all white Little Rock branch of the University of Arkansas. I continued to be invited regularly to serve as an adviser in connection with the federal Title III program that supported so-called developing colleges, until 1995. I thus was able to maintain contacts with the college and to follow its development over five decades. In 2002 I was awarded an honorary doctorate by the college.

When we spent the summer of 1964 in Fayetteville, restaurants, hotels, movies, hospitals, and most other institutions were still segregated in Arkansas as they were in other Southern states. After Congress enacted the Civil Rights Act in 1965 which outlawed segregation in public places and institutions, there was general compliance with the law. When I traveled to Little Rock in January 1966 with a black colleague, we had no problem renting a double room at a major hotel, something that would still have been impossible two years earlier.

In the meantime the conflict between students and administration at Buffalo intensified. The most immediate issue was the Vietnam War. Student protests turned against military related research and the reserve officers training program (ROTC). At the same time, students demanded a role in the formation of university policies.

The protests began in 1964, just at the time when I came to UB. In the beginning, the protests were peaceful, for example, there were sit-ins in the Administration Building when the university cooperated with the government's demand that students take special examinations to be eligible for student deferments from the draft. I participated in one such sit-in. Soon, however, there was a direct confrontation with the campus police when Dow Chemical, which produced napalm, wanted to conduct job interviews on campus. In 1968 students demolished the laboratory of a research project for the navy and the following year they trashed the ROTC barracks. The protests succeeded in bringing about the suspension of ROTC training. In the spring of 1969 students occupied the Administration Building and raised not the red flag of socialism, but the black flag of anarchy. After twenty-four hours, the administration called in the police, who, however, refused to enter the building. A "peace keeping group" consisting mostly of faculty, in which I participated, persuaded the students to leave peacefully.

In February 1970 (three months prior to the shootings of student protesters at Kent State University in Ohio) a full fledged student uprising spread across the campus. After students had blocked a basketball game by sitting on the floor of the court demanding better conditions for black athletes, a group of radical students marched to the Administration Building. They demanded an audience with acting president Peter Regan, but he refused to meet with them. His predecessor Meyerson had taken a leave of absence during the unrest and did not return. In September he became president of the University of Pennsylvania in Philadelphia. The Meyerson Era was a thing of the past. When the students began to smash windows, Regan called the police, who for the first time entered the campus. The students then barricaded themselves in the Student Union. The police stormed the building, and fighting resulted that lasted until late in the night.

The violence of the confrontation was fueled by the deep resentment the townspeople and the city administration held toward the radical students, as well as by the radical students' desire to provoke precisely such a confrontation. The hatred had some anti-Semitic overtones among the police because a number of the leaders of the radical students were Jews from New York City, not from Buffalo. Because of the brutal manner in which the police proceeded, the radicals succeeded in gaining the sympathy of many moderate students. During the days that followed, there was chaos on the campus, classes were boycotted, entrances to buildings blocked, and windows smashed. After a few days things seemed to return to normal. Yet on the following Sunday morning the Buffalo police occupied the campus in riot gear. That afternoon there was a large peaceful protest march, in which many professors and people from the city took part. On Tuesday evening a second ugly confrontation occurred between students and police, with many injured on both sides. That Friday the University Senate, which at this point included all teaching personnel, called upon the president to ask the police to leave the campus in order to avoid further clashes.

After Regan not only refused to do this and declined to meet with a delegation of the University Senate, a group of professors and teaching assistants assembled that Sunday afternoon for a sit-in in the conference room in front of the Regan's office, in order to initiate a dialogue. The group made certain that they neither blocked the hall nor the entrance to the president's office. The lawyer who advised us was of the opinion that the sit-in did not violate any law. The police also admitted us into the building when we explained to them what we intended to do. The group consisted mostly of young people; the well known French scholar and author Raymond Federman and I, both of us in our midforties, were the oldest.

I had expected the afternoon to be boring and had taken material along for reading. After a short interval, an assistant from the president appeared and told us that that he would have us arrested if we did not leave the room within five minutes. We decided to stay. The police was unprepared and waited for vans to take us away. After half an hour my history colleague Michael Frisch asked whether we could go to the bathroom. An officer was assigned to accompany us. The officer was obviously uncomfortable and said that he would have no objection if we disappeared through the bathroom window, an offer that we, of course, declined. Frisch then returned to the conference room.

When I too wanted to return, the officer refused to let me in. He had noticed my German accent and told me that he did not want me to jeopardize my American visa, having mistaken me for the German professor who was in our group and who had left earlier. However, there was the young South African novelist, John Coetzee, in the group who actually lost his visa because of the incident. Coetzee many years later received an honorary doctorate from the university, and a few years ago the Nobel Prize for Literature. I decided to go to the police station to await the arrival of our group. When I arrived a number of my colleagues were already there to see what they could do to help. Wilma and Jonathan were also there. A colleague had phoned Wilma to tell her that I had been arrested. The Buffalo district attorney asked for five hundred dollars bail in cash from each of us, a sum that was difficult to raise on a Sunday afternoon. Nevertheless, by early evening we had the money, but the judge let all of us go on our own recognizance. Shortly afterwards, the Buffalo court sentenced all of us to thirty days imprisonment and fines, but the appeals court in Rochester reversed the sentences and accused the Buffalo authorities of having violated our right of assembly.

Slowly calm returned to the campus. Students called for a strike and many refused to attend classes as long as the police occupied the campus. While many professors canceled their classes, I moved my seminar to our living room and my lecture class to a storefront across the street from the campus. Further confrontations between students and police occurred only in early May, when the United States intervened militarily in Cambodia and a wave of demonstrations broke out on campuses throughout the country. A new climax was reached in Buffalo after the Ohio National Guard had killed four demonstrating students at Kent State University on May 4th. Immediately thereafter the Buffalo administration closed the university and sent the students home before the final semester examinations.

Shortly after our arrival in Buffalo, I was elected to the Board of Directors of the Buffalo branch of the NAACP and until 1975 also headed the education committee. The branch in Buffalo was less active than those in Little Rock and New Orleans. The situation was also different from that in the South. Here it was not a question of challenging segregation laws, but rather of discrimination in employment and housing, mistreatment by the police and other forms of inequality, and the registration of voters. I am still a member of the Board of Directors of the Buffalo NAACP, the only white member. However, my situation is different, as I am not teaching in a predominantly black institution and live in a predominantly white suburban neighborhood.

In August 1969 we visited Israel with the children for the first time. I had always wanted to go there, but not as a tourist. I was waiting for an invitation from a university that never came. So we finally went as tourists after all. We visited my cousin and her husband in Haifa, went on a two day tour of Galilee, and took the bus from Haifa via Afula through the occupied West Bank and through Nablus and Ramallah to Jerusalem. When I tried to take the same trip once more by bus from Haifa through the West Bank to Jerusalem in 1996, I was told that this was no longer possible.

We were very interested in the relationship between Israelis and Palestinians. An Israeli woman who spoke Arabic accompanied us on a walk from the Hebrew University campus on Mount Scopus to a nearby Arab village. She spoke to an elderly man on the street who invited us to his house, introduced us to his family, and served us coffee. He spoke of his life under British, Jordanian, and Israeli rule without bitterness.

After our visit in Jerusalem we had hoped to spend a week in a guest house on a kibbutz, but the travel agency had changed our reservations and placed us at a hotel on the beach near Netanya. We did not want to be there, where we felt isolated. We thus decided to make an excursion on our own by bus to Tulkarem, a medium sized Palestinian town immediately across the pre-1967 border with Israel. The people there were very friendly, but we could not communicate with them until we met a teacher who spoke English. He took us to a café, where Wilma, who was wearing short sleeves, was the only woman. He talked with us about the situation in the West Bank. He hoped for reunification with Jordan and was confident that this would happen. After that, we spoke with a young man who also spoke good English and took us on foot through the town. He had been driven out of Jaffa as a child, and did not expect to ever return there, but hoped for a Palestinian state.

Our impressions of Israel were very mixed. We had assumed that much in Israel would be familiar to us since we had friends and relatives there. Somehow I had imagined it as a mixture of an Eastern European, Yiddish, and Central European German-speaking culture. This may have been the case in 1948, but it was no longer so in 1969. In the meantime, approximately half of the Jewish population had come as refugees from the Arab states or from Iran. The young generation of European descent spoke Hebrew. In many ways the country seemed very strange to us, much more Oriental than we had expected. As tourists we were unable to make contacts that would have been possible if we had been invited. I felt very much at home with three professors at the Hebrew University who invited me for lunch, J. T. Talmon, whose book about the totalitarian aspects of the French Revolution I had used in my courses; Shlomo Avineri whose book about the young Marx we had discussed in my seminar about Marxism as an intellectual tradition, and Yehoshua Arieli, who had come to Palestine from Karlsbad in Bohemia as a young man in the 1930s, and had received his Ph.D. in American history at Harvard with Oscar Handlin, and was very active in the organization Security through Peace, the predecessor of Peace Now.

When I was in Israel a second time, in 1996, to attend a conference at the Hebrew University, and when Wilma did research in Tel Aviv and Jerusalem in 1979 and 1990, we saw a different side of Israeli life that was more familiar to us. In 1969 I had been shocked by the gulf between rich and poor, the Hatikvah section between Tel Aviv and Jaffa, and the slums along the old Israeli-Jordanian border in Jerusalem that we had not expected in a country that from 1948 until 1977 was governed by Social Democrats. By 1996 the slums across from the Old City in Jerusalem had been replaced by modern buildings, but the gulf between rich and poor had grown. We were also disturbed by the chauvinism of many of the people with whom we spoke, the maps without the borders of 1949, and the prejudices of many against the Arabs, which did not bode well for a lasting peace.

After our return from Israel, in August 1969 we traveled to Prague, where in August 1968, exactly one year after the Soviet occupation, a colloquium on Fascism, that Bedřich Loewenstein had already planned for a long time, was to take place at the Academy of Sciences. I had assumed that under the new circumstances the conference would be canceled, but it took place nevertheless, with a number of distinguished guests from the West, including Akexander Mitscherlich, Ernst Nolte, Peter Pulzer, and David Schoenbaum. It was a strange atmosphere in Prague. On the intellectual and cultural level little had changed. In the movie theaters the Czech film "All Good Countrymen" played which took issue with the collectivization of agriculture under the Communists. All of the Czech historians who attended the meeting expected that within a few weeks they would be dismissed from their positions and a new Ice Age would begin. And that is exactly what happened.

WILMA

After our first stay in Göttingen, we returned to New Orleans for the 1962–63 academic year. We neither liked the social atmosphere nor the climate, and we were glad when we were offered positions in Chicago, Georg at Roosevelt University and I at Loyola University, another Jesuit institution. There I taught almost exclusively upper level undergraduates and graduate students. I got along very well with the students, the colleagues and the chairman.

We lived in Hyde Park, the section around The University of Chicago which theoretically had a liberal attitude toward blacks. This turned out to be pure hypocrisy. The public school that our children attended, segregated the pupils racially by dividing them into different academic "tracks", and segregation in housing also remained. Since we had been students there in the forties, Hyde Park had become a well-to-do enclave surrounded by black slums. It was the only area in Chicago where blacks and whites could live together, but only wealthy blacks. We decided on Hyde Park because of its multi-ethnic character, because of the proximity of

The University of Chicago and because of Ray School, the only public grade school in Chicago with about the same number of students of both races. We also appreciated the many cultural opportunities, including the library and the bookstores. But we were afraid of the high crime rate, especially after dark. In our neighborhood, a child was found murdered, his body dumped in a garbage can.

The Chicago school authorities sabotaged integration at Ray School in any way they could. According to statistics, 49 percent of the students were white, 43 percent black, and the rest mostly Japanese, but the individual classes were composed on the basis of IQ tests, and were divided into classes for the "gifted" and for "less gifted." The gifted classes consisted mostly of white children and a few black children from Hyde Park; the "less gifted" were made up of children from Woodlawn, the neighborhood that was turning into a slum. Physical education classes were effectively segregated as well. Many parents disliked this situation and therefore founded the Ray School Parents for Integrated Classrooms. An analysis of the IQ test results showed that a number of the black children from Woodlawn actually belonged in the "gifted" classes. The school's atmosphere also created hostility among the students.

The school kept strict control over who entered the school building. The fact, that I was refused permission to show our friend Marki Thompson of Fayetteville, Arkansas, an enthusiastic teacher, the school from the inside suggests that the administration had some things to hide.

After eleven years in the South I found people in the much-praised North less friendly, and I preferred the sometimes condescending attitudes of Southern whites toward blacks to the aggressiveness I observed in the North, where people of both races had many fewer opportunities to meet in their daily lives.

I started to do what could be called scholarly work rather late. Through a Czech colleague, I found out about the Czechoslovak Society of Arts and Sciences, a kind of academy of sciences abroad, and was able to present a lecture at its conference in 1964. The article that resulted from the presentation was my first publication. It dealt with Vojtěch Rakous (1862–1935), the most important Czech-Jewish storyteller and writer of whom I had been fond since my childhood. He wrote funny stories about village Jews in the second half of the nineteenth century who lived harmoniously with their Czech Gentile neighbors. The opposite pole to these people were the conceited, rich city Jews, who of course spoke German. Rakous' antipathy extended to the German speaking rabbis and teachers of religion. He was very disappointed when in 1897 he experienced a strong Czech wave of anti-Semitism. His realization that he had idealized his fellow countrymen is evident in his later stories. It was, by the way, my Bavarian born and raised mother who introduced me to Rakous.

At that time I read much prose, Czech as well as West and East German, which I reviewed for *Books Abroad* (later renamed *World Literature Today*), and I wrote summaries of historical articles for *Historical Abstracts*.

When toward the end of our second year in Chicago Georg was offered a position at the State University of New York at Buffalo, I wanted him to accept.

When, through the mediation of the dean at Loyola University, I received an offer from Canisius College in Buffalo, another Jesuit institution, there was no doubt that we would move to Buffalo.

As an undergraduate school, Canisius had good standards, not only in the social sciences and in the humanities, but also in the physical sciences and in the school of business administration. My relationships with colleagues at Canisius remained largely superficial, and I met with some hostility. Judy Mendels was the only member of the Modern Language faculty who had something of a record as a scholar. Apart from Georg, there was almost no one in Buffalo with whom I could discuss my scholarly interests. One exception was and still is Regina Grol at Empire State College, who largely works on Polish topics.

When I came to Canisius, the chairman of the Department of Modern Languages did not make a secret of his anti-Semitism. His successor was an Austrian who had served in the Luftwaffe and was convinced that I would have to consider him a Nazi. The third chairman did not like women. The fourth and last made vague remarks about my teaching methods, but never told me concretely what he meant. During the Vietnam War, I was stereotyped by colleagues at the college generally as a "peacenik" and probably a Communist sympathizer, which I never was. My peace activities were also mentioned pejoratively in my personnel file. Nevertheless, after one year I was promoted to associate and eventually to full professor. Since I was one of the few professors who in those years were active scholars, I frequently received faculty grants, but I was very much underpaid. The often heard remark, "You with your rich husband at UB", offers a clue. I got along well with the students, especially the German majors. After some time, one of my courses was replaced by the directorship of the fellowship office, where I advised students who where headed for graduate school.

During the years I taught at Canisius, 1965–91, the college underwent major changes. The Catholic Church's list of prohibited books, the Index librorum prohibitorum, was abolished, and the crucifixes disappeared from the classrooms. Gradually the number of required courses in religion and philosophy decreased. The year I arrived was the first year women students were accepted at the college on an equal basis. I was also the first woman professor with children. The number of women on the faculty increased, as well as the number of Protestants and Jews on the faculty. A Protestant minister, a Reform rabbi, and for a while a Buddhist woman, taught religious studies. In the administration and on the faculty there were fewer priests, and when a Jesuit professor left the order to marry and was permitted to continue in his position as professor, no one was surprised.

Soon after we arrived in Buffalo, I joined the Womens's International League for Peace and Freedom ("WILPF"), which since its founding during the First World War has worked for peace and international understanding. At that time we were mainly concerned about the Vietnam War. I was vice president and then president of the Buffalo branch. But often, when I was driving home after a meeting, I asked myself if we had accomplished anything. The answer was no. I asked myself if it had at least been a stimulating evening among friends. Again the answer was negative. The most vocal members seemed to consider arguments normal. I knew that it would have been better if I had spent the evening with the children, although they were reaching an age when they no longer were very interested in their mother's company. There was one member who was convinced that one of us was an agent of the FBI, and gradually I came to realize that she meant me. On the other hand, I did meet one of my best friends there, Halina Kantor. Halina had escaped from Poland as a child and later lived with her husband at the Highlander Folk School in Tennessee. Because of the Vietnam War she moved to Toronto with her husband and children. Then there was, and still is, Miriam Becker, who still in her high eighties is very devoted to causes of peace and social justice.

Gradually I found out that in WILPF sympathies for the Soviet Union and its foreign policy interests predominated. After I returned from my first trip to Czechoslovakia in 1966, I listened to a report by a WILPF member about the country. She had not had the opportunity that I had to be in touch with people there, and so saw everything very differently and was enthusiastic about the achievements of socialism.

Some further experiences led me to lose interest in the organization. During the seventies, we were repeatedly asked to make donations for the followers of Salvador Allende who were persecuted by Chilean general Augusto Pinochet. When I suggested to the head office in Philadelphia that they also support the dissidents in Czechoslovakia, I was told that WILPF was not interested in being another organization of Red-baiters.

In Buffalo one of my first friends was Hanne Strauss, a former refugee from Frankfurt. Through her we met two wonderful human beings, David and Adelheid Miller. David, a physician, was head of the Department of Internal Medicine at the University, and Adelheid was a social worker at Roswell Park Memorial Institute, the cancer hospital in Buffalo. In Germany her family had been Nazis, but from the late thirties on, when the Millers came to Buffalo, they were untiring in their devotion to helping Jewish refugees.

Through Hanne we also met our family doctor Hans Henschel, who originally was from Berlin, the kind of doctor of whom one now can only dream. Through her we also met Virginia King, who until her death in 1998 (from a long-ignored and untreated cancer of the esophagus) contributed much to making our house a home. It was always a pleasure to have her with us. She always took part in our family celebrations. Hanne was exactly the same age as my mother. She did not have my mother's critical mind, but she was full of *joie de vivre* and very sociable.

We lived in Amherst, a suburb of Buffalo, for the first time in a large house of our own, in an attractive neighbourhood with many trees. The children were quickly acclimatized. All three, but especially Jeremy and Danny, were influenced by the atmosphere of revolt of the late sixties, each in his own way. Jeremy became co-founder of the "underground paper" in his high school, which reported on the major issues of the day, and later he was editor of the school paper, which was printed in our basement. He was preparing for college, where he intended to major in philosophy. He was accepted by Columbia, but decided on Carleton College, a small liberal arts college in Minnesota.

Dan and his two best friends, Tim Block and Mike Owsowitz, who are still his best friends, wanted to found an alternative free school following the ideas of Summerhill, where children would develop without authoritarian methods. With his parents' consent, Timmy founded an alternative institution at his house, where well-known professors such as Leslie Fiedler and Edgar Z. Friedenberg occasionally taught. At the age of fifteen, Timmy lectured at the university about his ideas on pedagogy. Later he took the high school equivalency examination, eventually received a Ph.D. in biochemistry, and is now a professor at the medical school of Drexel University in Philadelphia and a leading researcher into Hepatitis B. Mike works as a psychological counsellor, at Buffalo State College while working on a Ph.D. in psychology and performs in the local music scene.

We were worried that Dan would quit school. At the end of the eleventh grade, he declared that he was fed up with school, and that it was boring. He took a course at the State College, completed his diploma by attending summer school, and was admitted to Canisius for the following year.

I was not much in favor of many of the student activities of 1968 or of the professors who wanted to recapture their youth by participating. Many mainly wanted to shock, also by their very appearance, while I felt that one was more likely to win over conservative citizens by showing them what goals we in the peace movement shared with them.

In Buffalo, I also began to devote more time to scholarly work. I also did some work on Karl Kraus, not in order to know more about him. I actually had had enough of him, but because I felt like contradicting the Krausians. I reworked my dissertation, so that it could be published in 1967, and wrote a few articles about Kraus.

If my work on Kraus had little to do with Germanic studies, this was even truer of my later work. I returned to the Bohemian and Moravian Jews, collected literature about them, and copied texts. I interrupted this work when, under the influence of our trips to the GDR, I read East German literature and wrote a fairly long article in which I pointed out the most important literary trends and deviations from them. The sources for my work on the Bohemian and Moravian Jews were at first largely belletristic, but my interest focused on social and cultural history. At its core were people from the heart of Europe: Czechs, Germans from the Czech lands, Jews, and Austrians. Slowly the contours of my book, *Die Juden in Böhmen und Mähren* (The Jews in Bohemia and Moravia) emerged, an anthology of texts from the last two hundred fifty years.

Chapter 7

THE SEVENTIES AND EIGHTIES

GEORG

There was considerable apprehension before the beginning of the fall semester in 1970. The spring semester had seen an escalation of the conflicts and confrontations that had built up on the Buffalo campus since the mid-sixties. There were rumors that radical students would be armed. In late August there was an ominous portent of what was to come, when a violent splinter group of the SDS detonated a bomb in the Mathematics Research Center at the University of Wisconsin in Madison, and two researchers were killed. But everything was quiet when the academic year began, not only in Buffalo, but throughout the country.

In Buffalo the years of the progressive administration of Martin Meyerson were over. The new president Robert Ketter from the UB engineering faculty was committed to making the university serve the economic and professional needs of Western New York as the old University of Buffalo had done. The bitter joke went around that while Meyerson had wanted to make the university the Berkeley of the East, Ketter was rapidly turning it into the Brockport of the West, a small state college east of Buffalo. The new UB lacked the intimacy and focus on liberal arts of the old UB. Emphasis was now on computer science, business administration and applied natural sciences, studies of importamce for economic development. Money also became scarcer than it had been in the sixties, and there were financial cutbacks in the humanities. In the fall of 1964, when I was interviewed, the history department had only 15 faculty members. By 1972 there were 38, and there was talk of a department of 70 in a university of 40,000 students. During the '70s, the department lost several of its best people to Harvard, Columbia and the Universities of Michigan, Indiana, and Maryland. The African specialist was not replaced nor was the Roman historian. The specialist for the

Muslim Near East, Stephen Humphreys, who soon became a leading Islamist, was not given tenure, because medieval and early modern Islamic studies were considered too exotic. While we had four medievalists in the '60s, none were left a decade later. There were no new appointments for the next two decades, with the result that the number of faculty members fell to 22. The philosophy department, which once had the reputation as the center of phenomenological studies in North America, suffered even more severely. It also lost one of the most important philosophical journals, *Philosophy and Phenomenological Research,* because of budget cuts, although it would not have cost much to maintain it. Nevertheless, the spirit of the sixties was not entirely gone. The English department was able to preserve much of its strength and played an important role in the launching of a comparative literature department that pursued new trends from structuralism to critical theory.

I was little affected by the changes in the university. I taught the courses in German political history for the last time in 1970 when William Sheridan Allen came and I was then able, as agreed when I was hired, to turn to my actual interest in intellectual history. I taught seminars at the undergraduate and the graduate level in methods of historical inquiry. Some of my students' papers were of such quality, that they were published in major journals. I also regularly offered historiography courses in which the classical heritage of historical writing served as a background for an examination of current trends. Broader questions of the theory of history remained pivotal to the discussion of diverse orientations in historical writing. The writing of history for me was inseparable from the political and intellectual context in which it was pursued. On the undergraduate level I regularly taught a course in European intellectual history since the eighteenth century Enlightenment, in which we read not only theoretical texts, but also literature as a reflection of basic outlooks of the time.

Two seminars were particularly close to my heart. Every Monday evening the seminars met in our living room, which provided a relaxed atmosphere for the twenty or so participants with coffee and cake. From the early 1970s until the late 1980s when he retired, I taught a seminar with my colleague from the German and Comparative Literature departments, Peter Heller, who had fled his native Vienna in 1938. Our approaches and outlooks were very different. Heller was largely apolitical and insofar as he was political, was relatively conservative. His interest in literature was primarily aesthetic. His publications concentrated on Franz Kafka, Friedrich Nietzsche, and particularly Sigmund Freud. As a child, still in Vienna, he had been analyzed by Freud's daughter Anna Freud. My outlook was more political and further to the left. The first seminar we offered jointly was on the writers who had emigrated to the West during the Nazi period. Other seminars dealt more generally with Weimar culture, including one on films in the last years of the Weimar Republic, 1930–33; another on the cultural scene in Vienna of the turn to the twentieth century, using Carl Schorske's *Fin de Siècle Vienna* as a basis for discussion. Together with other colleagues in the German, English, and Philosophy departments, we obtained a grant from the National Endowment for the Humanities and had sessions with Peter Gay and Carl Schorske in our living room.

Starting in 1968 I began to teach a seminar on "Marxism as an Intellectual Tradition" on the graduate and undergraduate level. The initiative for the course actually came from the chair of my department who felt that there was a need for such a course because of the intense interest of students in Marxism in the turbulent late 1960s. The undergraduate course involved readings of major Marxist writings, beginning with Karl Marx's conception of alienation in his early works, to selections from *Capital* and Friedrich Engels' very different *The Origins of the Family, Private Property and the State,* the first and for a long time the only Marxist work that took the role of women seriously. The course focused on various forms of twentieth-century Western cultural Marxism—Antonio Gramsci, Georg Lukács, E. P. Thompson, and the Frankfurt School, headed by Max Horkheimer and Theodor Adorno—which entailed not merely an economic critique of capitalism, but a critique of modern civilization. In this connection we read Herbert Marcuse who, with his rejection of a performance-oriented society, appeared as the signpost to an alternative world free of the inhibitions and hangups of Western civilization. We also read Michel Foucault's *Madness and Civilization,* with his indictment of the repressive character of an allegedly enlightened modern society, which in the name of liberating human beings used science, medicine, psychiatry, and penal reforms as means of domination and forced conformity.

I also saw the dual side of modernity, the extent to which progress had not only given humans greater freedom, but also made possible the mass destructions of the twentieth—and as it seems now the incipient twenty-first–century—and new forms of direct or indirect controls. However, I also continued to believe in the Enlightenment ideals of human dignity and self-determination. I agreed with Foucault that the modern world's conception of sanity was off base, but did not agree that there was no distinction between sanity and insanity and that therefore the world of the medieval village fool, with whom the book opens, was preferable to that of the modern world inspired by Enlightenment that seeks rational, that is reasonable, solutions.

The graduate seminars had different topics and readings each time they were offered. The first one in the fall of 1968, included students from both the philosophy and the history department, and was the most exciting. The history students were for the most part relatively apolitical, interested in the course primarily from an academic perspective; the philosophy students on the other hand were directly involved in the controversies on campus.

Two philosophy students stood out in the seminar, Robert Cohen and Paul Piccone. Cohen, who had been expelled from the University of Wisconsin, had become the rabble-rousing leader of the radical students in Buffalo. Piccone, who avoided such tactics, had founded what was to become one of the most important Marxist theoretical journals in America, *Telos,* dedicated not to revolutionary activism but to philosophical critique. We read and discussed the early Marx, selections from the later Marx and from Marcuse's *Eros and Civilization* and *One Dimen-*

sional Man. Despite the sharp theoretical and political differences between the historians and the philosophers in the seminar, the atmosphere was surprisingly cordial and conducive to serious study. In the seminars that followed I always chose books of significance for the Marxist discussion that had just appeared in English, such as Marx's *Grundrisse* of 1857, an early not previously published draft of *Capital*, in which the humanistic elements of Marx's economic theory are apparent. Antonio Gramsci's *Letters from Prison,* written in Mussolini's prisons by the leader of the Italian Communist Party, stressed that the defeat of the party in Italy by the Fascists could not be explained in orthodox Marxist categories, but that cultural factors had to be considered, among them the "hegemony"—Gramsci's term—of the establishment over the consciousness of the workers. We also read Georg Lukács' *History and Class Consciousness,* first published by Lukács in 1923 but promptly withdrawn by him under pressure of the Comintern (Communist International) because of his unorthodox stress of the Hegelian idealist elements in Marx's thought. The book was not released again until 1967 and was first translated into English in 1972. One of the most successful seminars involved the discussion of Martin Jay's *The Dialectical Imagination* (1973) on the Critical Theory of the Frankfurt School. Each week we read a chapter in Jay's book and then the works that he discussed. Several times we devoted a whole semester to reading all of *Capital,* vol. 1, after first reading selections from the early Marx. While my colleague Paul Zarembka in the philosophy department, an Althusserian Marxist who considered Marx's early works to be pre-scientific, skipped the first two chapters of *Capital* as not directly relevant to what he considered to be Marx's scientific analysis of capitalism as an economic system, I spent considerable time on the first chapter in which Marx examines capital not merely as an economic system but also in terms of human needs leading to the conclusion of the chapter in which the irrational basis of capitalism is portrayed as the fetishism of commodities, irrational because it views the economy abstractly in terms of the maximization of profit, not concretely in terms of what it means to human beings.

These readings gave me an opportunity to define my own position on Marxism. I never considered myself a Marxist. I viewed Marx's conception of history to be speculative and schematic. I could not accept the economism of orthodox Marxism. Even before I knew of cultural Marxism, I held that cultural factors played an important role in the shaping of societies. I also felt that the definitions of class, even by so-called Western Marxists like Lukács and E. P. Thompson, were too simplistic and neglected the impact of religion and ethnicity as well as of traditional conceptions of status, gender, and morality on society. And, of course, the Leninist formulation of Marxism with its authoritarian and terroristic aspects was totally abhorrent to me. I considered Marx himself a dogmatic but unsystematic thinker, especially as his political views are concerned. Marx' and Engels' idea of the withering away of the state, and Marx's sympathy for the Paris Commune, seem almost to point in an anarchist direction, while Marx's famous speech in Amsterdam in 1872, and Engels' preface of 1895 to Marx's "Class Struggles in France 1848–1850," point in a social democratic direction. On the other hand,

Marx' glorification of the Jacobin phase of the French Revolution with its Reign of Terror constitute a justification of revolutionary violence that foreshadows Lenin and Stalin.

Yet I also saw positive aspects in Marxist theory, particularly in its critique of existing conditions under capitalism, not only on the economic and political level, but also with respect to society and culture. At the core of Marx's theory of knowledge is his insistence, which he voiced very early in his stinging critique of traditional materialism in his "Theses on Feuerbach" (1845), that reality must never be viewed in purely empirical terms, as an "object," but must take into account the human activity that shapes it. But Marx was by no means consistent in his critique of positivism. He and especially Engels again and again asserted that their analysis of society and economics constituted a strict science that "discovered the law of the development of human history," as Engels summed up Marx's work at his graveside, comparing Marx with Charles Darwin. The dialectic as conceived by Marx also involved a contradiction. On the one hand it pointed to the limitations of positivistic science and emphasized the need to see the human world in terms of a broader context of social relations, while on the other hand it viewed the dialectic as a scientific system of history, as a development to a predetermined end. But, nevertheless, at the core of Marx's thought was the ethical notion of human dignity, of humans freed of the "alienation" imposed on them in existing societies. Thus the subtitle of *Capital*, "A Critique of Political Economy," must be taken very seriously. It is a critique in a double sense. On the one hand, it is an empirical study of traditional political economy since Adam Smith and David Ricardo, pointing to the dysfunction of capitalism as an economic system, and on the other hand it criticizes political economy because it abstracts the economy from human needs. It is this humanistic critique of modern society that I consider to be Marx's most valuable contribution.

While teaching my courses on Marxist thought, I took the Critical Theory of the Frankfurt School very seriously, particularly the writings of Max Horkheimer in the 1930s and his critique of a one-sided scientific positivism. Horkheimer stripped Marx of his optimistic philosophy of history and stressed the critical aspects of his thought. He and his associate Adorno proceeded to show how the capitalist market economy has permeated every aspect of culture and everyday life. I parted with them when in the *Dialectic of the Enlightenment,* written in American exile in 1944, they, like Foucault, made the Enlightenment responsible for the barbarism of the twentieth century. Thus they argued that the Enlightenment had paved the way to totalitarianism and to the Holocaust. Horkheimer and particularly Adorno, with his elitist conception of culture, moved dangerously close to the anti-rationalism of Friedrich Nietzsche and Martin Heidegger that fed into the ideology of the right. In this way the left and the right merged again. For Horkheimer and Adorno the core of the Enlightenment was the instrumentalization of reason to organize all of society along scientific lines. But this overlooks the fact that a very basic element of the Enlightenment, I would even say its basic element, was the belief in the dignity of all human beings and the commitment to create a world in which humans using their reason can free themselves from arbitrary authority. Of course, there has also been the danger that in the search for a just world the end justifies the means, as has been the case in revolutionary movements of the left in much of the twentieth century. Yet the ideas of the Enlightenment cannot be blamed for the totalitarianism of Stalin's Russia, Mao's China or Hitler's Germany. They have to be understood in terms of power struggles and entrenched authoritarian structures and traditions, which have little to do with the Enlightenment or even with Marx. Fully cognizant of the deficiencies of Marxism, including those of Western Marxism, I nevertheless see in Marxist thought an important challenge of exploitative political, social, economic, and cultural realities. From the perspective of the early twenty-first century, I am aware that the world is much more complex than the one Marx and Engels perceived in the nineteenth century, or that Western Marxists perceived in the twentieth century.

In January 1970, I accepted a visiting appointment at the University of Rochester to teach the graduate seminar in European Intellectual History, which Hayden White, who had just left for Wesleyan University, was supposed to have taught. I met him shortly after I arrived in Buffalo. I had liked his book, *The Ordeal of Liberal Humanism,* co-authored with Willson Coates, which I considered by far the best textbook on nineteenth and twentieth-century intellectual history, and was also impressed by his two articles in *History and Theory,* "The Burden of History" and his essay on Foucault, that I considered brilliant although I disagreed with him on many points. I visited him in Rochester for the first time shortly after I arrived in Buffalo, and we then met occasionally to discuss our work. We both signed a contract to co-author a small book on the idea of progress in which each of us was supposed to write a longer essay and then reply to the other. I soon completed my essay, but White never wrote his. He was busy with work on his book, *Metahistory. The Historical Imagination in Nineteenth-Century Europe* (1973), one of the most important and influential works of the last third of the twentieth century on the theory of history. White's thesis, simply stated, was that history is a form of literature, that it is in no way a scientific enterprise, and that it must be judged by literary criteria, not by criteria of historical truth. Proceeding from facts, which he concedes can be established empirically, the narrative of the historian consists of interpretations that defy examination as to their truth or accuracy. Selecting four major historians of the nineteenth century, Ranke, Michelet, Jacob Burckhardt, and Alexis de Tocqueville, and four major philosophers, Hegel, Marx, Nietzsche, and Benodetto Croce, White argues that there is no basic difference between works by historians allegedly based on research, and writings in the philosophy of history. I agreed with him that histories necessarily take the form of narratives and that they have a literary character. But this does not mean that these narratives are indistinguishable from works of fiction. Insofar as they are based on research, they seek not to invent but to recapture the past. Admittedly this past can never be reconstructed as it was. It is always seen through the mind of an historian, so that subjective and ideological factors enter into the representation of the past. Thus, every account of the past is incomplete. It is, however, not arbitrary, but subject to generally accepted criteria of logical inquiry.

In the fall of 1969 White left the University of Rochester to accept a position at Wesleyan University. Perez Zagorin, the chair at Rochester, asked me to teach White's graduate seminar in European intellectual history in the spring semester of 1970. The University of Rochester is slightly more than an hour's drive from Buffalo, so I could easily combine this with my teaching in Buffalo. Soon Zagorin offered me a full-time position as White's successor. This was still the time when departments could make appointments without a national search. I declined but agreed to teach one seminar a semester until White's position was filled. Thus until the end of the spring semester 1971, I drove to Rochester each Monday. One student whom I found particularly challenging was Russell Jacoby, who wrote several papers for me, including a critique of psychoanalysis from the perspective of Critical Theory, which became part of the first of his several important books, *Social Amnesia. A Critique of Conformist Psychology from Adler to Laing* (1975). At the University of Rochester I entered a world completely different from that of the university in Buffalo where, in the spring semester of 1970, all hell had broken loose. In Buffalo many windows had been smashed and many walls were covered with revolutionary graffiti, while in Rochester all was quiet. With its high tuition, the University of Rochester as a private school recruited a different student body than Buffalo. Some of the students in my Rochester seminars were Marxists of some sort or other, but they were committed to the theoretical critique of the existing order, not to open confrontation. To be sure, in Buffalo the history students were also relatively passive compared to those in sociology or philosophy. Yet among both my Buffalo and my Rochester students there was an interest in Critical Theory. When students in Buffalo had asked me to arrange discussions on Sunday afternoons, Rochester students soon joined us and we then met alternately in Buffalo and Rochester.

In the following year, Eugene Genovese, the new chair, renewed the offer that Zagorin had originally made. With its exciting faculty Rochester seemed very attractive. Genovese was about to publish *Roll Jordan Roll. The World the Slaves Made,* and Herbert Gutman, who had been my office neighbor during my first year in Buffalo, was also there, working on immigrant working class culture as well as on the black family in slavery and freedom. Both Genovese and Gutman were cultural Marxists. Genovese was strongly influenced by Antonio Gramsci, Gutman by E. P. Thompson, and both stressed the role of slaves or workers as active agents in shaping their own destiny. Genovese had earlier been a member of the Communist Party, but became increasingly conservative both politically and in his approach to history. In the 1990s, together with his wife, Elizabeth Fox-Genovese, a social historian of the Old Regime, he co-founded the Historical Society, that was intended as an alternative to the American Historical Association and its alleged cultural radicalism and historical relativism. Christopher Lasch and Perez Zagorin emerged as critics of the new culturalist historical relativism.

There were a number of reasons why I decided against accepting the offer from the University of Rochester. I was on good terms with everyone in the department in Rochester. Every Monday I had lunch in the elegant faculty club with one of my potential colleagues. But the department was terribly split, not only on ideological lines but also because of personality conflicts. Gutman had been instrumental in recruiting Genovese, but the two soon became bitter enemies. Had I gone to Rochester, I would have been drawn into these conflicts. Moreover, I felt at home in the Buffalo department, and still was optimistic about its future. There was also Wilma's position at Canisius College, and finally, my active involvement in the Buffalo draft counseling center was very important to me. As we mentioned in the previous chapter, Wilma and I had already been active in the opposition to the Vietnam War in Chicago as members of a peace group that sponsored demonstrations and teach-ins and that placed ads in the local newspapers and in the *New York Times*. We continued these activities in Buffalo as a matter of conscience, without being convinced that they were in any way effective. Wilma joined the Women's International League of Peace and Freedom, and was elected president of the Buffalo chapter, but was soon disillusioned by bickering in the group that prevented it from making a difference in the opposition to the war. In 1967 I became one of the founders of the Greater Buffalo Draft Counselling Center.

There were two major groups in Buffalo that were opposed to the draft, each in a different way. One was Draft Resistance, part of a national movement that encouraged young men to destroy their draft cards and to take refuge abroad in Canada or Sweden. Canada was merely a few hundred yards from Buffalo across the Peace Bridge, and at the time was still willing to take in draft refugees. Our draft counseling center took a very different approach. We dissuaded persons subject to the draft from going to Canada, except as a last resort. Instead, we counselled them to explore the legal alternatives, such as conscientious objection, as well as medical and hardship exemptions. A number of my colleagues volunteered to do counseling. The Quakers (Friends) in Buffalo supported our efforts and let us use their Meeting House from Monday morning until Saturday evening. At this point we were a congenial group of well-meaning academics with little training in selective service law and regulations. The Friends recruited a young Quaker, Larry Scott, to organize and professionalize the counselling. Scott moved into the Friends Meeting House with his wife and began to train the counsellors. To begin with he had someone from the staff of the Central Committee for Conscientious Objectors (CCCO) to come from Philadelphia to conduct an intensive one-week training session, which included the thorough study of regulations. Almost none of the original counsellors took the course. Instead, a large number of young people came, many of them intent on applying for conscientious objector status themselves. Soon about forty volunteers counselled as many as three hundred young men a week. I committed myself to counsel at the Friends Meeting House every Tuesday and Thursday evening. I also met applicants at my office at the university and at home. We prepared applicants for their meetings with the draft board, and discussed their written statements in which they explained the nature of their pacifist beliefs and how they arrived at them. We then set up a trial session. They had to make it clear that they were in principle opposed to all wars, not only to a specific one. We advised them that in the event that they were turned down by the board, to follow all the steps required under the selective service law, such as submitting to the physical examination and reporting for induction. At induction they would be asked to take a step forward and with that step they would be in the armed services. We suggested to them that at this point they disobey and refuse to take this step. They could then be arrested and charged with a criminal offense, but from then on it would be up to the government to prove that they were not conscientious objectors. Buffalo was fortunate in having two federal judges who were sympathetic to defendants and either acquitted them or sentenced them to alternative civilian service. A fair number of draft resisters came to us to refuse induction in Buffalo from federal districts in the South where they were likely to receive sentences of as many as five years, until eventually new regulations required that they report for induction in their home districts. Jehovah's Witnesses, who as a matter of conscience refused even civilian service, faced jail sentences. Canada for us was a last resort when all legal channels failed.

In retrospect I am not entirely happy with what we did. Our counselling center was a visible sign of opposition to what we considered a criminal war. But our clientele consisted almost exclusively of middle-class students, and in their place socially and economically less advantaged young men were sent to Vietnam. The procedure by which applicants had to explain their beliefs in writing discriminated against those who had fewer literary skills. We tried very hard to reach out to the black community, but with almost no success, even though the Friends Meeting House was in a largely black neighborhood. And we had no black counselors. I am also aware that few of the persons I counselled were pacifists, even if they pretended to be. They were against the war in Vietnam, or in many cases, like most middle class kids, just wanted to get out of the army. I was deeply disappointed when a good friend of Daniel, whom I had counselled, joined the Israeli army—shortly after he was recognized as a conscientious objector in the US.

Both our sons Jeremy and Daniel applied for conscientious objector status. Jonathan turned eighteen shortly after the draft ended. Jeremy had no problem being recognized. Daniel, who was also deeply committed in his opposition to war, had been active in peace causes since he was ten. Both had impressive letters from teachers, community leaders and friends, and in both cases our rabbi Daniel Kerman, who knew them well, testified for them. Daniel was turned down. For a long time conscientious objectors had to present a traditional theistic belief or affiliation with a peace church, but a short time earlier, the Supreme Court had decided that deeply held beliefs did in fact constitute a religious outlook. Nevertheless, the board decided that Daniel's pacifism was purely political. In a bizarre statement it justified its decision in poor English in the following words:

> "The registrant states that his views of being against participation in war are religious views. However, it seems to the local board that the registrant's claims are strictly due to political happenings. He indicated that his parents fled from Nazi dominated Europe. His parents were then involved in the civil rights movement in the South. He also indicated that his parents were very peace oriented as were the three rabbis in the synagogues he received religious instruction were peace oriented. He further states that he was in West Germany when the Eichmann trial began and that it was an emotional experience for his parents. He states that he participated in several peaceful marches during the Cuban missile crisis. The local board feels that on the information above, that the registrants views are only political because of his parents involvement when he was young. He states that his rabbis were peace-oriented. Therefore, since his views are political, according to LBM 107, he does not qualify for a C.O. classification." The vote was 5 to 0 to deny Daniel C.O. status.

At the time, applicants who had been turned down had to face induction unless they had a sufficiently high draft lottery number to avoid being called up. Daniel did not yet know what his lottery number would be. He had just completed his freshman year, taking courses both at Canisius College and UB, and decided to transfer to York University in Toronto for the remainder of his undergraduate studies. He received the lottery number of 349 out of a possible 365, a number which would never be reached, as most other eligible nineteen year olds would have to be drafted in order to reach his number. He could have legally returned to the United States, but decided to go to law school in Canada and make his home there. Today his views have become more conservative, while Jeremy's and Jonathan's have not. Jeremy also received a high draft number and thus did not have to perform alternative service.

In the fall of 1971 Wilma, Jonathan, and I went to Göttingen on a sabbatical. Before going to Germany I asked to be trained as a counsellor for objectors in the military. This was an opportunity for the Buffalo Draft Counseling Center to extend its services to persons in the armed services. I went through a training course in Buffalo conducted by a CCCO staff member from Philadelphia. In Germany I worked with American military for the first time. One of the two German draft and military counseling organizations referred several American soldiers to me who, for the most part, merely wanted information. But I worked closely with two cases, a non-commissioned military police officer and a lieutenant stationed at a nuclear installation, both of whom decided to apply for discharges on grounds of conscience. The military police officer came several times with his wife to see me in Göttingen, and I set up mock hearings in which two persons from the German organization participated. Both cases resulted in honorable discharges.

When I returned to Buffalo in the fall of 1972, I for the first time dealt with young soldiers, including several women, who had joined the military because they hoped to receive vocational training, and then realized that the reality which they confronted was very different from what they expected when they enlisted. Now we were reaching the people with whom we had always wanted to work, including an occasional African American or Latino, and one Native American from a nearby reservation.

We had joined the Reform synagogue, Temple Beth Am, when we first came to Buffalo because we wanted our children to have a liberal Jewish education. We were very impressed with the rabbi, Daniel Kerman, a real Mensch with a social conscience with whom we could communicate well. But in all the years we were members we had little in common with the members of this relatively affluent suburban congregation. We were disappointed in the quality of the religious instruction. Jeremy met individually with Kerman, which was good, and he also remained the only one of our children with an informed interest in Judaism. Daniel and Jonathan were taught by uninspired women from Israel whose main qualification was that they spoke Modern Hebrew, but who knew little about Judaism. The result was that both Daniel, who skipped many of the classes and together with a friend passed the time in a nearby pizza parlor, and Jonathan, were thoroughly alienated.

Kerman shared our opposition to the Vietnam War and had the courage to participate in anti-war demonstrations on the Sabbath, without incurring criticism from the congregation. But Israel was another matter. He largely agreed with us, but refrained from making his views known publicly. He encouraged me to conduct a small study group on Sunday mornings on the historical background of the Israeli-Palestinian conflict. When the Quakers called for a dialogue between Arabs and Jews, I proposed to Kerman a four person panel, including a Jewish student from Tel Aviv University and a Palestinian student from Bir Zeit University on the West Bank. Kerman agreed, but would continuously find reasons for postponing the discussion until both students had returned home. I then suggested a discussion between Kerman and George Hourani, a professor of medieval Arab philosophy, after the Friday evening service. Kerman agreed and was even enthusiastic about the idea. Hourani was a distinguished philosopher, an Oxford Ph.D., a Lebanese Christian who had taught in Jerusalem from 1939 to 1949. In Buffalo he established a program in medieval Jewish philosophy at the university. Hourani was committed to Jewish-Arab understanding, but understandably also saw the Palestinian side. After the discussion was announced in the Buffalo newspaper, some members of the congregation began a hate campaign against Hourani, claiming that he was associated with radical Palestinian groups committed to the destruction of the State of Israel, which was an outright lie. A few hours before the discussion was to take place, Kerman called me and told me that he was under considerable pressure from some members of the congregation to cancel the session. He had not yet made up his mind, but he hoped that I would understand if he called off the discussion. I told him that if the discussion was cancelled, I—and I was sure Wilma too—would leave the congregation. When we arrived for the evening service, still not certain about Kerman's decision, we found an unusually large number of persons present, including some Arab students. There was general disappointment, including among many of the congregants, when it became clear that there would be no discussion. Wilma and I then resigned. Kerman came to our house to persuade us to change our minds, said that the time had not yet come for the discussion, but promised to start a program of education. We have since then not joined a congregation in Buffalo, but instead have attended services at Hillel, the Jewish student association.

In Buffalo I directed doctoral candidates for the first time. The first dissertation was by Zdenka Gredel-Manuele, a young woman born in Croatia, who spent the war years as a child in Germany before coming to the United States. She wrote on historical studies in post-war Germany, both East and West. Her work included a good deal of oral history, interviews with historians in both Germanys. Clarence Pate, an American with a German wife, followed with a study of the controversial, nationalist historian Hans Rothfels comparing the continuities in Rothfels' work before his forced emigration from Germany in 1939 and after his return to West Germany after the war. In retrospect the question may be raised whether this study, relying on published works, was too early considering that Rothfels' papers were not yet accessible. Next came a dissertation by an African student, Micah Tsomondo, a refugee from Rhodesia, an intellectual biography of Kwame Nkrumah, examining European influences on his African socialism. Tsomondo was one of the brightest students I have taught, had a classical British education which included Latin and Greek, and wrote an eloquent English. After completing his doctorate, Tsomondo taught at the University of Maryland in College Park, but in 1980, immediately after Zimbabwe became independent, returned there and had an impressive career as undersecretary of labor in the Zimbabwe government and as Zimbabwe's representative at the International Labor Organization in Geneva. He died tragically in a traffic accident in Zimbabwe about ten years ago.

I was very interested in attracting good foreign students to Buffalo since it was difficult for us to recruit the best American students who were more likely to receive funding at the Ivy League schools or at the more prestigious state universities. In fact a majority of my doctoral candidates have been foreign. In the 1970s and 80s there was Peter Walther from West Berlin, who wrote about the German historians who fled to the United States during the Nazi period. He is now a researcher at the Humboldt University in Berlin. Then there was Sang-Woo Lim, who had served time in jail in South Korea because of his involvement in student protests and afterwards was not permitted to continue his studies there, but did so well on the Graduate Record Examination that we offered him a doctoral fellowship. He wrote a thesis on the émigré sociologist Albert Salomon and now has a professorship at Sogong University in Seoul. Next came Liang-kai Chou from Taiwan, who wrote on the historiography of British labor and who is now a professor in Taiwan; then Lixin Shao from Beijing who wrote on Nietzsche in China and remained in the United States. Supriya Mukherjee from Calcutta and New Delhi, who was very much interested in German Jewish culture and in educational reform movements in Germany, wrote on the German Jewish psychologist William Stern. Henry Darcy, my oldest doctoral student, had fled Nazi Germany to Belgium as a political refugee, escaped to France when the Nazis invaded Belgium, was handed over to the Germans by the Vichy French, and imprisoned in Buchenwald concentration camp until its liberation in 1945. He wrote a dissertation on the Lex Heinze, a vice and morality law sponsored by the government under Wilhelm II and bitterly opposed by the Social Democrats.

During my period as chair of the department from 1981 to 1984, the director of graduate studies rejected two Asian women applicants, Supriyah Mukherjee who had accompanied her Indian husband who was a doctoral candidate in the economics department, and Shih-deh Chang who had accompanied her husband Liang-kai Chou. I concluded that both were highly qualified candidates, and overrode the director of graduate studies. Later I had to intervene under the next director of graduate studies, to rescue an African American candidate, Robert Wright, whose eight-hundred page dissertation on the Pan-Africanism of W. E. B. DuBois was rejected and who was dropped from the doctoral program for what I thought were arbitrary reasons partly based on personal antagonisms. I thought the dissertation was excellent. I was particularly impressed by Wright's treatment of DuBois' early studies in Germany were he studied under the so-called "Socialists of the Chair" at the University of Berlin, who were political conservatives, but advocates of social reform to win the allegiance of the working class, and also knew the famous German sociologist Max Weber. Through contact with the German Social Democratic Party, Du Bois became acquainted with Marxist thought. DuBois' later development, Wright argues, cannot be understood without this German phase. Wright's dissertation was ultimately approved.

I also had a number of good dissertations by Americans in the 1970s and 80s. The one by Walter Peterson about the German journalists in Parisian exile between 1933 and 1940 was excellent. Peterson has been a teacher at the J. F. Kennedy School in Berlin for many years. A study of the German League for Human Rights in the Weimar Republic was written by Richard Cohen, who had followed me from Rochester to Buffalo and obtained both his doctorate and a law degree and decided to make law his career.

I also succeeded in establishing a graduate student exchange program with the Technical University (Technische Hochschule) in Darmstadt, Germany, which proved to be important for the preparation of our doctoral students. In 1968, when we were searching for a historian of Germany, I suggested that we bring Helmut Böhme to Buffalo for an interview. Böhme had just published an important book on the unification of Germany in 1871 in which he placed less emphasis on the role of Otto von Bismarck than had almost all histories on the topic, and focused instead on the role of economic factors, particularly trade, which led to the primacy of Prussia. I was fairly certain that because of his liberal views, and as as a student of Fritz Fischer Böhme would have difficulty obtaining a post in Germany. Fischer at the time was highly controversial in Germany because in his book, *Germany' Aims in the First World War* (1961) he had placed the prime responsibility for the outbreak of the First World War on Germany and seen a continuity between Imperial Germany's annexationist aims then and the Nazis' aims in the

Second World War. We offered Böhme the position, but to our and his surprise he was offered a professorship at the Technical University in Darmstadt, and soon afterward was elected to its presidency as the youngest university president in Germany. We have been good friends ever since.

When we visited Böhme in Darmstadt in the summer of 1974, he suggested that we exchange advanced students between our two history departments. While neither of us had money for an exchange, we found a solution: we would exchange fellowships. The student from Buffalo going to Darmstadt would vacate a fellowship in Buffalo and vice versa. My chair approved, and the program started in the fall of 1975 on a very small scale with no bureaucracy involved. Böhme and I made the selections. The exchange proved to be of great advantage to both sides. We sent our students to Darmstadt before they took their qualifying examinations for their Ph.D.s to perfect their German and to become acquainted with the German scene, and in consultation with the staff there to explore topics for a dissertation. The Darmstadt students were able to travel from Buffalo to American archives. As long as the exchange was so small, Wilma and I befriended the students from Darmstadt, friendships that in several cases have lasted until now. Wilma supplied the Darmstadt students with necessities for their temporary households, which were returned to our basement when they returned to Germany to be available for the next set of exchange students. After a few years the exchange was formalized and a contract signed. Responsibility was taken out of my hands and situated in the Office of International Education, although I was still consulted. Later the exchange was extended to include the entire university. Darmstadt was increasingly interested in sending natural scientists, computer specialists, and architects to Buffalo, but for some years a spot was reserved for an historian; Buffalo, in turn, sent primarily persons in the humanities who had a working knowledge of German. We were quite successful in obtaining money from various foundations and agencies, especially from the German Academic Exchange Service (DAAD), for our students to do their dissertation research in Germany. The program was seriously crippled by our administration in 1998, when it began to require that our students pay full Buffalo tuition for the time they are in Darmstadt, where there was no tuition. In Buffalo these students would have had a tuition waver and a stipend; if they went to Darmstadt they would have no Buffalo funding and hence would find it difficult to pay the Buffalo tuition.

In 1968, my book *The German Conception of History. The National Tradition of Historical Thought from Herder to the Present* was published. The book addressed two basic problems: It examined the claims to scholarly objectivity of the German historical profession, on which much of its international prestige rested, and showed to what extent a nationalist ideology colored and distorted its writings. Furthermore, it questioned the philosophical assumptions of this tradition, often labeled as historism *(Historismus)*, which denied that there are any universal standards of right or wrong, such as human rights, but that every historical epoch must be judged on its own terms. Claiming to be free of all metaphysical presuppositions, the practitioners of this tradition assumed that the political and social system as it existed in Germany under the Hohenzollern monarchy represented a higher moral order. While theoretically rejecting the idea of progress, they in fact hailed the unification of Germany under Bismarck with its authoritarian and militaristic aspects as the high point of history. They not only rejected Enlightenment conceptions of human rights as unhistorical, but also repudiated Western conceptions of democracy.

In the United States my book was treated as essentially an academic work. Walter Simon, in a nasty review in the *American Historical Review*,[1] asserted that I was seeking to establish a direct line from Martin Luther via Bismarck to Hitler, although the English version of the book did not even treat historians in the Nazi period. Nevertheless it tried to show how the historians contributed to an intellectual atmosphere that made it easy for many Germans to accept Nazism. In the long run the book did not do badly in the United States either. It went through a second revised edition and remained in print until very recently. To my surprise the Deutsche Taschenbuch Verlag (dtv), the largest publisher of scholarly paperbacks in Germany, decided to bring out a German edition under the title *Deutsche Geschichtswissenschaft* early in 1971. The title that the publisher chose, and that I did not see until the German version appeared, suggested that this was a history of the German historical profession, while in fact it was an examination of the basic assumptions of this profession, not of their actual writings on history. In Germany the book played a very different role than in America. There had been no similar critical examination of the philosophical and political assumptions of the German historical profession. Historians who came from this tradition, trained in the Weimar Republic or in a few cases even still in the *Kaiserreich* (German Empire), were still firmly entrenched.

But a younger generation born between 1929 and 1941, who grew to intellectual maturity after the war, began to question the political and philosophical ideology of this establishment. They looked critically at Germany's national past, saw the failure of Germany to follow Western societies on the road to democracy, and returned to Enlightenment ideals of human rights. They saw it as a tragedy that the rapid economic modernization of Germany in the last part of the nineteenth century was not accompanied by the transformation of an outdated political and social system. Bismarck's unification of Germany by "blood and iron" under the hegemony of an authoritarian, militaristic Prussian monarchy was now seen not as the glorious high point of German history, but as a tragedy. This new generation turned to the West not only politically but also intellectually. Some of the leading historians in this generation were: Hans-Ulrich Wehler, perhaps the most influential and articulate among them, Hans Mommsen, Wolfgang Mommsen, Dietrich Bracher, Dieter Groh, Jörn Rüsen, Gerhard A. Ritter—no relation of Gerhard Ritter, the leading establishment historian—and the somewhat younger Jürgen Kocka. I established contact with all of them and Rüsen and Kocka became particularly good friends. Wehler coined the term "Historical Social Sci-

---

[1] Vol. 74 (1968–69), 1019–1021.

ence" to denote an approach that moved away from a state oriented history of the old school to an analysis of the social structure in which states function.

A crucial concern of the younger historians was the troubling question of how it was possible for the Nazis to come to power and carry out their terrorist and genocidal policies. Particularly Wehler and Kocka were strongly influenced by empirical social science, as it was practiced particularly in the United States, but also by the sociology of Max Weber, who placed greater emphasis on cultural factors. Although none were Marxists, they viewed social inequality as a major factor in political conflict. For Wehler the Critical Theory of the Frankfurt School was very important, particularly the work of Max Horkheimer, which rejected a positivistic social science that approached the objects of its studies primarily empirically, without asking what they meant in terms of human needs.

My book was taken seriously in Germany, even if there were some dissenting voices who felt that I carried my critique of the German tradition too far. My name now was much better known in Germany than in the United States. For many history students the book became required reading. However a few days after the publication of the book in Germany, I received a letter from a young German historian, Thomas Nipperdey, who later wrote a monumental history of modern Germany and challenged the critical assessment of German history by the historians I have just mentioned. In his letter he complained that I had dealt with the German historians from the perspective of their ideologies rather than their substantial works based on serious research. I replied that a history of historiography must not limit itself to a critique of ideology, but that the ideology of the historians with whom I dealt had colored their scholarly work.

At about the same time a registered letter arrived from Robert Servatius, the attorney who had defended Eichmann in Jerusalem and who had represented former Nazis in West Germany, on behalf of his client Walther Hubatsch, who had been an active Nazi historian before 1945. In the German edition, but not in the American version, I had briefly mentioned historians who had written history in the service of the Nazis and included Hubatsch. Although Hubatsch denied this, there was solid documentary evidence that he had been affiliated with Walter Frank's *Reichsinstitut für die Geschichte des Neuen Deutschlands* (the Reich Institute for the History of the New Germany), a Nazi institute committed to rewriting the history of Germany from a racist National Socialist perspective. All this was true. But I had made an embarrassing mistake in listing Hubatsch in a footnote as the recipient of three grants from the institute although he had received only one. I had misread a list of grants issued by the institute in Helmut Heiber's monumental study of Frank's Institute. Heiber had correctly listed the first grant and then marked two further ones with "—" which I assumed referred to Hubatsch, but apparently referred to two anonymous recipients. Servatius asked for a court injunction against the distribution of the book. The matter, however, was resolved when the publisher agreed to insert a note in each book to the effect that Hubatsch was not the recipient of these other grants, and I agreed to publish a note in the *Zeitschrift für Zeitgeschichte* (Journal for Contemporary History) admitting my mistake. The matter was thus settled. In my book I had mentioned that Hubatsch had been commissioned to write a history of Germany for the West German army, but very soon after my book appeared the army withdrew his book from circulation. I do not know whether this action was directly related to my book, but it may very well have led Hubatsch to bring charges against me to clear himself. In the meantime, I learned what I had not known before, that in 1943 Hubatsch had edited the posthumous book, *Volk im Feld* (Nation at War—nation understood here in racial terms) on the Nazi campaigns in France and in Russia by the Nazi historian Kleo Pleyer, who had fallen on the Russian front. In the book, which was widely circulated among the German troops, Pleyer not only justified the brutal treatment of prisoners of war, but called for the "Ausrottung des Judentums" (extermination of Jewry). I intended in the second edition that appeared in 1972 to acknowledge my mistake, but to maintain my allegation that Hubatsch was affiliated with Frank's institute and that he edited the Pleyer volume. The editor at dtv, who had been very supportive of me in this matter, asked me to arrange a personal meeting with Hubatsch. Wilma and I saw him in his office in Bonn, where I confronted him with further archival evidence of his links to Frank's institute and brought up the Pleyer book. He said that he would not undertake anything further, but referring to the historians I listed as Nazis, he commented that after all he had been in good company. I was disappointed when the editor decided not to include my reference to the Pleyer book in the new edition.

The Max-Planck-Institute for History in Göttingen became increasingly important for my work, more so than the university. I have never had an official affiliation with the institute, but since 1961 I have been a steady guest, always having at least a table at which I could work and sometimes, when space was available, even an office. The Institute library contained most of the books and journals I needed; the rest were mostly in the University library. At the institute I found not only researchers with whom I could discuss my work, of whom several became good friends, but a steady stream of visitors from all corners of the world, including quite early scholars from Eastern Europe and East Asia. I know of no comparable meeting place elsewhere. In the sixties I became well acquainted with Dietrich Gerhard, a student of Friedrich Meinecke, who had emigrated to the United States during the Nazi period, divided his time between Washington University in St. Louis and the University of Cologne after the war, and after his retirement in 1962 came to the Max Planck Institute to direct a comparative project on Europe during the Old Regime. In 1971 Rudolf Vierhaus came as director and brought young scholars who worked on proto-industrialization, the transformation of the countryside on the eve of industrialization. Beginning with the examination of material life, they moved to a broad examination of village life with an emphasis on family life, social relations and daily life. Using computers, they examined the economic transformation of the countryside in the process of industrialization and at the same time explored how those affected by this process reacted to and influenced this process. This approach called for new methods of understanding the cultural setting in which these reactions took place. Thus, the same historians who had begun in the 1970s with the analysis of economic and demographic developments, and in the 1980s turned to an anthropological study of everyday life, to what came to be called *Alltagsgeschichte,* about which I shall say more later. Vierhaus, whose historiographical and political outlook was more traditional than that of the young people he had brought, deserves credit for the stimulating and open atmosphere at the institute. We very much appreciated him also as a person who had time to follow and discuss both my and Wilma's work.

In the 1970s I moved away from my concentration on German historiography in the nineteenth and the first half of the twentieth century to two topics, one a comparative survey of contemporary historical writing, the other historical thought in the Enlightenment with a focus on Germany, but placing the German Enlightenment in the broader context of the European Enlightenment. My study of the Enlightenment did not result in a book, but in a number of articles and a volume, *Aufklärung und Geschichte* (The Enlightenment and History) which I coedited, the result of a conference at the Max Planck Institute for History in 1980. It did not seem to me that there was a smooth transition from eighteenth-century Enlightenment to the historicism of the German Historical School of the nineteenth century, as had often been argued, but rather that some of the historians of the eighteenth century, foremost among them A. L. Schlözer, had an approach to social history and the history of everyday life and a world historical perspective that the much vaunted German historians of the nineteenth century did not have. In their focus on the political aspects of the nation and on its rejection of methods of social analysis, the latter seemed to me much more provincial and one-sided than a good deal of the historiography of the eighteenth century and of historical writing in Western Europe and America in the nineteenth century.

The journal *History and Theory* asked me to prepare a special issue of the journal on contemporary historiographical trends. I submitted the draft manuscript, assuming it would need to be cut, but received a letter from *History and Theory,* and from the Wesleyan University Press, the publisher of *History and Theory* that they would like to publish the manuscript uncut as a book. The book appeared under the title, *New Directions in European Historiography* (1975). In it I examined four important currents: the French *Annales* circle, West German Historical Social Science, varieties of Marxism in the Eastern bloc with a focus on a non-dogmatic social and cultural history in Poland indebted to the *Annales,* and a chapter together with my Buffalo colleague Norman Baker on new trends in British historical writing with special attention to the Western Marxist school. A rewritten version appeared then in German as a dtv paperback with a new chapter on developments in American historiography by my Buffalo colleague Michael Frisch. Translations also appeared in Italian, Danish, Greek, Chinese, Japanese, and Korean.

I began moving between two orientations in German social and cultural historiography, the so-called Bielefeld School of Historical Social Science at the newly founded University of Bielefeld and its journal *Geschichte und Gesellschaft* (History and Society) with Hans-Ulrich Wehler and Jürgen Kocka its chief editors, and the practitioners of *Alltagsgeschichte* (History of Everyday Life), represented by Hans Medick, Alf Lüdtke, Jürgen Schlumbohm, Peter Kriedte, and, before he returned to America, David Sabean. My sympathies lay between these two orientations.

The Bielefeld School proceeded sociologically, interested in social structures and processes, quite aware of social conflict, and never forgetting what had gone wrong in Germany. In their emphasis on processes of modernization in industrial societies with their impact on politics they differed markedly from many of the *Annales* historians, who also concentrated on structures with much less concern about change, and took refuge in the premodern, preindustrial world, which French historians could do much more easily than German historians because of the latter's sense of responsibility for what had happened.

The advocates of *Alltagsgeschichte* felt strongly that the social science historians paid too little attention to the fate and life experiences of individual human beings. Wanting a history with a human face, they turned away from the macro-history of social science history to what they called microhistory, a history that concentrated on small topics. Instead of sociology, economics, and statistical demography, they turned to cultural anthropology and semiotics in seeking to grasp the sense of meaning in a culture, seeing in symbols a key to understanding. Family relations, work, and mentalities all played an important role for them. Many turned away from the modern world, but the works of Medick and Sabean, each of whom examined pre-industrial society and culture in a small village, took into consideration the impact of the emergence of a capitalist industrial economy on the transformation and dissolution of these small communities.

Alltagsgeschichte was not a specifically German phenomenon, but had its counterparts in Italian *microstoria* and the history workshops in Great Britain and Scandinavia. A good deal of *Alltagsgeschichte* in Germany dealt with every day life under the Nazi dictatorship, particularly the work of Alf Lüdtke and of Lutz Niethammer, while others dealt with the Holocaust. Beginning in the 1980s, historians of the Memorial oral history group in the Soviet Union undertook similar studies of life under Stalinism and thereafter, based on the testimony of witnesses. Inevitably, the social and cultural history of these two orientations had to converge, and it largely did by the 1990s.

My own perspective on historiography became increasingly comparative and international. Since my doctoral studies I had always followed the discussions in France and frequently went to Paris to present my work, and occasionally also to Great Britain and the Netherlands. I already mentioned my contacts with Jerzy Topolski in Poland. In 1978 Wilma and I were guests of the Institute of History at the Academy of Sciences in Budapest for ten days. Since the two historians who invited and accompanied us were old time Communists, we were probably given a one-sided view of historiography and political attitudes. When we returned to the Hungarian Academy of Sciences in 1986 at the invitation of Ferenc Glatz and his associate Attila Pók, much had changed. The atmosphere was much more open, and contacts with the West were now well developed. I was particularly impressed by Gyorgy Ránki, an innovative economic and social historian, who divided his time between Budapest and the University of Indiana. My book, *The German Conception of History*, was just being translated into Hungarian.

Wilma and I traveled frequently to Czechoslovakia, but the historians there had either gone into exile or been dismissed from their positions. Francis Carsten in London, who in the 1930s had funneled money to the Social Democratic resistance in Nazi Germany, asked my colleague William Allen and me to organize the collection of money in the United States for Czech dissidents.

Beginning in 1980, I also had increasing contacts with East Asia. Soon after the end of the Cultural Revolution, Buffalo established an exchange program with Beijing Teachers College. In 1982, when I was chair of our department, I was asked whether we would be willing to take a historian from Beijing Teachers College for half a year as a guest, and I readily agreed. The visitor, Professor Qi Shirong, although very reserved, fitted well into the department and gave seminars on his research on British appeasement policy in the 1930s. In the summer of 1984, Wilma and I went to China for six and a half weeks as part of the exchange. We lived at the Friendship Hotel for foreign scholars. I gave two lectures at Beijing Teachers College, two in Zhang Zhilian's seminar at Beijing University, and two at the Chinese Academy of Social Sciences. Zhang had previously participated in my seminar in Buffalo. He was a highly cultured gentleman, educated in Paris and Oxford prior to the establishment of the People's Republic, an expert on the Enlightenment and on the French Revolution, and not at all the kind of doctrinaire Marxist we had thought we would encounter in China. I spoke about currents in contemporary Western historiography and about Western Marxism. There was always a lively discussion, mediated by an interpreter. After having lectured in East Berlin and Leipzig earlier that year, I was struck that with one sole exception, there were no questions couched in Marxist language. The democracy movement was already in full swing. A group of students at Beijing University asked me to spend an afternoon with them, which I did. About thirty students attended. Their main interest was in Western literature of which they knew but which was not accessible to them, including Karl Popper and Milton Friedman. Another group of students visited us in our hotel accompanied by an interpreter, which took courage because they had to register at the entrance. I had a particularly intense conversation with a student from East China Normal University, Wang Qingjia, who had come from Shanghai to attend my lectures in Beijing and invited us to visit him in Shanghai, which we did. An active correspondence followed and I was instrumental in his obtaining a doctoral fellowship at Syracuse University. We have become very good friends and are now working on a joint project. Wilma lectured on German literature at the Foreign Language Institute and was impressed on how well the students had been trained in both German language and culture. We interrupted our stay in Beijing for a two-week tour of the country, flying to the ancient capital of Xian, from where we also visited the nearby terra cotta soldiers. From there we took the train to Kaifong, where there had been a Jewish community from the Middle Ages until the mid-nineteenth century of which there are almost no reminders left today, and on to Nanjing where I gave a lecture at Nanjing University. From Nanjing we proceeded to the two beautiful cities of Souchou and Hanchou and to Shanghai. Our friend Akira Hayashima, whom we had met in Germany, where he had obtained his doctorate from Theodor Schieder in Cologne, had arranged for us to spend a week in Japan on our way home, and there I met with the Japanese circle for modern German studies in Kyoto and the Japanese *Annales* circle in Tokyo.

The following year I was invited to South Korea by Prof. Lee Min-Ho, a historian of Germany whom I had met at the Max Planck Institute for History. The Korean translation of the *New Directions in European Historiography* had just appeared. In Seoul I addressed the Korean association of European Historians and then spoke to a large student audience at Taegu University. Interestingly, in contrast to my audiences in Beijing, many of the students at Taegu, judging from their questions, were Marxists. From Seoul we flew to Taiwan to visit my student Liang-kai Chou and his wife Chang Shih-deh in Taichung, who arranged a meeting with historians in Taipeh.

In 1986 Jürgen Kocka invited me to participate in a project on bourgeois society and culture in the nineteenth century from a comparative European perspective to be held at the ZiF, the Center for Interdisciplinary Research at the University of Bielefeld, from the fall of 1986 to the summer of 1987. Kocka had invited historians, philosophers, specialists in literature, art, and architecture, sociologists, political scientists, and anthropologists from a host of countries in Western and Eastern Europe, the United States, and Israel for the year or parts of the year, and for the first time also two scholars from East Germany, the social historian Hartmut Zwahr and the cultural anthropologist Wolfgang Jacobeit. The GDR permitted them to participate in this project, but forbade their wives from joining or even visiting them. We were all housed on the campus of the ZiF, located a five-minute walk up the hill from the University of Bielefeld. There were apartments for the participants, a library, and a swimming pool where I swam every evening. Before our time the famous cultural historian and anthropologist Norbert Elias had been a fellow at the ZiF for several years and had been interviewed in the swimming pool by West German television. There was a conscious attempt to create a community, with formal meetings on Tuesday mornings at which one of the participants presented a paper, and there were many occasions for informal exchanges. My task was to pursue a comparative study of the German and French historical professions in the second half of the nineteenth century in the context of different political and intellectual cultures.

In Bielefeld I established contact with the local Jewish community. It was a sad handful of people, almost none originally from Germany, who had a bad conscience about being in Germany and eschewed all contact with Germans. An exception was Frau Florsheim, born in 1900 in nearby Dortmund, who had returned to Germany from Palestine after the war and despite her age was active in speaking to school classes about Judaism and in establishing contacts with various church and other community groups in Bielefeld. Since no one in the congregation knew how to conduct a Passover seder, the president of the congregation asked me to conduct it. When he found out that Frau Florsheim had invited several non-Jews to the seder, he wanted the invitations to be cancelled. After I told him that I would not conduct the seder if they were not welcome, he reluctantly gave in, but I was never again informed of any activities of the congregation. The second seder we held at our apartment with the Wehlers, the Kockas, Frau Florsheim, and the Hungarian historian Gyorgy Ránki, a survivor of Auschwitz.

In the spring of 1980 I received a communication from Charles Carbonell, a French historian, and Lucian Boia, a Romanian, asking me to join them in organizing an international commission on the history of historiography at the International Congress of Historical Sciences in Bucharest later that year. The International Committee of Historical Sciences, the world association of historians, supported their plan. The founding meeting was well attended. To my pleasant surprise there was also a Chinese historian, Zhang Zhilian, present and willing to work with the commission. We had a good mixture of historians from the West and from the socialist countries in the East. We adopted bylaws and elected a "Bureau" (steering committee) of seven persons, with Carbonell from Montpellier, Hans Schleier from Leipzig in Easr Germany, Andrzej Grabski from Lodz, Lucian Boia from Bucharest, Bianca Valotta-Cavallotti from Milan, Karl-Georg Faber from Saarbrücken in West Germany, and myself from Buffalo as members. I was pleased that the Bureau consisted of members from both sides of the East-West dividing line. Wolfgang Mommsen objected to my nomination to the Bureau, saying that the committee needed a real American, to which Richard Vann, the editor of *History and Theory*, responded: "Iggers is as American as apple pie." At the several conferences we organized in the 1980s, members from the East, including China, the Soviet Union, Poland, Hungary, Romania, and East Germany as well as members from various Western countries participated. The commission also launched a journal, *Storia della Storiografia* (History of Historiography), published in Milan, and later in Turin, with articles in English, French, German, and Italian. At a time when there were still Cold War confrontations, the commission made possible discussions and cooperation across ideological divisions.

Chapter 8

OUR CONTACTS WITH EAST GERMANY (1966–1990)

GEORG

In the summer of 1966 we were in Göttingen with our children and a new Mercedes that was very inexpensive because of the favorable exchange rate. We wanted to drive to the area from which Wilma came in Western Bohemia, to see her old friends. This was her first trip to Czechoslovakia since her émigration in 1938. We thought that we would not be able to take the shortest route through the German Democratic Republic, and would have to take the longer route through Bavaria. Nevertheless, I applied for a transit visa through the GDR and to my surprise we were allowed to stay overnight in Halle. We knew no one in the GDR, although some names were familiar to me from their publications. The only name in Halle that rang a bell was Leo Stern, who occupied a leading position at the university, interestingly still called Martin Luther University, and was one of the most influential historians in the GDR. Stern, who was born in Bessarabia and grew up in Vienna, fought in the International Brigade in the Spanish Civil War, and spent the war years in Moscow. I wrote him that I would be staying overnight in Halle and would like to meet him and his colleagues. I received a telegram that he would unfortunately be out of town, but two of his colleagues would meet me.

It was a strange feeling when we turned off from the busy autobahn to Berlin, passed the border controls, and entered the GDR. There was little traffic and the towns through which we passed were remarkably empty and dark. We reached Halle about midnight and with the help of a hitchhiker we had picked up, found our hotel, zum Weltfrieden (World Peace). The hotel had a sign outside: "Weltfrieden zur Reparatur geschlossen" (World Peace closed for repairs). We had no choice but to look for the expensive Interhotel, which we had hoped to avoid—at that time foreign tourists were not compelled to stay in the Interhotels. The people at the Interhotel already knew about us and directed us to the modest but comfortable hotel zum roten Ross (Red Horse).

The next morning, two of the Halle historians appeared at the hotel, Professor Tillmann, the chair of the history department, an expert on German policies in the Near East before and during the Nazi period, and Professor Hübner, who wrote on the political role of the Prussian Junkers (landed nobility.). They were accompanied by a chauffeur who took Wilma and the children on a tour of the city. Tillmann, Hübner, and I walked the short distance to the university. The only American historian who had preceded me in Halle was Herbert Aptheker of the American Communist Party. I was thus the first non-Communist American historian to visit the history department in many years. I was received very cordially. When I expressed a desire to become acquainted with historians in the GDR, my hosts invited me to come again the following summer for the ceremonies commemorating the hundred fiftieth anniversary of the merger of the Universities of Halle and Wittenberg. They told me that two historians in nearby Leipzig, Hans Schleier and Werner Berthold, who had both worked extensively on German, and particularly West German, historiography, had expressed an interest in meeting me. I was well acquainted with their work. They could not have known about me except for a few articles that I had written. The one that had made the greatest impression on them was my article, "The Idea of Progress. A Critical Reconsideration," which appeared in *The American Historical Review* in 1965.

Travel to Leipzig required a special permit. We were taken to the police station where we immediately received the stamp for Leipzig. I am convinced that there had been prior communication between Halle, Leipzig and Berlin, and that the Stasi (secret police) had files about me. However, my attempts to obtain them have been futile until very recently. In Leipzig we were met by Schleier and Berthold and his young assistant, Günter Katsch. This was the beginning of a friendship with Schleier and Berthold that lasts until today. Berthold was, and still is, a convinced Communist from a working class background, who was grateful to the GDR for having made possible his university education and career. Schleier was quite non-ideological, and it was only after 1989 that he could express his true democratic convictions.

Berthold had just published a critique of Gerhard Ritter, the doyen of the West German historians, which differed from my own critique in its harsh, dogmatic language. Schleier was working on a book on the democratic historians in the Weimar Republic. We talked with Berthold and Schleier all afternoon about a variety of topics, while Katsch entertained our children. The differences between Berthold's Marxism and my frank critique of its GDR form became obvious. However, we also found common ground in our critical assessment of the nationalistic conception of historical thought that had dominated the German historical profession since the early nineteenth century. Berthold invited me to Leipzig the following summer, to give two lectures there, one based on my yet unpublished book on the German tradition of historical thought, the other on my assessment of contemporary currents in historical writing in the United States. I was surprised that the Halle and Leipzig historians, who hardly knew me, invited us to visit the following summer. It undoubtedly had something to do with the isolation of historians in the GDR from the West. Invitations to and even communications with West German historians would have been very difficult or even impossible for GDR historians. Despite the criticism I expressed of the authoritarianism of the GDR regime, they invited me because of what they knew about my involvement in the civil rights movement, my opposition to the Vietnam War, and my willingness to talk with them. This became apparent in three documents I received after 1989, not from the Stasi files, but from the Ministry of Higher Education. One from the Karl Marx University mentioned my criticism of the Soviet occupation of Czechoslovakia, but nevertheless also said that it was important to invite me for discussions because I took them (the GDR historians) seriously. They also could justify the invitations because, in their view, I was a victim of fascism who had to flee from Nazi Germany. The fact that I spoke German also helped.

We then proceeded to Bohemia. On the way we made a detour to Merseburg to see the cathedral. While we were parked at the central square, a small crowd of teenagers assembled, astonished by our Mercedes with West German plates. A young man told us that he just completed his apprenticeship. In forty-seven years when he would turn sixty five, he said, he could travel to the West.

The next year, 1967, I spent three weeks in the GDR. In the meantime I had also received an invitation to come to East Berlin. The Six Day War had just taken place in the Middle East. When I woke up the first morning in Halle, I witnessed a large demonstration by members of the Communist youth organization, the Free German Youth, who in their uniforms looked remarkably like Hitler Youth. They were carrying placards with the slogan "Aggressor Israel". I seriously considered leaving, but then decided to stay. I was also shocked by what I saw in the party newspaper *Neues Deutschland* (New Germany). Its headline Auschwitz in the Desert closely resembled the headlines in the neo-Nazi *National- und Soldatenzeitung* (National and Soldiers' Newspaper) that I had just seen in West Germany. Yet a little later in the day, at a lunch with Halle colleagues and guests from elsewhere in the GDR, I heard quite different views. Although the official line vehemently opposed Israel and expounded an anti-Zionism that bordered on anti-Semitism, the people at my table were relieved by the Israeli victory. The philosopher Hermann Ley from East Berlin, known for his study of atheism, was jubilant, announcing that he had just learned that Jean-Paul Sartre had come out in support of Israel.

I attended a Soviet-GDR conference on the scientific-technical revolution. The irony, of course, was that the scientific-technical revolution was an important topic in the Eastern block where it was not taking place, while it was in process in the West where there was much less talk about it. I found most of the papers and the discussions that followed largely uninteresting because of their dogmatism and their ritualistic use of Marxist language. I tried unsuccessfully to get into conversations with the Soviet participants, but there was a language barrier. My Russian was insufficient and their German or English was nonexistent. Nor did they seem particularly interested.

Among the participants I met a young Polish historian, Jerzy Topolski from the Adam Mickiewicz University in Poznań. Topolski's field was the economic history of early modern Poland. He had spent considerable time in Paris at the circle around the *Annales* journal, and his approach to history represented a Marxism deeply influenced by the *Annales*. He wrote extensively on the theory and methodology of history, mediating between Marxist and Western conceptions. Through him I gained insight into a profession that was much more diverse and sophisticated than the dogmatic historiography of the GDR. Topolski visited Buffalo in the fall of 1968 in conjunction with the meeting of the International Economic History Association in the United States, along with his Warsaw colleague Andrzej Wyczański, whose work on Polish economic history had been published in the *Annales*. Because of student riots in Poznań in 1968, my visit there had to be postponed. Topolski came to Buffalo several times thereafter and I to Poznań. Through him I met other Polish historians interested in the theory of history, such as Andrzej Grabski.

While West German cities for the most part had been rebuilt, much of Halle was still in ruins. My hosts took me to the edge of town where a huge apartment project, Halle Neustadt (Halle New City) was under construction. I was told that the top floors consisted of two-story apartments for the intelligentsia who were entitled to more space. At the time this was the pride of the Halle authorities, since people desperately needed better housing. The project was actually very drab.

A high point of the Soviet-GDR conference was a bus tour to the Wartburg, the castle where Luther was given refuge and where he translated the Bible. Two young students accompanied me and the only other Western guest, a Danish physicist. They wanted to know what the five-year research plans were for the United States and Denmark, respectively. A lively discussion ensued throughout the trip, with us explaining to their astonishment how research was organized and carried out in Western countries. At the end of the conference there was a sumptuous banquet with all sorts of delicacies and tropical fruits. The next morning when I went to a state grocery store to buy supplies for my train trip to Amsterdam, I discovered that no fruit was available.

From Amsterdam we drove to Berlin in a rickety rental car which broke down in the middle of the GDR. We had been told how poor the workmanship of socialist repair stations was in the GDR and how difficult it was to obtain spare parts. We were lucky to find a small private garage that was able to fix our car.

In Berlin, I met several of the most important GDR historians. Except for Ernst Engelberg, who was in a sense the czar of the historical profession who enforced ideological conformity, all saw the shortcomings of the GDR regime, particularly its authoritarian aspects, and yet considered themselves loyal citizens of a socialist state. The two most impressive of them were Fritz Klein and Jürgen Kuczynski.

Fritz Fischer had told me that I must absolutely look up Klein in East Berlin. Klein was a good example of what was possible and impossible in the GDR. He came from an upper class Protestant family. His father had been a journalist for a very conservative, nationalistic paper in the Weimar Republic but no Nazi, and died mysteriously in the early days of the Nazi regime. After the death of both of his parents Klein was brought up in a Social Democratic family that was opposed to the Nazis, and who later were also critical of the dogmatic and authoritarian aspects of the Communists. Klein served in the German army on the Russian front, and came back totally disillusioned about the Germany that had made the Nazis possible. He was a loyal dissident until the collapse of the GDR, a man of integrity. Trusted in both the East and the West, he was called out of retirement in 1990 to head the Institute of History of the GDR Academy of Sciences in its final days. In 1953 he became the first editor of the official GDR historical journal, the *Zeitschrift für Geschichtswissenschaft* (Journal for Historical Science), but was dismissed a few years later because of his insistence on scholarly standards and his commitment to opening the journal for discussions with non-Marxist and Western historians. Nevertheless, he kept his position in the Academy of Sciences. The academy in the GDR, as in other socialist countries, was centered on research, and possessed greater prestige than the teaching universities, but was also a place where scholars who were not quite trusted, were isolated from students.

Klein was very open with us when we met him, although he was quite aware of the limitations of the GDR. When he asked Wilma what first struck her in the GDR, she told him that in a book store window she had seen all sorts of books glorifying the leaders of the GDR and GDR society generally, while in the United States during the Vietnam War critical literature predominated. We were struck by Klein's openness when he replied that he fully understood this contrast. The United States, he said, was a stable society. In the GDR everything was shaky. At the time Klein was co-authoring a three volume work, *Deutschland im Ersten Weltkrieg* (Germany in the First World War), which proceeded from Marxist assumptions of the economic foundations of domestic and international politics, and came to similar conclusions about the role of the German government in the outbreak of the First World War, as did Fritz Fischer. Fischer's study had relied heavily on government documents that Klein and his co-authors Willibald Gutsche and Joachim Petzold had provided concerning extensive empirical data on the role of industry. The three volumes, published the following year in 1968, were positively reviewed in major American, British, and French journals because of their solid research that was recognized as valid contributions to the study of the First World War. However, the work was virtually ignored in West Germany, where it was generally viewed as East German propaganda. It is still considered significant and was republished in 2004. Klein was one of the first East Germans allowed to accept a research fellowship in the United States at Johns Hopkins University, and during his tenure there in 1975 visited us in Buffalo.

From Berlin we proceeded to Leipzig where I gave two lectures. I spoke to a small audience of invited distinguished guests from the various corners of the

GDR, Berlin, Jena, and Halle. My first lecture dealt with the historiographical situation in West Germany. I presented an account that was different from the official GDR one as represented by Berthold, which portrayed the West German historians as "NATO historians." I tried to present a balanced picture, on the one hand stressing the ways in which German historiography continued the nationalist tradition into the 1960s, on the other hand pointing at reorientations in historical thought in West Germany in the 1960s that broke with this tradition. I not only pointed to Fritz Fischer's controversial thesis of the continuity of German war aims in the twentieth century leading to the Nazis, but also at to new generation of young democratically oriented historians such as Hans-Ulrich Wehler who found the roots of Nazism in social and political structures that resisted democratization. A counter-lecture was then delivered by Gerhard Lozek, spokesman from the party institution, the Academy for Social Sciences of the Central Committee of the Socialist Unity (Communist) Party, not to be confused with the Academy of Sciences of the GDR. This was followed by two hours of heated discussion. Berthold argued that I failed to recognize the Bolshevik Revolution as the turning point of the twentieth century.

Later that week I gave my second lecture on trends in contemporary American historiography. Again I attempted to present a balanced picture, beginning with consensus historians of the 1950s and then looking at critical voices in the 1960s, including the New Left historians. This time the commentator was Alfred Loesdau, the specialist in American history in Lozek's party institute, who had moved from West to East Berlin in the late 1950s. While Lozek's comments had been articulate and sophisticated, even if in part misguided, Loesdau was dogmatic and poorly informed, strictly following the party line. He knew little about the American scene and argued that I had given a totally false picture of historical writing in America and that the American historians were agents of the government who overwhelmingly and uncritically supported the imperialist policies of Washington. His lecture was devoted to Charles Beard, the great liberal historian, whose writings long predated the 1960s, and called Beard a Fascist because as a pacifist he had opposed America's entry into the Second World War. It was easy to refute his arguments. Unlike Lozek, who was well informed about the historiographical scene in West Germany, Loesdau was a pure propagandist who frequently wrote for West German publications friendly to the GDR. Nevertheless I would send him American publications that I hoped would help to enlighten him. The official GDR historical journal, the *Zeitschrift für Geschichtswissenschaft* covered my speech, but distorted its content, giving the impression that I had talked only about the "reactionary"—their word—German historicism that dominated West German historiography.

The most impressive historian we met in Leipzig was Walter Markov. Markov, who had received his doctorate at the time of the Nazi accession to power, had spent ten years in Hitler's prisons. After the war he attempted to obtain his *Habilitation,* the second doctorate required for teaching on the university level but was turned down at the University of Bonn in West Germany while several former

Nazis were admitted without any problems. He then went to Leipzig where he soon became a professor of history. He was one of those committed Communists who were uneasy about the dictatorial aspects of the GDR, but like his Leipzig colleagues, the famous philosopher Ernst Bloch and the literary scholar Hans Mayer, he believed that the GDR was a better society than the capitalist West German Federal Republic where there had been no radical cleansing of old institutions and where former Nazis were soon restored to positions of power and influence. Because of his independent stance, Markov was expelled from the Communist party (the Socialist Unity Party) in 1952 as an alleged Titoist, but was not removed from his professorial chair. He quickly attained an international reputation as a leading Marxist historian of the French Revolution who wrote history from below, and who after a two year stay as a visiting professor in Nigeria in the early 1960s, founded the field of African studies in the GDR. I remained in contact with him until his death in 1993. In the midst of the Stalin period, Leipzig, with Markov, Bloch, and Mayer, provided a stimulating intellectual climate. Bloch and Mayer left the GDR in the early 1960s, Markov stayed.

Berthold tried to make us feel at home. He arranged for Wilma to meet a professor of German literature, who was married to a ship's carpenter and proud of her proletarian lifestyle. Jeremy and her son spent hours playing chess in Clara Zetkin Park, named after the German Communist activist. Berthold's assistant, Günther Katsch, took Wilma and me to a concert and then to the famous Auerbachs Keller, the tavern where a famous scene of Goethe's *Faust* takes place. The historic center of Leipzig had been beautifully restored, but much of the rest of the city, with many stately apartment houses of the late nineteenth and early twentieth century, looked drab and in disrepair, hiding the beauty of these buildings that was only restored after unification.

From Leipzig we made two excursions, one to Dresden, once one of the most beautiful cities in Europe, that had been destroyed in the fire bombing in 1945 a few weeks before the end of the war. Little had been rebuilt. The main street, named after the Communist leader Ernst Thälmann who was murdered by the Nazis, consisted of new buildings in the typical austere GDR style. We stayed in the historic Gewandhaus, the old clothiers' guild house, which had been beautifully restored as a hotel. When we stayed there again in 1985, it was dreadfully run down. The second trip was to Weimar, home of Goethe and Schiller, the almost sacred center of German classical culture, the historic parts of which had been largely restored. Since the hotels were booked up, we stayed in nearby Erfurt. The center of this city had remained intact. In Erfurt we visited Fritz Klein's co-author Willibald Gutsche and his wife, who followed the party line much more closely than did Klein. They received us cordially, but refused the gift we had brought, namely coffee which was rare and expensive in the GDR, saying that they had everything they needed in the GDR.

Before leaving Weimar we visited Buchenwald concentration camp, which was now a museum. It had not been an extermination camp like Auschwitz, but was primarily intended for political prisoners, although many thousands died there.

A large number of the prisoners at Buchenwald were Communists, but by no means a majority. There was, however, little indication that there had been other prisoners there as well, and there was no mention of the Jews who had been brought there after the pogrom on November 9–10, 1938. The centerpiece of the museum was a display celebrating the liberation of the camp by the Communist prisoners in May 1945, an actual uprising which, however, was only possible when the American troops, who were given no credit for the liberation, approached the camp and the Nazis fled.

We then proceeded to Czechoslovakia, to Wilma's corner in Bohemia and to Prague. The thaw that had begun there already in the mid-sixties was apparent, leading to the Prague spring two years later.

We subsequently lost touch with the Halle historians, but Berthold regularly invited me to lecture whenever we were in Göttingen. I always chose topics about new trends in the West such as E. P. Thompson's cultural Marxist approach to the history of the working class, Herbert Gutman's similar cultural approach to American labor and immigrant history, Eugene Genovese's Marxist approach to American slavery, women's history, critical voices in America, and the social and cultural history of the French *Annales* school, which was virtually unknown in the GDR unlike in Poland where it was taken very seriously. In 1969 the history department at the Karl Marx University in Leipzig wrote a letter to the Ministry of Higher Education in 1969 asking for permission to invite me to deliver a lecture, despite the fact that I had voiced criticism of the Soviet occupation of Czechoslovakia. Permission was granted. On the other hand, the rigid limits of free expression were very obvious. Discussions in closed circles were possible, but open criticism could be severely punished. A philosopher we had met in Dresden, Dieter Kraa, who in a faculty meeting in 1968 had criticized the Soviet invasion, was promptly suspended from his position, assigned translation work in his home, and finally permitted to leave for West Germany, one might say expelled, after his sister in West Germany paid a hefty sum. He was still more fortunate than others who landed in prison.

By the 1960s, the GDR was less repressive than it had been during the Stalin era, but it remained an authoritarian state that severely repressed dissident opinions. Yet there were areas where independent thought was possible. There was much greater freedom in the realm of literature, which often presented critical pictures of socialist society, or at least its GDR variety, than among historians who were much more closely controlled and much more obedient than the novelists and dramatists.

On our next visit to the GDR in August 1969 the contradictions of GDR society were very obvious. We went from Prague to Leipzig by train, changing in Dresden. In Dresden we were held up in the station for almost two hours while our books and papers were examined, and questioned about the purpose of our trip. The GDR authorities were afraid of liberalization in Czechoslovakia even a year after the Soviet occupation. Nothing happened to us, but Kraa, who had been waiting for us at the station, was interrogated. In Leipzig we were welcomed as warmly as before. In Berlin, Leo Stern who had now moved to the academy, arranged for our children Jeremy and Daniel to visit a school in Berlin for a day, where they were asked all sorts of questions about America by the curious students. Our friend Jürgen Lenz, a novelist who had left Hamburg in the mid-1950s for East Berlin and now was thoroughly disillusioned, told us that Günter de Bruyn would read from his just published novel, *Burians Esel* (Burian's Ass), at an international students meeting, international here meaning students from the Communist block and a few sympathizers from the West. De Bruyn's novel portrayed a weak man torn between two women, far from the heroic image of socialist society. In the lively discussion that followed, there was general agreement that socialist realism belonged to the past. Interestingly, the most outspoken critic of socialist realism was a young woman from the Soviet Union.

During our stay in Berlin, a Jewish woman who had just left Israel for the GDR wanted to interview me on my views on the Vietnam conflict. I was willing to grant the interview only under the condition that I could listen to the tape before it was broadcast, to make sure that it was not edited. She could not guarantee this, so there was no interview.

Someone in a semi-official capacity urged us to witness the voting at a nearby polling place in the elections for the GDR legislature, to see how democracy functioned in the GDR. Obviously she wanted to show us what a farce these elections were. Voting was compulsory. All voters received a ballot that they dropped into the ballot box without marking it, thus giving approval to the official list. While we were there, no one went into the voting booth to mark their ballot, which would have taken courage.

During the 1970s, I received no official invitations to visit East Berlin, although we frequently visited as private individuals and kept in touch with those we met on our first visit. However, I was regularly invited to Leipzig, where our closest contacts were Werner Berthold and Hans Schleier. Schleier was at the Academy of Sciences in East Berlin, but lived in Leipzig. We frequently corresponded about our work. I sent him drafts of my articles on nineteenth- and twentieth-century historiography and we discussed his work on Hedwig Hintze, the first woman to complete a *Habilitation* in history, Hintze was an expert on the French Revolution and the French Enlightenment, and one of the few democratically oriented historians in the Weimar Republic. Of Jewish origin, she had fled from the Nazis to the Netherlands. She was offered a professorship at the New School for Social Research in New York, but was refused an American visa and died in 1942 just before she was to be deported. She was ignored in West Germany for a long time after 1945, largely because she did not fit into the conservative nationalistic tradition of historiography, and received recognition only in the 1990s. In his book on the German historians in the Weimar Republic, published in 1975, Schleier was the first historian, in East or West Germany, to focus on Hintze. In the book Schleier, largely avoiding Marxist rhetoric and dealt with the most important liberal democratic historians in Weimar Germany. In 1975, when I began to edit, together with my American colleague and friend Harold Parker of Duke University, the *International Handbook of Historical Studies,* the first book of its kind that dealt not only with historical writing in the West but also in the rest of the world, including sub-Saharan Africa and East Asia, I asked Schleier whether he would contribute a chapter on East Germany. He had to ask for permission, which to my surprise he received.

In the late 1970s, the Western Association of German Studies (WAGS) was founded by Gerald Kleinfeld at Arizona State University. Its goal was to bring together scholars in various fields who studied German history, literature, and culture. At first conceived as a regional organization of the western United States and western Canada, it rapidly attracted persons from all of North America as well as from West Germany and Austria. Soon the name of the organization was changed to the German Studies Association (GSA). In 1981, I suggested to Kleinfeld that the association also invite scholars from the GDR and he agreed and asked me to arrange for the participation of East Germans. The Central Institute of History at the Academy of Sciences of the German Democratic Republic accepted our invitation and agreed to pay for the trans-Atlantic flights provided the GSA would assume the expenses in the United States. The first visitor to attend the GSA meeting in El Paso in October 1982 would be Hans Schleier.

In the spring of 1982, I attended a conference on current trends in historical theory that the Italian historian Pietro Rossi had organized in Turin. Virtually all the important theorists were there, including historians and philosophers from the Soviet bloc, as well as Wolfgang Küttler from the Central Institute of History at the Academy of Sciences in East Berlin where he headed a work circle for the history and theory of historiography. The most outspoken and controversial theorist at the Turin conference was Hayden White from the United States, who in *Metahistory. The Historical Imagination in Nineteenth Century Europe* (1973), viewed history merely as a form of imaginative literature, poetry if you will, and denied the possibility of any objective knowledge of the past. Küttler and I had an opportunity to talk about the conference and particularly about White on the train from Turin to Milan. Küttler assumed that someone who held White's anti-rational and anti-scientific positions, which Küttler identified with Nietzsche and Heidegger, must be politically on the far right. He was surprised that White considered himself an outspoken leftist and had played an active role in the opposition to the Vietnam War. In fact, White liked to say that he was a Marxist, which made little sense in view of his emphatic rejection of the sort of scientific explanation of the historical process that is associated with orthodox Marxism. For him it meant a critique of market capitalism as a repressive social and economic system which had created an inhumane culture in which scientific rationality served as an instrument of exploitive control. Küttler turned out to be anything but an orthodox Marxist. His goal was to make certain that Max Weber was taken seriously in the GDR as an addition and even a corrective to Marx.

Shortly after I returned to Buffalo from Turin, the Central Institute of History at the Academy of Sciences in East Berlin informed me that Küttler would accompany Schleier to the GSA. They planned to talk about the status of historical theory in the GDR. I asked Jörn Rüsen, the most promising of the younger West German theorists of historiography, to deal with the status of the discussions in West Germany. I would moderate. The three first came to Buffalo, where I arranged an evening at a colleague's house to which about forty colleagues and students came. Schleier and Küttler read their papers, which they had prepared in East Berlin, and that appeared rather schematic. But then the discussion became lively. My colleague, William Sheridan Allen, a specialist on the Third Reich, began by asking what would happen if an historian in the GDR would be confronted by the same sources as the Yale historian Henry Turner had been, which forced Turner to conclude that the Nazi Party received most of its money from its rank-and-file members and much less from high finance, which was directly contrary to GDR doctrine. Now Schleier and Küttler talked very frankly about what was possible and what was proscribed in GDR scholarship. From there we proceeded to the GSA meeting in El Paso, which provided an opportunity for further discussions. From then on the meeting of East and West German historians first in Buffalo and then at the GDR became an annual event.

In 1983, the historians Willibald Gutsche, Klein's coauthor, and Dietrich Eichholtz, came to Buffalo and to the GSA meeting in Madison, Wisconsin. Gutsche's topic was "German Imperialism and the Pre-History of the First World War", and Eichholtz's topic was "Monopoly and the State in the Time of Fascism," The formal presentations were disappointingly doctrinaire. Even more disappointing was the extent to which they felt they needed to defend the official GDR party line. We talked until three in the morning at our house along with Jörn Rüsen and my former chair at Roosevelt University, Jack Roth, and then had a similar discussion at the home of Erwin Knoll in Madison. Knoll was a refugee from Nazi occupied Vienna, a pacifist, Quaker, and editor of the *Progressive* magazine. The Soviets had just shot down a Korean commercial airliner with over three hundred passengers. While Wilma and I, Rüsen, Roth, and Knoll were critical of the way in which the Cold War was pursued by both sides, Gutsche and Eichholtz blindly defended Soviet and GDR policy.

The visitors who came in following years were more flexible. In 1988, Schleier, Küttler, and Rüsen again visited us, this time changing their roles, with Schleier and Küttler examining the historiographical developments in West Germany and Rüsen those in East Germany. I also took Schleier and Küttler to an NAACP meeting where they were confronted by very critical questions from an African-American public about human rights in East Germany and in the Soviet Union, that they had not expected from a black audience. A somewhat similar confrontation took place when Walter Schmidt, the chair of the Institute of History at the academy, delivered a lecture before a largely Jewish audience about the historical treatment of the Jews and the Holocaust in the GDR, a topic that until the 1980s, had been largely neglected. In 1985, independently of these exchanges, Jürgen Kuczynski, the grand old man of East German historians, visited us. After trying for many years, he had finally received a visitor's visa. He attended the meeting of the board of directors of the International Economic History Association and visited Immanuel Wallerstein, the author of the Marxist-inspired *World Systems,* and then to Buffalo, where we conducted my seminar in our living room.

In 1983, I for the first time received a formal invitation from the Institute of History at the Academy of Sciences in East Berlin to give a lecture; from then on I was invited annually. The Academy arranged for us to visit other parts of the GDR, including Erfurt where it put us up at the elegant Erfurter Hof hotel.

Incidentally, much more attention was paid in Erfurt and elsewhere in the GDR to the 500th anniversary of the birth of Martin Luther than to the 100th anniversary of the death of Karl Marx. Luther, for many years had been considered a villain who supported the brutal suppression of the Peasants Rebellion and the execution of its religious leader Thomas Münzer, who had been the champion of the poor against the rich and powerful. The GDR now wanted to use the German national past to legitimize its regime. After my talk in Berlin, Ernst Engelberg, a powerful hardliner among the GDR historians, who had just returned from the Soviet Union, confided to me that he found the country in a severe economic crisis, and that the Soviet Union was destroying itself by competing with the United States on the world scene and in outer space.

My talk in Berlin took place on a Friday afternoon and I asked my hosts to take me to a Jewish Sabbath service that evening. I was uncertain whether they could or would fulfill this request. They took Wilma and me to the synagogue in the Ryke Strasse, at the time the only one in East Berlin. This was not an Orthodox synagogue, but as soon as Wilma and I sat down together as we were used to in America, we were separated and Wilma was sent to the women's section. There were only about forty worshipers, many of them quite young, in some cases children and grandchildren of high Communist functionaries who were seeking their Jewish roots. I was struck two years later when I attended the Kol Nidre service at the beginning of Yom Kippur to see in the row behind me Stefan Heym, one of the leading writers in the GDR, who had sought refuge in the United States and served in the U.S. Army during the war, but moved to the GDR in protest against McCarthyism. While there was a fair number of persons of Jewish origin in the GDR, some in high positions in the party, by the mid-1980s there were only about 400 persons who identified themselves as Jews, approximately half of them in East Berlin. We were very impressed by the cantor, Oljean Ingster, who had spent his youth as a slave laborer, was largely self educated, and managed to keep the congregation together without making serious concessions to the regime. After the regime fell, he was honored by the Federal Republic with the Federal Cross of Merit.

The mid-1980s saw a gradual thaw. It was possible to express ideas that previously would have been forbidden. But the dictatorship remained firmly entrenched, as did the Marxist-Leninist dogmatism. Nevertheless there were openings. We became acquainted with four very different sorts of people. There were the academics who piously towed the party line. Then there were members of the Christian peace movement who later played an important role in the protests in the summer and autumn of 1989, which led to the fall of the GDR. And then there were

Waldtraut and Gerd Klitzke, librarians at the *Deutsche Bücherei* in Leipzig, the German National Library, who were neither affiliated with the church nor party members. Waldtraut was assigned to help Wilma in the library and she and her husband Gert soon became close friends, something the authorities did not view with favor, with the result that Waltraut was never again asked to accompany visitors from the West in the library. A fourth group consisted of ordinary people we met in restaurants, taxis, and trains, almost all critical of conditions in the GDR. The fact that they dared to talk openly in public places reflected a striking difference from the Nazi regime, where most of the population supported the regime and criticism often resulted in imprisonment, and from earlier times in the GDR where people also were fearful of the consequences of being openly critical. As to the academics, we were struck by the gulf between their public and their private opinions. By the mid-1980s, many, even a stalwart like Werner Berthold, voiced more and more doubts about conditions in the GDR.

An example of this new openness was a conference that Wolfgang Küttler organized in 1984 on the seventy-fifth birthday of Ernst Engelberg, on "Marxist Typology and Idealtypical Methods," the latter referring to Max Weber, in which Marx and Weber were no longer seen as irreconcilable opposites, but as complements to each other. Küttler invited the two Weber scholars from West Germany, Wolfgang Mommsen and Jürgen Kocka, to the conference. Mommsen was an outspoken critic of the GDR and Kocka, although more willing to take East German scholarship seriously, nevertheless was critical of its Marxism. I also was invited, but could not attend because Wilma and I were in China, but I sent an essay that was published in East Berlin together with Mommsen's and Kocka's contributions in the proceedings from the conference. This was a new development, that non- and even anti-Marxist essays by Western scholars would be published in the GDR.

There was also a notable shift in the official East German conception of German history. Until then a sharp line had been drawn between the small number of Germans who had been considered forerunners of a revolutionary tradition that led to the establishment of the German Democratic Republic, and a reactionary tradition going back to Luther and Frederick the Second, the latter no longer called Frederick the Great, and Bismarck. Now historians were urged to see the past more sympathetically, and to include Luther, Frederick, and the generals of the war against Napoleon that was now stylized as a national uprising, the movement led by Prussia that led to the creation of the German Reich as part of a national history and of the heritage of the GDR. In a sense, of course, this new view of history prepared the way to a new state imposed orthodoxy.

At the same time, a new social history emerged which, while proceeding from Marxist ideas of class, moved relatively independently from the narrow economistic interpretation of doctrinaire Marxism to a more empirical approach. In 1977, Hartmut Zwahr from the Karl Marx University in Leipzig published his study of the formation of the Leipzig working class, which proceeded on anthropological and empirical sociological lines, utilizing Leipzig city directories and the city archives and exploring family structures. In a very interesting section on the choice of godfathers, he showed that the class lines between workers and the middle class were much more porous than they had been portrayed in older East German Marxist histories. Zwahr's book immediately received attention in the West and was also published in West Germany. He was the only East German to be invited to an international conference of social historians in Konstanz and given permission to attend. Only a very limited number of scholars were "travel cadres", who were permitted to travel to the West. In 1980 he and Helga Schultz founded a discussion group dedicated to problems in empirical social history, in some ways similar to the Working Circle for Modern Social History in West Germany, but carefully avoiding the term social history that was still taboo, because it was claimed that a dialectical materialist approach did not need empirical substantiation. In 1980, Jürgen Kuczynski published the first of six volumes of his *Geschichte des Alltags des Deutschen Volks 1600–1945* (History of the daily life of the German people). In his introduction he was critical of East German historians who focused on political battles and argued that they could learn a good deal from social historians in the West, particularly from Fernand Braudel and the French *Annales* circle. Like them, and without losing sight of class distinctions, he argued, Marxist historians must deal with "what people ate, how they dressed, how they were housed, what they thought about every day, how they worked, how they rested and slept, what it was like when they became ill, into what circles they married, what the relationship of the children was to their parents, what happened with old people, etc." In fact, an increasing number of East German historians in this period became aware of the shift of social history in the West to the study of culture.

As yet, there were few direct contacts between East German historians and historians in the West. As a matter of fact, much of East German historiography seemed to be extremely provincial, not even Marxist in a profound sense, but following the guidelines of the party. This was beginning to change among the small but nevertheless important groups of social and cultural historians. Studies of the working class, such as Dietrich Mühlberg's work on everyday life in Berlin around 1900 and several regional studies, such as the team study of life in the countryside around Magdeburg on the eve of industrialization, reflected this new orientation. Here ethnological studies were combined with economic history in a way that was not done in regional and local histories of daily life in the West. Thus the Marxist concern with the material bases of society and culture proved to be fruitful. Jan Peters studied church seating and the enforcement of Sunday laws as an indicator of social networks of power. Helga Schultz, who had begun as a relatively orthodox Marxist, in her book on the history of Berlin in the seventeenth and eighteenth centuries commissioned by the East German Academy for the 750th anniversary of the founding of the city, wrote a broadly comprehensive history in the spirit of the *Annales,* beginning with an examination of social structure and demography and proceeding to politics and culture and ending with an examination of the position of Jews and that of women. In 1987 she was chosen by the academy as their representative at the German Studies Asociation. We had a very interesting discussion with her in Buffalo after she read from her introduction to the diary of an eighteenth-century master baker in Berlin. Our students, who had expected her to present a Marxist analysis, were surprised that she presented a much more complex picture of society than they had expected from a Marxist. We had hoped to invite Zwahr too, but he did not receive permission. As a matter of fact, all the persons who visited us came from the academy, none from the universities. We did succeed in getting Rita Kuczynski, a philosopher and novelist, then daughter in-law of Jürgen Kuczynski, who had resigned her position at the academy to have greater freedom to write, to come to Buffalo and to the GSA at the same time as Schultz.

At this time, I decided to assemble a collection of essays in English by the new GDR social historians, to make their work known in the West. I had previously published an anthology in English of articles by West German social historians. Jürgen Kocka, to whom I showed a list of the articles I proposed to include, commented that they were interesting but not at all typical of historiography in the GDR. I agreed but replied that this was the very reason why I had chosen them. The book appeared only in 1991 and at the same time also as a German paperback.

In 1995, a particularly negative review by Alexander Fischer of my collection of writings on social history in East Germany, and of a similar volume by the German-American historian Konrad Jarausch, appeared in the *Historische Zeitschrift*, the leading journal of German historians in the Federal Republic. Both volumes sought to give a balanced picture of historical studies in the former GDR, pointing out on the one hand, the ideological distortions, on the other hand serious scholarly contributions. Referring to both of us, Fischer expressed his surprise that "North American" historians should still see anything valuable in a "historiography which was identified long ago as one of the main supports of a totalitarian system." The review was particularly surprising since in 1988 Fischer had published an article of mine in a collection on historiography in the GDR that closely resembled the introduction of the volume he now condemned. At that time Fischer, who was a professor of Eastern European history in Bonn, took scholarship in the GDR seriously. After the collapse of the GDR as director of the Hannah Arendt Institute for the Study of Totalitarianism in Dresden, he made a hundred and eighty degree turn and now condemned all aspects of GDR scholarship as mere propaganda in the service of the regime. I wrote him to express my surprise, but did not realize that he was in the last stages of cancer. While it is possible to reply to reviews in the *American Historical Review*, this is not the case with the *Historische Zeitschrift*. I urged Lothar Gall, the editor of the *Historische Zeitschrift*, to publish an article or a series of articles that would examine GDR historical scholarship. I was able to obtain a grant to hold a symposium in 1996 with a broad spectrum of East and West German historians. The proceedings of the symposium were published in a special issue of the *Historische Zeitschrift* in 1998, edited by Jarausch and me together with Matthias Middell, a young East German historian, and Martin Sabrow, a young West German historian.

I always complained that my lectures in the GDR were restricted to an invited audience. Finally, in 1986, I gave a lecture in a public auditorium in Leipzig. In the discussion, the question of American foreign policy came up. I commented that both the United States and the Soviet Union had pursued, and were pursuing, imperialist aims. Afterwards Berthold told me that he was very embarrassed by my remarks and that he might not be able to invite me again to be a guest lecturer. In the fall of 1985, I spoke, with Berthold and Zwahr, before a large student gathering about the World Historical Congress that had taken place in Stuttgart, West Germany along. One of the students asked me whether students at Buffalo had free access to Marxist literature, which of course I was, of course, able to answer in the affirmative.

Shortly afterwards Peter Schäfer, the specialist for America at the University of Jena, asked me to deliver a public lecture to a student audience. Schäfer was an independent thinker and always had a subordinate position in the department. He was never permitted to go to West Berlin to use the American collection at the John F. Kennedy Institute of the Free University, perhaps because his two daughters had escaped from the GDR to West Germany. Only after the fall of the GDR did he become a full professor. The lecture hall was full with perhaps a hundred fifty students and some faculty. Schäfer had asked me to speak about current American historiography. I decided not to talk about what was being written, but how it was being written. I spoke how the American historical profession was organized, the relative independence of the individual historians, the diversity of historical interpretations from the consensus historians on the conservative side of the spectrum to the New Left on the other side, and the new trends in social and cultural history including the rise of ethnic and women's history. After I finished, a student stood up and condemned my talk as a *kleinbürgerlich* distortion of reality, *kleinbürgerlich* (petty bourgeois) being a standard term in the GDR vocabulary to discredit divergent political opinions. According to this student, history is written in the United States in the service of the imperialist aims of the government and high finance. I pressed him to define the term *kleinbürgerlich* and to back up his portrayal of American historians as lackeys of the establishment. He stuttered and the students applauded me. I then apologized to Schäfer for possibly having caused him embarrassment, but he assured me that he agreed with my presentation. On the other hand, I was disappointed when I read the draft chapter on current American historiography that he had written for a volume on historical studies in the West that was being prepared by a group of historians in the GDR. The volume, which was actually published, prided itself on its openness in no longer referring to the historians with whom it dealt as *bürgerlich* (bourgeois), but as non-Marxists. In his text he made the nonsensical claim that the Communist Party of the United States marked an important turning point for American historiography. As for women's history, which after all by that time was well developed in the United States, he mentioned only two names, Angela Davis, who had become famous in the violent racial confrontations of the late 1960s and by the 1980s held a leading position in the U.S. Communist Party, and Bettina Aptheker, the daughter of Herbert Aptheker, also of the U.S. Communist Party. The book as it was conceived, despite its claim of openness, reflected a continuing attempt to view historical studies in the West from the perspective of an unreformed GDR ideology.

Part of the thaw was also that we now could stay with friends, in Leipzig with the Klitzkes, in East Berlin with the Küttlers, and in Erfurt with the Gutsches. Of course our overnight stays had to be registered in the "House Book" that could be inspected by the police.

We spent the fall of 1985 in Leipzig. Wilma had received a three-months grant from IREX (the International Research and Exchange Commission), a U.S. government agency, comparable to the Fulbright Commission, but for the socialist countries. Since I had a sabbatical, I was able to accompany her. I decided to devote myself to GDR historiography and to interview historians. When I asked Küttler to let me present my findings to his work circle on the theory and methods of history at the academy in East Berlin, he consented. The following March I talked about my evaluation of historical studies in the GDR. My assessment was partly positive, partly very critical. I thought that the new trends in social and cultural history were to be welcomed, and in fact should be better known in the West. On the other hand I expressed my disappointment about the direction in which the heritage and tradition orientation, which had been hailed for its openness, went. The officially sanctioned historiography now saw the tradition from Luther to Bismarck in a positive light. Thus, Luther was now seen as a great liberator and modernizer, with little attention given to the medieval aspects of his thought and to his intense hatred of Jews. But what particularly disturbed me was how the nineteenth century movement for German unification was now hailed as progressive. Its spokesman, the philosopher J. G. Fichte, and the physical fitness enthusiasts Ernst Moritz Arndt and Friedrich Ludwig Jahn, after whom innumerable streets were named in the GDR, were hailed as national heroes, with little attention paid to their racism, their conception of Germany as a community of blood that excluded and despised Jews, and their xenophobia and militarism. Engelberg, who had visited the Soviet Union and had given me the first volume of his Bismarck biography that interestingly, had just been published simultaneously in the GDR and by the conservative Siedler Publishing House in West Germany. This biography was a major work, based on thorough research and free of the polemics that had characterized earlier studies of Bismarck in the GDR which contributed to its positive reception in West Germany. Engelberg saw the way Germany was unified under Prussia and Bismarck's role in it very differently from Marx and Engels who had looked at Bismarck very critically and had encouraged the Socialist members of the North German parliament to oppose the war against France in 1870. Engelberg, without referring to Marx and Engels, argued that Bismarck's decision to unify Germany through military force may have been wrong from a moral point of view, but was right from a historical perspective because the unification of Germany was a necessary step in the onward development of Germany. Without mentioning Engelberg by name, I said that the new "heritage and tradition" orientation was dangerously close to conservative, nationalist historians in West Germany and avoided the critical examination of the German past that had led to Nazism and the Holocaust, undertaken in West Germany by historians such as Fischer, Wehler and Kocka. Engelberg had intended to come to my lecture and had invited Wilma and me for coffee at his home in the afternoon. Unfortunately—or perhaps fortunately—he became ill and could not come. I sent him a copy of my talk and a few days later received an irate letter from him. He understood that he was included in my critique of East German historiography, but referring to my view of German history, he accused me of not having overcome "our joint émigré resentments." He had spent the Nazi years in Turkey. Küttler told me the morning after my talk that his colleagues had welcomed the talk because I said things that they thought but did not dare to say. My talk was subsequently published in German in *Geschichte und Gesellschaft* (History and Society), the leading social science journal in West Germany, and in English in *History and Theory* in the United States.

The Leipzig stay gave us an opportunity to observe daily life. We stayed in the home of the widow of a physician in Taucha, a town at the northeastern end of the streetcar line. We had a bedroom without a desk, and poor lighting. We spent our days at the Deutsche Bücherei library at the other end of town which closed at 10:00 P.M. and ate out, lunch at the canteen in the library, supper in nearby restaurants. Doing our laundry was difficult; the laundries always had an excuse for not accepting our clothes. One day they only gave out laundry but did not take it, the day on which they were supposed to accept washing, the apprentices were taking examinations, on a third day the employees had gone on an excursion. Friends, who heard of our trouble, offered to wash our clothes for us. In fact, working morale was generally very low; it was difficult to obtain services or to be served. Workers in stores and restaurants knew that they could not be fired and that there were few opportunities for advancement. When Wilma wanted to buy a shirt for me, she was sent from one sales lady to the next and ultimately back again to the first. Another time when we had waited for a long time in a restaurant to be served and saw the waitresses all sitting at a table, we asked when we would be served, and were very rudely informed that they were having their meal. Distribution was poor. When I went to a bakery one morning to buy bread, I was told that they had no bread but that they had nice cake. It was easier to shop in the HO state supermarkets, where most basic foods were available, but there was much less of a selection than in the West. Fresh fruit was hard to get. Fruits that had to be imported were not available. Green oranges from Cuba did not appear until Christmas. The price structure was very different from the West. All basic items were amazingly inexpensive, as was public transportation. Rolls cost 5 Pfennige, as they had before the war, compared to about 30 Pfennige in Göttingen in the West. Streetcar rides cost about one tenth of what they cost in the West. Good seats in the theater cost a fraction compared with in the West, although it often took connections to get tickets. All this was possible only with gigantic subsidies that ultimately forced the state into insolvency. Everything that was not a basic necessity was expensive. Color televisions cost 6,000 M as compared with 300 or 400 DM in the West, but nevertheless people bought them. They made down payments for the small Trabant cars for which they had to wait for many years, and also for telephones. Rents were incredibly low, but the government did little for the upkeep. Therefore, houses were very run-down, and many could be called slums. Tenants repaired their apartments at their own expense, provided they could find the necessary materials. Wilma received 800 M a month, which was approximately the average wage in East Germany and a third of the comparable wage in the West, and free rent. In addition, IREX deposited U.S. dollars in our Buffalo bank account that we never touched. There were special Intershop stores where you could obtain imported goods for hard currency. However, all in all, the standard of living in the GDR, although considerably lower than in West Germany, was not bad. There was no unemployment, there were no homeless, there was access to medical services, although the quality was not up to Western standards, and there were subsidized summer camps, child care, theater and music, which in the long run the state could not afford.

It was a delight to work in the Deutsche Bücherei. Compared to such state libraries as the Bibliothèque Nationale in Paris, it was remarkably unbureaucratic. One received books within about twenty minutes, while in many European libraries one had to wait until the next day. The staff was very helpful. The library was open to the general public, although, as was to be expected in an authoritarian state, some material was not available to the general reader. We could use anything we wanted.

I met not only the established historians at the university, but also Karl-Heinz Blaschke, an avowed non-Marxist historian whose work on the social history of Saxony was respected but had been rejected on ideological grounds. After losing his position at the Saxon archives in Dresden, he was denied public employment and earned a meager living teaching at a church school.

One was very much aware of the fact that one was living in a dictatorship. There were rigid restrictions on travel to the so-called capitalist countries. Although in the 1970s GDR citizens were able to travel to Poland and Czechoslovakia without a visa, travel to Poland was curbed after the beginning of the Solidarnosc Movement in 1980. The media were strictly controlled, with newspapers, radio, and TV, all following the official line. However, in most of the GDR with the exception of the area around Dresden, West German TV signals could be received, and radio everywhere, so that the GDR public was well informed. A very popular program during our stay was the American series *Dallas* on West German TV. The first time we ever saw it was not in the United States, but at the house of our landlady, who was very critical of the GDR and admired the West. This uncritical admiration of the West and of Western ways of life was widely shared. Her son, a student at the university, was just as critical, but had joined the party in the hope of being invited to a scholarly conference in the West and then defecting. Werner Berthold was also a fan of *Dallas*. He helped to persuade the tenants in his apartment house to raise money for a special antenna, so that Western signals could be received more clearly. He defended his enthusiasm for *Dallas* by explaining that the series presented the sordid side of capitalist everyday life, which, if it had been produced by GDR television, would not have been believed.

We enjoyed our three months in Leipzig. We had friends such as the Klitzkes, the Schleiers and Berthold. I was included in activities at the university. We enjoyed the theater and the music. Wilma was invited to speak at the Clara Zetkin Teachers College. But we found our contacts with the Jewish community depressing. The year before we went to Leipzig the *Aufbau,* the German Jewish refugee paper in New York, had an article about the Leipzig Jewish community. Before the Nazis came, Leipzig had a vibrant Jewish community of 17,000 to 18,000 members. In 1984 there were only fifty left, almost all elderly. In the fall of 1985, when we came, there were fewer than forty left, death having taken its toll. It was a pitiful collection of people. The policy of the GDR with regard to the Jewish religious community was ambiguous. On the one hand membership in any religious community could raise serious obstacles to career advancement. On the other hand, the GDR did not want the Jewish community to die out entirely, and the Leipzig congregation was therefore subsidized by the state.

At the Yom Kippur service we met Timotheus Arndt, a Protestant theological student, and then his father, Pastor Siegfried Arndt, both of whom worked very closely with the Leipzig Jewish community. They were also active in the organization *Kirche und Judentum* (Church and Judaism) which was very similar to the Society for Christian Jewish Cooperation in West Germany. Its meetings were very well attended. The elder Arndt had migrated from West to East Germany in the 1950s, not out of sympathy for the regime but because he felt he was needed as a Protestant pastor. After applying for three years for permission to immigrate to the GDR, he was finally given permission. However his children, as Christians who did not join the Communist youth organization, would not attend university and instead attended the Protestant seminary in Naumburg. Only later in the 1980s was Timotheus permitted to study at the Humboldt University in East Berlin, and after the fall of the GDR he obtained his doctorate in Jewish studies there. He now teaches at the University of Leipzig—no longer called Karl Marx University. Pastor Arndt's work with the Jewish community was widely recognized and he was honored in Israel during GDR times. Father and son participated in the Monday evening peace vigils at St. Nicholas Church that prepared the way for the mass demonstrations in the fall of 1989 that led to the peaceful revolution that toppled the regime. Shortly before his death in 1997 Pastor Arndt, with tears in his eyes, confessed to us that he had been a convinced Nazi, had joined the Hitler Youth in 1931, two years before the Nazi accession to power, and realized what the Nazis were all about when he served as a soldier on the Russian front. He viewed his subsequent life as atonement for his participation in the Nazi Movement and as a soldier in Russia.

The Committee for Conscientious Objectors (CCCO) in Buffalo had asked me for a telephone number where they could reach me in an emergency, and we gave them the number of our American friends, Irene and Howard Schultens in

Göttingen. While we were in Leipzig, CCCO wanted me to assist an African American soldier who had been arrested in Mannheim in West Germany. The Schultens gave CCCO the number of Werner Berthold who passed it on to me. Since I could not go to Mannheim, I found someone who could. Word went around now like wildfire that I worked with American soldiers who wished to be released from the armed services. I was asked to talk to a small group of students at the Karl Marx University about the peace movement in the United States and spoke critically not only of United States, but also of Soviet policies.

A few days later while Wilma and I were sitting in the restaurant at the Leipzig train station, a woman at our table who overheard our conversation, put a "Swords into Plowshares" armband of the independent peace movement in front of us. She then asked whether we would be willing to come to the small Brandenburg town of Finsterwalde the following Sunday to meet with GDR conscientious objectors in her church. We agreed. She said she would speak with her pastor and would then call us to confirm. We knew that what we were going to do was illegal. We of course told no one except the Klitzkes, whom we could trust and who should know if we did not come back from Finsterwalde the following day. In the afternoon we met with twenty-eight young men who either intended to apply for service in the Volksarmee without weapons or to refuse service entirely. While the GDR did not recognize conscientious objection, serving without weapons as so-called construction soldiers (Bausoldaten) was an option. In the evening we met with adult parishioners. The pastor told us proudly that there was not a single spy in the audience; we could not be sure of this, but nothing happened to us. We wonder whether the Stasi (the secret police) had any information about our visit or whether they just decided not to pursue the matter. (We have still not received our Stasi files for which we first applied in 1991.) We spent the night with members of the congregation which, of course, was also illegal. The next morning we returned to Leipzig.

During my first invitation to the academy in East Berlin in 1983, I approached the director of the Institute of History, Horst Bartels, about the possibility of an exchange of doctoral students between his institute and our history department in U.B. He promised to look into it, but died shortly afterwards and we heard nothing more. Then on my visit to the institute in 1985 Fritz Klein asked me whether we were still interested in an exchange. I indicated that we were, and soon an arrangement was reached: in the fall of 1997, each side would send one candidate for one semester. It was important for us that our doctoral students should be able to do their research in the GDR and also have access to archives. The first exchange researcher from East Berlin, Jan Lekschas, came in September 1987. He was very different from what we expected an East German academic to look like, with long hair, a hippy appearance, very personable, who quickly made contacts with our graduate students and moved into an apartment together with an American student and a West German woman exchange student. Buffalo was a good base for travel to American archives, particularly in Washington, D.C. The following September Rüdiger Horn was supposed to be one of our exchange researchers. At the last minute we were informed that he would not be able to come because his wife was ill. We were disappointed because we had set money aside for him which now could neither be used nor moved to the following year. I called Klein who told me that there were problems in Horn's family. However, when we met Horn in East Berlin in the summer of 1989 and asked him how his wife was, he told us that his wife had never been ill. He was forbidden to travel because he had circulated a protest against the banning of the German-language Soviet magazine *Sputnik*, which reflected the new liberalism of Glasnost and hence was anathema to the GDR, which now felt isolated even within the Soviet bloc. Nevertheless, Horn now received permission to come to Buffalo, but we had no money for him, because the stipend had now been made available to Ralf Possekel, a student of Küttler, who came in August. Nevertheless our dean agreed that if I took money from my small research and travel fund he would match it. Thus Horn too came in August 1989, when refugees from East Germany were already flooding the Czechoslovak embassy in East Berlin and masses of East Germans were fleeing to Hungary. Horn was quickly integrated into our department. He was open and willing to talk about conditions in the GDR. Possekel too was well received, but more reserved. He had spent five years in Moscow as a student some years earlier. He told me that he had been a convinced Communist when he arrived in the Soviet Union and was soon cured. Incidentally in 1987 I approached Werner Bramke, the chair of the history department at the Karl Marx University in Leipzig, about a possible student exchange with Buffalo. Bramke was the first GDR historian to deal in an objective manner with Carl Goerdeler, the mayor of Leipzig, who had been a powerful member of a circle of conservative opponents of Hitler and was executed by the Nazis in 1945. Bramke expressed his own support for the exchange but also thought that it was still politically impossible. In the fall of 1988 he wrote me that the exchange was now possible if the money could be found. The plan failed to be realized amid the rapid changes after the fall of 1989.

The atmosphere was grim when we arrived in East Berlin the second week of June in 1989, a few days after the massacre on Tienanmen Square. The GDR government now saw its only two allies in China and North Korea. TV praised the action of the Chinese government, as if to warn East Germans how they might be treated. Küttler, who met us with a colleague at the Friedrichstraße train station, the crossing point from West Berlin, apologized for how the East German government reacted to the events in Beijing. On our way to the history institute we passed a church with a big sign announcing a service of mourning for the murdered Chinese students. Everyone we talked to openly expressed their concern, telling us that things could not go on as they had been, but that unfortunately they would. Hartmut Zwahr, whom I saw in Leipzig on my way back to West Germany, expressed the same sentiment. He told me that the present leadership that had served time in Nazi jails or fought in Spain would very soon be replaced by a younger generation who after 1945 had shifted from the Hitler Youth to the Communist Free German Youth. Unlike West Germany, East Germany had never honestly confronted the German past. This new generation, Zwahr feared, would govern the GDR for the next twenty years. He did not foresee that the GDR would be at an end.

On the way back from Leipzig to Göttingen I stopped once more with the Gutsches in Erfurt and asked them to drive me to Buchenwald. Wilma and I had visited Buchenwald a second time in 1985, at which time the exhibit had changed markedly since we had seen it in 1967. But in the spring of 1989 the *New York Times* had published an article by its correspondent Henry Kamm with the heading, "The Buchenwald Museum. No Mention of the Jews." I wrote a letter to the editor saying that while this was the case in 1967, it was no longer so in 1985 when we last visited the camp. As one entered the grounds, one was immediately confronted by a memorial for the Jews who had been sent to Buchenwald after the November pogrom. The new exhibit no longer focused exclusively on the Communists, although they had comprised a large portion of the prisoners. It now dealt with the many non-Communist political and nonpolitical prisoners from many nations, and contrary to Kamm, also the Roma. Kamm wrote me an irate letter claiming that I was wrong. Ingster had shown me a Temple bulletin from a suburban Boston congregation that also maintained that there was no mention of the Jews. I wanted to check once more in 1989, to see whether the exhibit had basically changed since 1985. It had not. There was a good deal to criticize about the GDR's attitude toward the Jews, but things were not as simple as they appeared in Kamm's article. For a long time GDR historians had kept silent on the Holocaust. Nazism was explained as a function of monopoly capitalism, and the popular support of the Nazis was denied. This changed slowly with Kurt Pätzold's book in 1975, *Verfolgung, Vertreibung, Vernichtung* (Persecution, Expulsion, Extermination). Gradually books dealing with Jews and with the Holocaust, such as Rosemarie Schuder and Rudolf Hirsch's *Der gelbe Stern* (The Yellow Star) in 1987 appeared. There began to be observances of the November 9 pogrom in various cities. Wilma was invited to a conference in East Berlin on the fiftieth anniversary in November 1988, organized by the Academy of Science. She was not impressed by the quality of the papers, no outsiders were invited to speak, and there was no provision for discussion.

In the fall of 1989 we had three East Germans in Buffalo. In addition to Horn and Possekel there were three East Germans, including Almut Nothnagle, the wife of my doctoral student Alan Nothnagle. Alan, who was active in the American peace movement and Almut, a Lutheran pastor and Ph.D. in church history from the Humboldt University, had met in 1987 in East Berlin. When Almut became pregnant with twins, the GDR authorities permitted Alan to stay with her provided he exchange twenty-five DM every day, as all Western tourists were obliged to do. After overcoming bureaucratic obstacles they were finally allowed to marry and she was permitted to emigrate legally with the children to the United States. In Buffalo she soon became minister of a small peace oriented church. During the fall we all listened every evening to the short wave *Deutsche Welle* from West Germany, following the rapid events leading to the opening of the wall. Rather than a united Germany, all three wanted a reformed democratic but socialist GDR.

Horn and Possekel returned to Berlin in December, and Almut the following year, as soon as Alan had passed his qualifying examinations and was ready to begin his dissertation research in Germany on a GDR topic.

I arrived in Göttingen from Buffalo early in February 1990 and immediately the next morning proceeded to East Berlin. The atmosphere was electrifying. The walls were plastered with posters from all sorts of political groups, from the right to the ultraleft. The following day the historical association of the GDR held an emergency meeting. Only members were admitted. Küttler and Schleier tried unsuccessfully to obtain permission for me to attend. Horn accompanied me to the Party University, where the meeting was held, but I was not admitted until Heinrich Scheel, the president of the association, recognized me and instructed the ushers to admit me, but advised me to sit in a corner where I would not be seen. Of course, all my acquaintances recognized me. Scheel, standing next to a statue of Lenin, opened the session by declaring that historians in the GDR had, on the whole, done respectable work during the forty years of the state's existence, but that history must never again be the handmaiden of politics. One of the young researchers from the Academy of Sciences, Stefan Wolle, sprang up and said: "Mr. Scheel, you sound like a pimp who wants to organize the prostitutes from the street into an association for the preservation of morality." There was a tremendous outcry to eject Wolle. Scheel expressed the unrealistic hope that the GDR association be integrated into the West German association. Elections followed, with the old guard being confirmed and the reform wing unsuccessful.

That afternoon I took the train to Leipzig and spent the evening with the Klitzkes, We talked until the middle of the night. The next morning we went to visit the Zwahrs. Hartmut had always been apprehensive when we met that the authorities might be eavesdropping. We would meet outside the *Deutsche Bücherei* and walk. Now I visited him for the first time in his apartment. His son Alexander showed me the wounds he had received from the police at a Monday evening demonstration. I had called Hartmut from Buffalo the morning after the wall was opened and renewed my invitation for him to come to Buffalo and to the German Studies Association; he immediately accepted. I then went to the Arndts who from the beginning had been involved in the Monday evening prayers at St. Nicholas Church. When I was leaving the Arndts, Werner Berthold and Günter Katsch accompanied me to the station. Berthold exclaimed that the GDR needed radical changes, but that they should have come from above as in the Soviet Union under Gorbachev; instead, they came from below with the masses destroying everything that had been built up in the GDR. Later we heard that soon afterwards Katsch made two suicide attempts, was committed to a psychiatric clinic, recovered, and started a new career as director of an all-German association of tenants of *Schrebergärten,* the plots of land in which city dwellers built their weekend cottages and cultivated their gardens.

In October 1990 the conference of the German Studies Association was held in Buffalo. On October 3, the last day of the GDR's existence, two emissaries from the GDR mission in Washington arrived in Buffalo and handed me a letter from

Lothar de Maizière, of the Christian Democratic Union, the first and only democratically elected premier of the GDR. It was sent a congratulatory letter informing me that I had been elected as a foreign member of the Academy of Sciences of the GDR. At the GSA there was a good representation of younger scholars from the GDR, as well as both Gutsches and both Zwahrs.

Our cleaning lady of many years who had become a good friend, Virginia King, was very active in her church in a very poor area of Buffalo. She invited the East German visitors to her church and arranged for them to come to the Sunday morning service, which was followed by a meal. Zwahr spoke about the Leipzig demonstrations, which reminded the black audience of Martin Luther King and of the nonviolent confrontation of the civil rights movement. During the meal one of the East Germans always sat between two members of the congregation. It was the first opportunity for the East Germans and the American blacks to meet.

Chapter 9

PRIVATE LIFE AND TIES TO BOHEMIA (1970–2006)

WILMA

As time went on we went to Göttingen more frequently and for longer periods: during the sabbatical year 1971–1972 with Jonathan, and the sabbatical year 1978–1979 without children. After for years renting apartments that happened to be available, we spent both sabbatical years and several summers with Irmgard Bokemeyer in Rauschenwasser. Especially for me Rauschenwasser was a unique and very positive experience. Irmgard had come from the GDR with her nine children in the fifties and taught home economics. She had built a large house near the village of Eddigehausen. As her children moved out, she housed students, guest workers and others who needed a place to stay. Sometimes her daughter Margot Kube lived there with her family, sometimes her son Michael with his family. I would call it a Christian commune. We had our own apartment, but everyone took supplies from a common pantry, did errands for the house and from time to time we settled accounts. That Irmgard took a sofa from Jonathan's room when she needed it was taken for granted, as was her willingness to house one of Georg's conscientious objectors and his wife. She did much for other people. She handled the correspondence for an illiterate man from Slovakia next door, and convinced the village of Bovenden to build housing for large families from the GDR. How could a super housekeeper and pious Christian remind me of my father? She did.

We made a great variety of friends in Göttingen. There were the parents of our children's friends, then colleagues from the university and the Max Planck Institute for History, Hannes and Dagmar Friedrich, the son and daughter in-law of Heide Friedrich, the Justus' whom I have already mentioned, and last but not least Irene Schultens and her husband Howard. They are expatriate Americans with a strong social and environmental conscience who had come to Göttingen several decades ago for his studies. As far as I know Irene has never had a paid job, but is always very busy. She takes care of lonely old people, works at the crisis center and helps raise her grandchildren. She introduced me to the "Göttinger Historikerinnen", a small circle of female historians who meet monthly to discuss their work-in-progress.

We are still in touch with people we met forty years ago, in contrast to Buffalo where some relationships that we thought would develop into real friendships have become increasingly empty. Some Buffalo acquaintances of the early years have moved away, and some friends have died or became very old. It seems to be a common experience that one does not lose many people when they die, but one loses them more gradually.

The Buffalo friend I miss most when I am in Gottingen is Thea Heberle, who has created a rich life for herself involving her children and grandchildren, work with recent immigrants, the study of new languages and relaxation.

My work on the Czech writer Vojtěch Rakous aroused my curiosity about comparable writers. Most of them are now largely forgotten, to some degree because the literary quality of their writings was overshadowed by a Czech-Jewish tendency to be didactic. One exception was Leopold Kompert, from the Judengasse ("Jewish alley") of Münchengrätz, a small town in Bohemia. His stories, which were published in mid-nineteenth century, dealt with the inhabitants of these small Jewish districts. His mother tongue was German, and like his contemporaries Ludwig August Frankl, Moritz Hartmann and others, he moved to Vienna as a young man. The impressions in his stories therefore stem from the years shortly before or shortly after the dissolution of the rural ghettos. Kompert's Jews spoke German and had fewer dealings with their Christian neighbors than those in Rakous' stories, who in many cases were the only Jews in the village. Kompert already deals with mixed marriages toward which he had a very conciliatory attitude. He idealized country life and was a vocal advocate of a minor movement that sought to convince Jews to become farmers or craftsmen.

All of my scholarly work—if one wants to call it that—rests on my love for, and my curiosity about the world from which I came. It is mainly rural, gently hilly, with mountains on the horizon. In Bischofteinitz/Horšovský Týn the language of communication was largely German. In Domažlice/Taus the language was Czech, and in Blížejov/Blisowa, where uncle Leo and aunt Ida lived, it was evenly divided between Czech and German. The problems among the nationalities did not seem worrisome and would not have become so if it had not been for the Nazis. To this day I pay attention whenever I hear Czech being spoken, wherever I happen to be, and I also am glad when I hear German spoken and guess that the speaker must have come from the "Egerland" about 60 years ago. Sometimes when I would ask whether they are from Bohemia, they would respond with anger about the post-war expulsions: "Don't you know that they drove us out?" "Oh yes, I was also driven out."

If my work on Kraus had little to do with Germanic studies, this was even more true of my later work. For many years I collected texts about the Jews in the Czech lands: how they lived, what they thought and how others reacted to them. Since I know little Hebrew, I began with the eighteenth century, when only religious documents were still being written in Hebrew. The sources for my work on the Bohemian and Moravian Jews were at first largely literary, but my interest focused almost from the start on social and cultural history. At the core of it were people from the heart of Europe: Czechs, Germans from the Czech lands, Jews, and Austrians.

For a long time I did not know what ultimately would become of the material. Gradually a plan for a socio-cultural history of the Jews in Bohemia and Moravia developed, in the form of selected texts with introductions, notes and a glossary. The hardest part was cutting and omitting texts. Unlike real historians I did not begin with a thesis that had to be proven, but finally one emerged: The Jews in the Czech lands never had the chance to conduct their lives to the satisfaction of all of the Czechs and the Germans. When they lived modestly, they were accused of being stingy, and when those who could afford a high standard of living and treated themselves to one, they were accused of being show-offs.

Through an acquaintance I got in touch with the Munich publisher Beck Verlag which agreed to publish the resulting book. It came out in 1986 and was reviewed in many publications in all German speaking countries.[1] It was published in English by Wayne State University Press in 1992 *(The Jews of Bohemia and Moravia. A Historical Reader)*, but the English-language edition has aroused much less attention than the German edition.

While I was working on the book during the 1980s it would have been very helpful to have access to the library and archive of the Jewish Museum in Prague, then called the State Jewish Museum. Although some foreign scholars gained access to those collections, for me they remained inaccessible, a reflection, I think, of the authorities' attitude toward the Jews and the place they should be accorded in the history of the Czechoslovak Socialist Republic. The persons in charge sometimes showed me their stony, sometimes their hostile faces; they could not even say that they were sorry.

On Marion Berghahn's suggestion I began to think about the title she suggested for my next work: *Women of Prague*.[2] I selected twelve women, Czech and German, Jewish and non-Jewish, with whom I could identify. I experienced a few surprises during my search: For German, non-Jewish women I found almost no suitable material. The few who had left anything in writing, had mostly written about their famous husbands or other "important" men. They seemingly had no

---

[1] *Die Juden in Böhmen und Mähren. Ein historisches Lesebuch* (München C.H. Beck, 1986); English: *The Jews of Bohemia and Moravia. A Historical Reader* (Detroit: Wayne State University Press, 1992).

[2] *Women of Prague. Ethnic Diversity and Social Change from the Eighteenth Century to the Present* (Providence and Oxford: Berghahn Books, 1995)

ambitions for themselves and, apart from conventional activities such as playing the piano, embroidering and French conversation, seemed only interested in preserving the status quo of their social class.

For the German, non-Jewish category I chose only Lola (Aloysia) Kirschner (1854–1934), who was a popular novelist in her time under the *nom de plume* Ossip Schubin. Her ancestors came from various ethnic groups, including Jews, but she was not Jewish. One would have expected to find German-Jewish women at the time of the Prague Circle in the generation of Franz Kafka and Max Brod, but almost all of those for whom one would have expected to find material had left Prague early and spent their most productive years abroad, before the Nazi period.

An important, highly educated woman, who stayed in Prague was Berta Fanta (1866–1918) who together with her sister Ida Freund conducted a philosophical salon and devoted herself almost exclusively to her intellectual interests. Among the people who joined her gatherings were Franz Kafka, Max Brod, Albert Einstein and Christian von Ehrenfels. Without her daughter Else Bergmann's informative memoirs, our information would be limited to brief references in various biographies and autobiographies. She was about to emigrate to Palestine to join her daughter and son in-law Hugo Bergmann when she died suddenly.

We know Grete Fischer (1893–1977) and Ruth Klinger (1906–1989) from their honest, detailed autobiographies. Both came from middle class Jewish families—and were totally different from each other. Grete Fischer was a talented writer, conservative, sensitive, careful and good, someone one would feel lucky to have as a friend. She lived in Prague, Berlin and London and loved old Prague so much that she did not want to see it again when after World War II it was again possible to do so.

About Ruth Klinger the saying "Fools rush in where angels fear to tread" comes to mind. A talented, beautiful actress, she rushed from one ill-considered affair or marriage to the next. Not all the tragedies in her life were her own fault. There was the pogrom against her parents in 1919, then National Socialism, her severely handicapped child, her hard life in Palestine and then communism in Czechoslovakia. She was the only one of the women introduced in this book who did not love Prague.

I found the richest selection of women among the Czech non-Jews: autobiographies, letters, memoirs, essays and more. The earliest whom I decided on was Magdalena Dobromila Rettigová (1785–1845), the famous writer of cookbooks, adviser of young people and Czech patriot. Her autobiography reflected the ideals of the time, Czech patriotism and progress through education. Opinions about her were divided: Some valued her because of her philanthropic activities and common sense; for others she was just a fat matron who wobbled self confidently through life.

Božena Němcová (1820–1862), as a writer, martyr, lover and patriot occupies a special position with the Czechs. Her letters give a clear impression of her sad life, and her novel "Babička" (The Grandmother) depicts the idyllic childhood she never had. She was beautiful, lived without regard to convention and suffered from the illnesses of her four children, political persecution by the Austrian authorities, her bad marriage and finally her terminal illness.

The next Czech woman, Josefa Náprstková (1834–1907), whom we know from her memoirs, was hard working, practical and reliable. She married Vojta Náprstek, one of the few Czech members of the upper bourgeoisie of his time, or rather, as she probably would have said, was married by him. Her ideals were those of her youth: hard work, frugality and an almost worshipful attitude toward her late parents.

After these three "early" women I introduce, after a pause of two generations, three more Czech women: Milena Jesenská (1896–1944), who as Kafka's friend is the only one among "my" women who has become known internationally, lived a life full of problems, despite the fact that initially she was very lucky. She came from a well to-do family, was gifted and, last not least, very attractive. After her youth as an "enfant terrible" and two failed marriages she became a writer and journalist, becoming the editor in-chief of Přítomnost (The Present), the best cultural-political journal of the time of the First Republic. During the time of the Protectorate Bohemia and Moravia that followed the German occupation in 1939 she wrote for the underground press and joined a secret military resistance organisation, which led to her arrest by the Gestapo in 1939. She died in Ravensbrück concentration camp in 1944.

Milada Horáková (1901–1950) was more conventional. After being jailed by the Germans for years, she was made the center of a show trial and executed by the communists. The indictment was totally fictitious, and the prosecution produced bushel baskets of letters from workers, demanding her execution.

The idea of writing a chapter about Jiřina Šiklova (1935–) came from the historian Vilém Prečan. I met him when he still lived in Hanover and there ran in his apartment a documentation center of Czechoslovak resistance to the communist regime. He collected literature which was published by Czechoslovaks in exile as well as samizdat manuscripts that were smuggled out of Czechoslovakia. There Jiřína played an important role. While about other women there was not as much material as one would have liked, there was plenty of material about Jiřina. I immediately felt at home with her, and soon considered her a friend. The morning I visited for the first time, a well known historian, Jaroslav Opat, also came to see her. That day the police had searched his apartment. The reason for his visit was to find someone from the West who would accompany him to a bank and to declare that he/she had given him an amount of Western currency that he needed to travel to Yugoslavia to visit the dissident Milovan Djilas. I went with him, and at the bank, thank goodness, I was only asked questions for which I was prepared.

Jiřina gave me all the material I needed: her letters from jail, where she had spent over a year, her various publications, the story of her divorce and so on. Although her life as a dissident had not been easy, she rejected the praise that came her way after the "Velvet Revolution", as well as the political posts that she was offered. As soon as possible she re-established the Institute for Social Work at Charles

University. The Center for Gender Studies which at first functioned in Jiřina's apartment now has its own larger quarters and is thriving.

In the years from 1966 on I had gone almost every year with Georg and the children to visit my friends in Western Bohemia and in Prague. I do not know why we did not go in 1968. That year many people wrote me euphorically and invited me to come and experience their new democracy. My contact with friends from the gymnasium continued uninterrupted.

Recently I read Milan Kundera's novel *Ignorance*. It deals with émigrés of 1968 who return to Bohemia, because it is expected of them, not because they want to. The friends of earlier times are a disappointment. Kundera here probably deals with his own experiences. His old friends and relatives are provincial, petty, coarse and sometimes even their language lacks refinement to his ears.

Kundera's experiences are rarely similar to mine. Franta, the only fellow student with whom I continued to correspond, asked many questions about our life and about politics. During the war Franta was a forced labourer in Germany. After the war, he worked as a border policeman and studied law on the side. During all those years he wrote me letters which were more faithful to the party line than they needed to be. When Georg visited him in 1964, we found out that he hated the regime as much as almost all my acquaintances. Some time in the seventies he left Růža and the children and moved in with a Slovak communist of whom he was soon afraid because he was convinced that she spied on him. They continued to live in two halves of their tiny apartment, and he became increasingly fat and depressed, and drank immense quantities of beer. When I told him that he was ruining his health, he said that he wanted to kill himself in that way, and that is exactly what happened.

Iva was very different. As the best student in our class she would surely have gone to university, if the universities had not been closed in the Protectorate Bohemia and Moravia. Her parents were gardeners and lived in the village of Kout na Šumavě (in the Bohemian Forest). Ivas husband was killed in an accident when their daughter was very little, and so she moved back to live with her parents. She worked in the office of a factory for many years, but spent most of her adult life working in her parents' beautiful garden. She is very much interested in economics and politics, and always asked me questions about the political situation in the West, about parties, historians and economists—often more than I could answer. I also stay in touch with her daughter and granddaughter.

My contact with Anita is similar. She taught school for many years and married a teacher. Since 1966 I have also visited her almost every year, mostly in the small village where they spend the warmer part of every year, or in Bor (Haid), in an apartment equipped with the comforts of town living. Some time in the seventies Anita and her husband, who had been in charge of a state-owned bee-keeping operation began increasing their own number of beehives. While Anita continued to teach, beekeeping, one of the few privately owned businesses permitted in communist Czechoslovakia, became their main source of livelihood. When Anita gave up teaching, around the time of the "Velvet Revolution", new tasks awaited her:

teaching German to adults in the area near the Bavarian border, and helping them find jobs on the other side of the border.

Anita is a wise person, the good soul of her village. Through her I became acquainted with other wise people from her class, for instance Vlasta Blacká and her husband Jakub in Domažlice, Catholics who had spent many years in jail because of their convictions, and Máňa Říhová, the resolute wife of the communist manager of what used to be our farm which had become part of a huge collective farm. Her husband was an enthusiastic communist, while she was outspoken in her rejection of the regime. I am very much in touch with her daughter Jana Tomášková who while mayor of Horšovský Týn/ Bischofteinitz awarded me the honorary citizenship of the town.

In 1968 many Czechs—many more than Slovaks—left the country, very much as they had in 1948. In contrast to the '48ers, many of those who left in 1968 had hoped a humane communism was possible, and that their country was moving in that direction. I met such refugees in America, almost all young scholars at the beginning of their careers. Among them were the mathematicians Tomáš and Pavla Jech, through whom I met their mother Božena. I have stayed with her during my annual Prague visits for over thirty years, and enjoy her friendship.

I think it was in 1987 that I was told that a Czech publisher was translating my book, *The Jews of Bohemia and Moravia*. A clandestine meeting was arranged, and I was told the book would appear in samizdat. After the Velvet Revolution I learned that the people who had approached me were close to the Jewish community, and that the book would definitely be published by the Jewish community or perhaps jointly with the publishing company Central Europe. I gave up expecting to hear from them long ago.

Of the many relatives I used to have in Prague, few were left. I had known Eva Dušková before the war as a small child. Her father died of pneumonia in Terezín, and she survived the concentration camps with her mother Gretka Freyová. Some of the drawings she made as a child in Terezin were included in an exhibit of children's art from the Holocaust. She would have liked to specialize in languages at university, but the powers that be decided that she would be a librarian. Her husband Milan, a Catholic, was not permitted to pursue his studies in music with some delay, because his father, a stove fitter, was considered a capitalist.

Bertik Brok, another cousin, had not joined his parents and sister when they emigrated to Canada in 1938. He spent the war years in various concentration camps, including Auschwitz, and survived, probably because he worked in one of Oskar Schindler's factories. He was not considered very bright by his parents and other relatives, and therefore not suited either for his father's enterprises or for university studies. After the war he pumped gas in the countryside, worked in a tire factory and finally for many years as a bellhop and receptionist in Hotel Central, across the street from his parents' former apartment house and fabric store. In his late fifties, Bertik married a woman 35 years younger than he and had four children with her. His family lived in a two-room apartment, while he continued to live in one room in his parents' apartment house. Whenever anyone expressed regrets about the loss of his parents' considerable property, he shrugged it off and remarked that he was no businessman, and probably would have lost it anyway. This changed after the Velvet Revolution. He became very optimistic about recovering the family property that had been confiscated first by the Nazis and then by the communist regime. He felt the matter was now a mere formality. In 1989 he was 81 years old, and lost his job at the Hotel Central due to his bad hearing. He now devoted himself intensively to the restitution, and became increasingly frustrated. The German magazine *Der Spiegel* and Hessian Radio dealt extensively with his case. His pension barely covered his rent. When he died that year of a heart attack, he was buried in the grave of his first wife from whom he was divorced and her second husband. There was not enough money for a plot of his own. Six years after his death his children received compensation from a Czech government fund, one of the largest amounts that had been awarded.

One of the most remarkable people who became a real friend was Ota Pavel, formerly Popper, a distant relative. He is the favourite writer of many Czechs. Originally a sports-writer, he had found his own themes and style by the time I met him about 1967. He often wrote about his father, a real "character" such as are frequently found in Czech literature, or about the river Berounka, the landscape around it, and fishing for carp in the river. Because of his gentile mother and because he was very young at the time of the Protectorate, he was not transported to Terezin. He was full of joie de vivre and had a good sense of humor, but he was manic depressive, and at times became seriously confused during his depressive phases. I saw him for the last time in 1973 when his wife Věra took me to see him in Říčany, where he was staying with his mother. He died a short time later of a heart attack.

Gradually I came to know so many people in Prague, scholars and others, that I unfortunately came to neglect many good people. Apart from the Prague historians Georg mentioned, the first Czech historian I met was Jan Havránek. I came to know him through Gary Cohen, who had written an excellent book about the Prague Germans, when I sought his advice about what historians I should visit. Jan was the inofficial adviser of many Americans and Germans working on Ph.D.'s in Czech history, and I wish he had been mine also. He was, as he said, after 1968 "not quite in and not quite out". He was not permitted to teach, but worked in the university archives and was able to help many scholars including myself. He died suddenly in 2003, before the publication of the second Festschrift in his honor, which was a cooperative enterprise of scholars from both sides of the iron curtain.

Miroslav Hroch is probably the best known abroad among the Czech historians I know. I met him in Bielefeld where he participated in a comparative project the middle class (Bürgertum) in nineteenth century Europe, in which Georg was also involved. Later I also met his wife Věra, a Byzantinist, and we became friends. Twice they took me along on excursions to parts of Bohemia which I had never seen. Věra has died in the meantime, but I have met Mirek during my visits in Prague and profited from his helpful suggestions.

During my first visit in Prague, I met Leo Brod and his wife Elisabeth. He knew the city very well. His interest in the Bohemian Jews was similar to mine, and he wrote stories about them which are situated somewhere between poetry and truth. The Brods, including their son Peter, became real friends. Both Brods senior have died, but my friendship with Peter, an encyclopedia with a human face, until recently in a leading position with the BBC Czech language service in Prague, and his wife Lea continues.

Through Leo Brod I met Kurt Krolop, the leading expert on Prague German literature. As a Sudeten German he was expelled in the immediate aftermath of the Second World War to the Soviet occupied zone of Germany and became a citizen of the GDR. Because of his interest in Prague German literature he wanted to study German literature in Prague with Eduard Goldstücker and was actually in charge of organizing the famous Kafka conference in Liblice in 1963. When the GDR demanded that he return, he hoped to prevent his extradition by means of a pro forma marriage to a Czech colleague, but he was forced to return to East Germany. He then worked for many years as an editor for an East German publishing company before moving on to the Academy of Sciences and a position that corresponded more to his interests. We used to meet in Halle and then in East Berlin. It was only after the Velvet Revolution that he was appointed to the post of professor in Prague. Already in the GDR he had become very much interested in Karl Kraus, the subject of my doctoral dissertation, whom I see much more critically.

During my work on the book *Women of Prague* I received good advice from the historian Zdeněk Šolle. Thanks to him I was able to use the unpublished memoirs of Josefa Náprstková, and to see the castle and grounds in Vrchotovy Janovice that had belonged to Karl Kraus' lover Sidonie Nádherný von Borutín, about whom I had seriously considered including a chapter in my book on the Women of Prague.

When I was searching for illustrations for the German edition of that book, Jan Havránek recommended the photographer Jiří Ployhar, whose name I have come across frequently since then in books about recent Czechoslovak or Czech history. When I went to a class reunion in Domažlice, he offered to take the train there and to hand me the material he had found. We met at the station and just had time for a cup of coffee. Mr. Ployhar remarked that my class reunion could be the subject of a film and suggested that I, a total stranger, borrow his valuable camera. Nothing became of the project he had in mind, but I treasure his generosity. Later, when I worked on the exhibition Myths of Nations for the German Historical Museum in Berlin, he collected illustrations for me, again refusing any payment.

Since the early nineties some things have changed in my life. In 1991 I retired and was looking forward to using my time as I please. Since 1990 we also have been spending about half of every year in Göttingen.

In February of 1990 I worked for a week on the literary estate of one of "my" women, Grete Fischer, in London where she had spent the last decades of her life. I stayed with Muriel, who died since then, and Ralph Emanuel, a couple of whom we have become very fond. Ralph is a distant relative of Georg's who found us through his genealogical research.

The following December I spent a week in Vienna with Christa, to help her with my month-old grandson Micha. Jeremy and Christa had met during the civil war in Nicaragua, where he was on a journalistic assignment and she was on vacation. Two intelligent, good looking people, why should that not work out? I think both sets of parents liked the idea. However, gradually irreconcilable differences emerged and Christa, already pregnant, returned to Vienna. Although we are sorry that Micha is not growing up in a household with both parents, we are pleased with his development and have a good relationship with Christa, as we did with her now deceased parents.

A short time later Jeremy, Dan and Jonathan went to Vienna to see Micha. In this trip they also visited my friends and relatives in Bratislava, in Prague and finally in the Bohemian Forest. In all places they made a video of people who congratulated me for my seventieth birthday and on the birth of grandson Micha. This turned out to be my best birthday present.

1993–1994 Georg had a Woodrow Wilson fellowship and we stayed in Washington. I was finishing work on my book about Prague women, but also took time out to enjoy what Washington had to offer. I also helped Georg's sister Lena find a suitable house in Baltimore. Lena was not a happy person—only in the last seven years or so of her life, after she had moved to an Orthodox Jewish neighbourhood in Baltimore, did she seem satisfied with her life. She moved there to please her two orthodox sons who are living in England. I think the difficulties with their parents helped Georg grow, but not Lena. If one did not know her well, one only saw what was peculiar about her: her chaotic messy house, her clothing. The house was always full of cats, dogs and strange domestic animals such as pet rats and snakes, and their smells. But I know few people as good and eager to help as Lena. She took care of a woman dying of cancer, a pregnant Hispanic student at the middle school where she taught for years in Los Angeles, a mentally retarded neighbor in Baltimore, and many cats and dogs. Her best friend was a Hispanic bag lady. She died early in 2001 and I miss her.

My sister Marianne is two years younger than I. She is a very successful economist. One of her themes is the professional status of women in international comparison. She retired from her professorship at the University of Illinois in Champaign-Urbana a few years ago, but continues to be active. Her late husband was an internationally known expert in marketing, also at the University of Illinois. She went to Champaign with him in 1948, raised two children and is very satisfied with her life which includes many friendships. Although I am frequently struck by how different we are, Georg is right when he says that we have many things in common. We are both very industrious. In her case, as she often says, it has to do with ambition, which is hardly the case with me. Marianne regards our great grandmother Franziska Abeles, who allegedly was always cheerful, as her model and emphasizes the positive in her life. This is surely more sensible than my attitude: I admit when something is pretty awful, even if it hurts.

In spring of 1997 I had a research grant at the recently founded Simon Dubnow Institute in Leipzig. My topic was the modest role that religion played in the lives of the Bohemian and Moravian Jews at the time of the First Republic. It was a continuation of the research I did in 1990 in preparation for my lecture at the University of Vienna about Jewish women and the role of religion in their lives in Bohemia and Moravia.

My main publications in those years were an annotated edition of the picaresque novel *Der jüdische Gil Blas* (The Jewish Gil Blas) by Josef Seligmann Kohn, originally published in 1837, the English edition of my *Women of Prague* in 1995 and the German edition in 2000. The latter is not a simple translation, but is reworked with the different German audience in mind.

We celebrated my eightieth birthday in March of 2001 in Göttingen. We invited Göttingen friends, and Jeremy, Danny and Jonathan came, as did Gert and Waldtraut Klitzke from Leipzig. Although I had wondered for a long time how to get out of a celebration, it turned out to be a nice day, with more proofs of real affection than I had ever expected.

In 1991 we stayed for the first time in our apartment in Schillerstrasse in Göttingen. Dagmar Friedrich had been in charge of re-modeling the first floor of this large one-family house, which is now a bright apartment with access to the large garden. I had fun furnishing it with things from flea markets and with furniture that friends could not take to their retirement homes.

And now again our children: Jeremy has arranged his work with the Minneapolis Star Tribune in such a way that there is time left for teaching at universities and colleges in the area, and for writing books and articles on themes related to journalism, ethics and food-and-culture. A few years ago, after he had travelled to some of the poorest countries in Asia and Africa, he wrote a series of articles about the politics of hunger, for which he was awarded a prestigious prize by the Overseas Press Club of America. He had written his dissertation about journalistic ethics and the commercialization of the press, which has been published as a book.

Dan is legal counsel of the Canadian Bankers' Association in Toronto and enjoys his work as a specialist in securities regulation, although we never expected him in that kind of company. He had married Maggie whom he met at university in 1973, at the age of twenty. Sarah was born in 1977, and when Sarah was a little over a year old, they separated. Maggie became a Jehovah's Witness. At the age of sixteen Sarah moved in with Dan and family. She studied drama for three years at York University, and now is manager of a 700-seat employee cafeteria at a large new casino in Niagara Falls.

Dan remarried in 1982. He had met Janet when both were working for the ombudsman of Ontario. Kelly, now twenty-two, worked for a year to earn money for an extended trip to Europe, where she fell in love with Prague and things Czech. After her first year at McGill University in Montreal, where she warmed her grandmother's heart by writing papers on Czech historical themes, she is spending her second year at the University of Toronto. Adam, now 20, spent the year after high school in an international youth exchange that included four months volunteering in schools in Newfoundland and then in rural Jamaica. He is an enthusiastic first year student at Trent University, and is particularly interested in international development studies and rowing.

Jonathan works as a Medicaid Examiner for the social services department of Erie Country where Buffalo is situated. His clients are people who need assistance with their medical, drug and hospital bills. Through this work he has come to know the problems of the disadvantaged.

In fall 2002, Jeremy and Carol Bouska were married. Their wedding gave us the opportunity to meet their friends and Carol's family. I don't think I could have done better picking a bride for him myself.

I worried for a very long time about the children's attitude toward me. And only what each of them wrote into the album which they gave me for my eightieth birthday convinced me that my efforts were not all in vain. With each I share something that is important to me: love of the world from which I came with Jeremy, my leisure time reading with Danny, and the joys and sorrows of daily life with Jonathan.

In fall of 1998 I was invited by Jiří Kovtun, the historian in charge of the Slavic division of the Library of Congress, to take part in a colloquium for the eightieth anniversary of the founding of Czechoslovakia. There I met Gordon Skilling, who had dedicated his life's work to the history of Czechoslovakia. Eighty-six years old, he still held monthly colloquia in his apartment in Toronto which I attended several times. He hoped that I would work with him to compose a portrait of Alice Masaryk, the president's daughter, similar to the portraits in my book on Prague women. He translated, and I edited the letters that Alice wrote to the Slovenian architect Josip Plečnik who was responsible for the modernization of the Prague castle in the nineteen twenties. Although Alice's letters may never see the light of day, because Plecnik's letters to her have been destroyed, I am grateful that I was able to work with Gordon Skilling, a credible admirer of Masaryk and a scholar who did not let old age keep him from working. He died in March of 2001.

In 1999 I worked—more than necessary, Georg thought—on a project for the German Historical Museum in Berlin. The project is a continuation of the Museum's 1998 exhibition "Myths of Nations." It was my task to show in texts and pictures how the Czechs remembered and continue to remember their national traumas between Thomas's Garrigue death in 1937 and the show trials of 1952. The most important themes are the Munich dictate, the German occupation of 1939, resistance and collaboration, the expulsion of the Germans and the Communist coup of 1948. The War and the Holocaust play a lesser role with the Czechs than in Germany, Poland and Israel. The takeover of Czechoslovakia by the domestic Communists was already planned during the war and its implementation was already noticeable in 1945. It was not forced on Czechoslovakia from the outside. Many of President Edvard Beneš' utterances during the war clearly supported the communist plans, although presumably he had not expected that the country was headed toward the kind of totalitarian regime that emerged in

1948. The expulsion of the Sudeten Germans was a trauma for the Czechs as well as for the Germans who were expelled. In official Czech literature the subject was mentioned rarely for over forty years. However, in the exile- and samizdat press there were many lively discussions about it, in which the damage inflicted to the Czech lands by the expulsion was discussed. New traumas, such as the Stalinist regime with its show trials, the Soviet occupation of 1968 and finally the division of the country caused earlier ones to fade in the collective memory. My interest in the topic goes far beyond the plans set by the German Historical Museum. It is as if I had owned a video camera and had used it for decades to document events and only now was finally able to view the videotapes.

In July of 2002, I gratefully received the honorary citizenship of my home town Horšovský Týn (Bischofteinitz) and two years later I was honored by the Czech Foreign Ministry with the state prize "Gratias Agit" (the Czech Republic "renders thanks"). We intend to continue staying for half a year alternately in Buffalo and in Göttingen, until something unforeseen interferes.

Chapter 10

AFTER THE COLD WAR
(1990–2006)

GEORG

The 1990s marked a turning point in our lives not only because of the changed political situation, but also because there were important changes in our personal lives. When Wilma reached sixty-five in 1986, she took partial retirement at Canisius College, teaching only two courses every other semester. After her seventieth birthday in 1971 she retired fully from teaching. After we returned from Germany in the summer of 1989, I investigated the possibility of my partial retirement, so that I could devote more time to research and writing and spend more time in Germany. The department chair at the time, Jonathan Dewald, wanted to keep me as a full member of the faculty and made a counter proposal. He suggested that I teach three instead of the normal two courses in the fall, and research seminar for M.A. and Ph.D. students in the spring at full salary. I could arrange the seminar so that I would spend the first three weeks in Buffalo to get the students started on their research projects, would then be free to go to Germany, and come back during the last two weeks of the semester to discuss the finished papers. During my absence the students would meet occasionally and keep in touch by E-mail. I would also be responsible for advising the graduate students who were working with me on theses or dissertations. This worked out very well.

The second great change in our personal lives was that now we were able to spend much more time in Göttingen. Since then, except for the academic year 1993 to 1994, which we spent in Washington, D.C. while I was a fellow at the Woodrow Wilson Institute, we have divided our time between Buffalo and Göttingen. We felt at home in Göttingen, where we had many friends and better opportunities for our scholarly work and more people with whom we could discuss it than in Buffalo. Göttingen is also a lovely small town with the cultural offerings of a larger city. In Buffalo we have been, and still are, dependent on each of us having a car. In Göttingen we can reach much of the city on foot, and there is good public transportation. Life is much simpler for us than in Buffalo. On the other hand in Buffalo we have Jonathan, whom we see almost every evening when we are there, and Daniel and his family as well as several of Wilma's favorite cousins nearby on the Canadian side. Our circle of friends and acquaintances has diminished over the years in Buffalo as they died, moved or just faded away, while in Göttingen we still are in close touch with friends we had made when we first came and with new friends, who are mostly younger than us. The university in Buffalo had become more fragmented and impersonal since the exciting days of the 1960, with the main campus no longer located in the city but in suburban Amherst, with no public transportation. The department also had become less cohesive than it was when I first came to Buffalo and more isolated from colleagues in other disciplines than had been the case on the old campus where we saw many of them every day at lunch in the faculty club. There was no such meeting place on the new campus. But I still enjoyed my teaching and the contacts with the students, most of all the Monday evening seminars in our living room, but also the many one-on-one meetings with students. We faced the dilemma that we felt very much at home in two places. Fortunately we did not have to choose between Buffalo and Göttingen but could enjoy both. While we remain in good health, we have not been forced to choose, but we are aware that sooner or later we shall have to.

For many years we had been renting apartments in Göttingen. During the 1970s we spent two full academic years and several summers at Irmgard Bokemeyer's house, a wonderful community that Wilma has already described. As Irmgard became too old to maintain the house, this was no longer possible, and we again rented. Dagmar Friedrich arranged for us to live at the house next door to hers, Schillerstrasse 50, with an eighty-nine year old woman who wanted to have someone in the house. It occurred to us that she might want to sell the house, and together with the Friedrichs we bought it. Both this house, which was built in 1912, and the Friedrichs' house next door built in 1912, reflect the style of the turn of the century. A wide treed boulevard divides the two sides of the street. The houses are wonderfully located, a few hundred meters from the former city wall and an easy fifteen minute walk to the *Gänseliesel,* the fountain of the girl with the goose, the Göttingen landmark in the square in front of the medieval town hall. We divided the three story townhouse into three apartments and kept the one on the ground floor; the other two were sold.

We were very pleased with our apartment. It has less than half the floor space of our house in Buffalo, but for our purposes it was adequate. It consists of a large living room with Wilma's office at one end facing the garden, a large bedroom, and a small office for me with a guest bed. The large former kitchen had been converted into a kitchenette large enough for Wilma and me to eat, and a miniscule bathroom. In addition we have a large storage room in the basement where we can store our excess books. Our living room steps lead to a beautiful large garden that we share with the owners of the other two apartments. With help of our friends we furnished our apartment with second hand furniture.

We now were residents of Göttingen in a very real sense. We had to apply every year for resident permits since we were staying for more than three months every year, which was a nuisance. Finally in 1995 I asked the visa official whether, since we spend so much time in Göttingen and had a home there, we might be able to obtain permanent residence permits. He replied that this would be difficult because we spent so much time out of the country. He then opened his desk drawer, took out the German constitution, the Basic Law of 1949, and read to us Article 116 that provided that all persons and their descendants who lost their citizenship during the Nazi period for political, religious, or racial reasons had a right to be reinstated as German citizens. In fact he was telling me that although he could not grant me a permanent resident permit, I was entitled to have my German citizenship restored. I did not want to endanger my American citizenship and I therefore obtained assurances from the American consular office in Hamburg that I would not lose my American citizenship if I accepted German citizenship, and obtained assurance from the German naturalization authorities that I would not have to surrender my American citizenship. German law forbids Germans to have a second citizenship, but there are exceptions such as persons falling under Article 116. Recently our son, Jeremy, who is an American citizen, and Kelly Daniel's daughter. Canadian citizen, have also become German citizens, which automatically makes them citizens of the European Union. Wilma's situation was different from mine because she had been a Czechoslovak, but never a German citizen.

The procedure for my re-naturalization was very simple. I was asked for three documents: my birth certificate, some documentation to prove that I fell under the categories listed in Article 116—in other words, in my case, that I was Jewish; I had a report card from 1937 from the Talmud Thora school in Hamburg, and our marriage certificate. The reason for the marriage certificate was that they were ready to offer Wilma German citizenship as well. I completed a simple questionnaire in which I was able to indicate that I did not intend to give up my American citizenship. Two months later I received my re-naturalization papers from the German consulate in Buffalo. We were told that since we had married in 1948 Wilma was entitled to German citizenship as the wife of a German under a law that had expired in 1953. She did not accept the offer, was then given a three year residence permit as my wife and a permanent resident permit after it expired. Our feelings were not the same. I considered myself an American and after all the years we had spent again in Göttingen also a German. I wanted to be an active citizen of both the United States and Germany. Wilma appreciated being in what was now a new and democratic Germany, but saw no need to acquire German citizenship and declined the offer. In 2003 Wilma, worried not only about American foreign policy but also about the threat to civil liberties under the Bush administration, applied for German citizenship. The official, with whom we had dealt for many years, saw no problem and told us to come back in a month. When we did he said that a problem had arisen. The regional immigration and naturalization office in Braunschweig had turned down her application. They gave an incredible reason, which reflected the fact that there are still unreconstructed Germans. They argued that I was not a German citizen in 1948 when we married because a law of 1941—a Nazi law-to be sure, had stripped all Jews of their German citizenship. Wilma thus did not become a German citizen again until 1995. Our good friend, Rudolf von Thadden, who served as the chief advisor on German-French relations in the Schröder government, intervened with an indignant letter and Wilma received her German citizenship without having to give up her American citizenship. Ironically Braunschweig had been the office which in 1932 had awarded German citizenship to the Austrian Adolf Hitler so that he could run against Hindenburg in the election for the German presidency.

In April 1990, we conducted two Passover seders, one at our friend's Irmgard Bokemeyer's house in Rauschenwasser with her grandchildren, all Christians, and the second at the Friedrichs with Hanna Vogt and Artur Levi, the Jewish lord mayor of Göttingen and his wife Liesl. On both evenings Thomas Kuczynski, the son of Jürgen Kuczynski, participated. Thomas at the time was the director of the Institute for Economic History, which his father had founded at the Academy of Sciences in East Berlin. During his visit in Göttingen he met with Rudolf Vierhaus to discuss the possibility of reorganizing the GDR Institute for Economic History as a Max Planck Institute. Notwithstanding its Marxist orientation, the GDR Institute for Economic History had an international reputation, and there was no comparable institute in West Germany. The treaty of unification between the two German states, which would abolish the East German academy, had not yet been concluded, and hope remained that the Institute for Economic History would survive. After reunification, everyone associated with the Academy was dismissed as of the end of 1991, and all of its institutes were closed. The journal of the institute, the very respected *Jahrbuch für Wirtschaftsgeschichte* (Yearbook for Economic History), survived, was reorganized in 1992 with an editorial board including distinguished West and East German economic historians, and continues to be published by the formerly East German *Akademie Verlag*.

I followed very closely the fate of the historians at the Academy and at the universities in East Germany after reunification. After all, I knew many historians who were affected by the changes. The West German Science Council set up committees to evaluate the various institutes of the Academy. Jürgen Kocka carried out the evaluation of the institutes in the humanities which included those for German and general history, but not economic history. Kocka sent me the draft of his report that I found very fair. His conclusion on the quality of East German scholarship resembled those in the introduction to my little anthology on social history in East Germany. A good deal of history written in the GDR was of questionable value, following party lines. But there were also very solid works, particularly in social and cultural history, some of which explored paths that had been neglected in the West. Kocka suggested that a serious attempt should be made to integrate historians who had done solid and imaginative work into the profession of a united Germany. Specifically he proposed seven new research institutes, one in history and one in the history of science populated with a mixture of East and West German fellows. Although the plan met opposition from West German quarters, Kocka found funding. The institute that interested me most was the Research Center for Contemporary History in Potsdam, that focused on the history of East Germany and that Kocka personally directed until it was well established. The staff of approximately two dozen people was divided equally between mostly young scholars from West Germany and others, younger as well as more established scholars from East Germany, for whom the positions could be a stepping stone for permanent appintments. Kocka also invited foreign historians and social scientists for shorter periods. I was a fellow at two different times, once for eight weeks in 1993 and a second time for three weeks in 1998. During my first stay I gave a series of lectures on current trends in Western historiography, more or less based on my small paperback which came out at that time, and I met with each of the East German fellows individually to discuss their projects. I felt uncomfortable about this second assignment, as I did not want to appear as someone from the superior West who judged their work. The position of the institute was precarious, and it was by no means certain that it would survive. Two counter-institutes had been established, one the Hannah Arendt Institute in Dresden for the comparative study of dictatorship, which suggested parallels between the Nazi regime and the GDR, and the other in Berlin, a branch of the Institute for Contemporary History in Munich, which at that time had taken a decidedly turn to the right. The conservative *Frankfurter Allgemeine Zeitung* ran an almost slanderous attack on Kocka, under the headline, "Kocka and the Cadres," insinuating that Kocka used the institute to bring in old party hard-liners. In 1998 when I was invited again for three weeks to work on my chapter on the GDR historians for this autobiography—the institute had borrowed correspondence with GDR historians from the archives of the Buffalo university library, the position of the Institute had changed fundamentally. It was now recognized as the leading center for studies of the GDR. A second successful research center was that for the history of science, understood in the German sense as including humanistic disciplines. Within a few years it was transformed into a Max Planck Institute. The new institutes offered opportunities particularly for younger scholars, but not permanent positions, so that many faced an uncertain professional future. A few of the outstanding historians found positions after 1989: Jan Peters at the University of Potsdam, Hartwig Harnisch at the Humboldt University, and Helga Schulz after a delay of several years at the newly re-established European university in Frankfurt an der Oder. Incidentally, I included work by all of them in my anthology on East German social historians. Hans Schleier, who lived in Leipzig, but had been attached to the Institute of History of the Academy, was appointed to a position at the University of Halle where he taught until his retirement in 1996, and Wolfgang Küttler became a fellow at the Max Planck Institute for the History of Science where he remained until his retirement in 2001. Others in their upper forties or older were less fortunate and were forced into early retirement.

The situation of historians who had been at the universities in the GDR was much more catastrophic. With few exceptions, almost all the historians I knew, including those who deserved much better, landed on the street. Only two of our acquaintances were able to keep their positions: Hartmut Zwahr, whose work had been highly regarded both in and outside the GDR, in Leipzig, and Peter Schäfer in Jena who finally received the professorship that he had been denied under the Communists. In the universities in the East almost all of the positions were occupied by West Germans. About half of all positions were eliminated for budgetary reasons to bring them down to West German standards, with the explanation that the East German universities had been overstaffed, but in fact the overcrowded West German universities were badly understaffed in terms of faculty student ratios. Virtually all East German faculty members had to compete against applicants from West Germany in order to keep their positions. In the majority of cases West Germans were appointed, often these were second-rank scholars who had not succeeded in obtaining permanent positions in the West, protégés of their West German doctoral mentors. There were a few outstanding Western historians like Lutz Niethammer and Gangolf Hübinger who went East, to Jena and Frankfurt an der Oder respectively, and Humboldt University in East Berlin became the leading university for historical studies after it had been cleansed of the old GDR faculty. At a time when there had been much discussion in West German about the reform of the universities, the unreformed West German university structure and mentality was superimposed on the East German universities, and the East German universities were now fully patterned on the West German university. Many of the newly appointed West German professors refused to move to the East, but commuted during the week from their homes in the West.

West German historians often brought ideas and approaches that reflected the state of historical studies internationally. In contrast, much of the Marxist historiography of the GDR had been rigid and isolated from the outside community of scholars. However, in some cases outdated West German outlooks replaced innovative Marxist approaches. One example is the institute that Manfred Kossok directed in Leipzig. Kossok had been trained by the historian Walter Markov as an African specialist and also became a leading Latin Americanist. Proceeding from Marxist questions, he developed a comparative study of social and economic structures in developing regions with an anthropological component. Kossok was terminated, his institute closed, and African studies now turned to an old-fashioned focus on philology, abandoning Kossok's broader social and comparative perspective.

I spent the summer of 1991 as a visiting professor at the Technical University in Darmstadt. The following summer I taught at the University of Leipzig, which only shortly before had shed the name of Karl Marx University. This was a period of transition. Gerald Diesener, a student of Werner Berthold, whom we had known since the beginning of his career in the GDR, then acting chair of the history department, had invited me. The old faculty were aware that they soon would have to go. The first West German professor had already been appointed by the Christian Democratic Saxon state government without consultation with the faculty.

By 1993 the change was complete and the new West German appointees had little contact with the older team. Diesener was also let go. The students I taught in Leipzig had almost all started their studies in the GDR. Most of the men had done their military service in the GDR army. I had two very good courses, a lecture course in historiography and a smaller intensive seminar in which I distributed the draft manuscript of my small book on twentieth-century historiography for criticism. The Leipzig students were much harder-working than those I had taught the year before in Darmstadt. This had a good deal to do with the fact that higher education in the GDR had been much more structured than in West Germany. In many ways, if one disregards the ideological structures of the GDR which by 1992 had disappeared, the GDR universities had closer similarities to the American universities, especially on the undergraduate level, than did the West German universities. In my Buffalo seminars I could expect my students to read the weekly assignments, and I also could expect this in Leipzig. I could not expect this in Darmstadt where students considered these assignments an imposition. Diesener's academic career ended with his dismissal in 1993, but he fashioned a new career. Together with his colleague Matthias Middell, who maintained a tenuous position in the university, he organized the Karl Lamprecht Society for comparative studies in world history that continued the work of the institute for universal history that was originally undertaken in the early twentieth century by Karl Lamprecht. He also founded an international journal, *Comparativ*, for comparative history, and launched a publishing house.

The 1990s in Buffalo were relatively uneventful. On the undergraduate level, I regularly taught a course in nineteenth and twentieth century intellectual history which relied heavily on literature as an indication of the intellectual climate, and a research seminar for seniors. All students selected their own topics, and the class followed the progress of each paper and discussed a draft before the final paper was submitted. On the graduate level, I taught the research seminars in spring and courses on European intellectual history and on historiography. Originally there had been three separate historiography courses on the graduate level, in European, American, and non-Western historiography. In my course we studied historiography from a comparative, intercultural perspective, focusing on changing conceptions of historical knowledge and method. The intellectual history course moved away from the older course of "Marxism as an Intellectual Tradition" to a broader discussion of trends in Western thought in the post-World War II period, leading to a critical discussion of postmodernism to which I invited colleagues from philosophy and comparative literature.

On my sixty-fifth birthday in December 1991 I received a *Festschrift*, a volume of essays in my honor. It made me particularly happy that the book was planned and initiated in 1987, before the wall came down, by three editors and friends, Hans Schleier from East Germany, Jörn Rüsen from West Germany, and Konrad Jarausch from the United States, a collaboration that was very unusual at the time. The contributions came from Western and Eastern Europe, the United States, Russia (Aaron Gurevich), and China (Zhang Zhilian). The volume was introduced by a thoughtful biographical essay by my Buffalo colleague, David Gerber, who in 1988 had carried out extensive interviews with Wilma and me, the transcripts of which are deposited in the University Archives in Buffalo. We did not know at the time that the interviews were in preparation for his biographical essay.

I continued to be active in the interdisciplinary Graduate Group of Modern German and Austrian Studies. In 1992 I organized, together with Helmut Böhme, who was still president of the Technical University in Darmstadt, an ambitious seminar involving history and architecture students and faculty in Darmstadt and in Buffalo, reflecting Böhme's interest in the emergence of modern urban centers since the second half of the nineteenth century. Fifteen students from each university participated. The focus was on two exhibitions that were held in 1901 that pointed in new directions, the Pan American Exhibition in Buffalo, which heralded the achievements of modern technology at the beginning of the twentieth century, and the exhibition "Documents of Modern Art" in Darmstadt that featured works of the *Jugendstil* (art nouveau). In both cases, we wanted to go from architecture and art to a broader exploration of political, social, and intellectual outlooks. As background, the students read Marianne Weber's account of Max Weber's trip to the United States in 1904, and Thorstein Veblen's account of Imperial Germany. Fifteen students from Buffalo travelled to Germany in mid-May with a member of the Buffalo German faculty after the end of the spring semester while school was still on in Darmstadt. They then spent two weeks in Darmstadt and nearby Frankfurt in the company of students and faculty from Darmstadt, and then proceeded to the centers of the *Bauhaus* in Weimar and Dessau in what until less than two years earlier had been Communist East Germany. We also stopped in Bitterfeld, which had been considered the most polluted place in East Germany, and was to be transformed into a nature park. In September, after our fall semester had begun and in Darmstadt it was still recess, fifteen Darmstadt students came for two weeks to Buffalo to study its important turn-of-the-century architectural monuments and then spent one week studying early twentieth-century Chicago. We were able to carry out this program thanks to generous financial support from the German Academic Exchange Service (DAAD) and additional contributions from the two universities.

In the meantime my contacts with East Asia intensified. Three of my books have been translated into Chinese and Korean and two into Japanese as well as a host of articles into all three languages. In 1993, the Japanese Society for the Advancement of Science invited me to visit Japan for three weeks. Our friend Akira Hayashima had been instrumental in arranging the invitation. In preparation for the trip, I read several recent Japanese novels. Wilma accompanied me and also gave some lectures. One very nice introduction to our visit was a letter we found in our hotel upon our arrival in Tokyo from a Japanese historian, Masayuki Sato, whom I barely knew at the time but who since then has become a good friend, inviting us to spend a weekend with him and his family in the university town of Kofu at the foot of Mt. Fujiyama. It was a very nice weekend. We stayed at the Satos' house where we also met his wife and three children. They tried to give us an insight into everyday life in a smaller Japanese town. Shortly after we arrived on Saturday afternoon, the Satos took us to a department store where we were able to observe the intense Japanese consumer culture. In the evening we were taken to a Japanese hotel for a meal in a small private room, and were able to watch preparations for a Japanese wedding in the lobby. The next morning Sato took us to a Shinto shrine for a name giving ceremony for a newborn baby. While Sato interpreted, the priest explained the service to us and allowed us to take photographs. We spent a very pleasant and interesting week on the campus of a Methodist university, where Akira Hayashima teaches, in Nishinomiya, near Osaka and Kobe, where we visited classes, spoke with faculty and ate in the student cafeteria.

In contrast to my many contacts in Eastern Europe and East China, I knew few people in Russia. During the Soviet period, I did not want to go there because of the travel restrictions. I did not want a guided tour by Intourist (the Soviet travel agency). In the other Communist countries in Eastern Europe and China, I corresponded freely with individual historians; my communications with colleagues in the Soviet Union were few and formal. In 1994, I received an invitation to teach an intensive one-week seminar on current trends in historiography in the fall workshop organized by the history department at Moscow State University together with the Max Planck Institute for History. I was told not to expect very much from the students who had been isolated from the discussions and the literature outside the former Soviet Union. I was pleasantly surprised when I met my small class of about ten students and saw how well informed they actually were. We had very good discussions. I assume that this was a select group, all of whom spoke good English. In contrast to East Germany, but very much like in other East European countries, there had been little change in personnel after the fall of communism. It is difficult to assess how much of a re-orientation there has been in the writing of history, although I assume that just as in these other countries, and in fact in China too, there has been an opening to historiographical currents from the West. The faculty lounge still had a large picture of Lenin. I have a photograph of myself standing next to the picture—and I was unable to receive a clear answer whether this picture was meant as an homage or as a joke.

I had two memorable meetings in Moscow, both with Medievalists who had managed to remain relatively independent in their work, closer in their outlook to the *Annales* than to Marx or the Party. Their careers had suffered as a result, but they had nevertheless been able to write. I had met Yuri Bessmertny already at the Max Planck Institute in Göttingen in the early 1990s. I also read his 1992 article in the *American Historical Review*, on being a historian in the Soviet Union. He came to my seminar to conduct a session on the *Annales*. The other was Aaron Gurevich, the author of *Categories of Medieval Thought*, which was widely recognized outside the Soviet Union as a major work. Like other scholars whose views were suspect, Gurevich was not permitted to teach and was isolated in the Academy of Sciences. I first met him at a panel that Natalie Davis had organized in 1988 at the American Historical Association. He had been invited already in 1987, but was not permitted to travel. I called him when I was in Moscow, and he suggested that I come at five o'clock. At the tiny apartment that he shared with his wife, daughter and teenaged grandson, we had a very good conversation, but when I got up to leave an hour later he said that he had assumed that I would spend the evening. We then went to the kitchen, where the four of us—he, his wife Esther, myself, and the student who accompanied me—incidentally Jewish as were several of the students in my seminar—passed the evening until the student and I left at midnight. We talked not only about history, but also about the Soviet Union, the strong Jewish identity that he and his wife Esther still shared after these many years, not a religious but still a cultural identity. Gurevich was almost blind at the time, and is now totally blind, but with the help of readers, mostly dedicated students, he continues to write. Esther has died.

The festival of Simchat Torah is the last of the holiday cycle beginning with Rosh Hashanah and concluding the Succoth (Tabernacle) holiday. This joyous festival begins with the reading of the final portion of the Torah, the five books of Moses, the death of Moses, and the creation of the earth in Genesis. All the Torah scrolls are taken from the arc and carried by congregants around the synagogue. Even during the Communist period, many Jews, sometimes harassed by the police, came to the Grand Synagogue. I told my Moscow hosts that I wanted to go there, and was taken by a non-Jewish student to whom the service seemed utterly strange. There was a huge crowd in front of the synagogue, but we managed to enter the building. We were met by three young persons who urged me follow them to the new, ultra-Orthodox Hassidic Chabad synagogue. It was packed with many young people. I was welcomed and immediately handed a scroll to carry in the procession.

I continued to be active in the bureau of the International Commission on the History of Historiography. Our journal, *Storia della Storiografia* (History of Historiograpjhy), which publishes articles in four languages, was separated from the commission and is now edited by a young Italian from Turin, Edoardo Tortarolo, with me as co-editor. There had been problems with the quality of the journal before the change, but it has noticeably improved. In 1995 I was elected president of the commission for a five year term. I organized two important international meetings. The first was in 1997 in Budapest, with the Hungarian Academy of Sciences our host, on the current state of historical theory. There were participants from Europe, East and West, North America, Latin America, South Korea, Taiwan, China, Japan, and Australia and leading theorists of historiography, including Hayden White, Jerzy Topolski, Frank Ankersmit, and Peter Novick attended. The second was in Oslo in 2000, where I was asked to organize and chair one of the three Grand Themes at the International Congress of the Historical Sciences on the "Responsibility and Irresponsibility of Historians." In preparation for this session I had given the keynote address in the summer of 1999 at a meeting of high school teachers from all over Europe, sponsored by the Council of Europe; a conference on this topic was organized later that same year in Kofu, Japan, by Masayuki Sato.

A good deal of my writing in the 1990s and thereafter examined trends of historical thought and writing in the second half of the twentieth century. The conception of objectivity in historical studies had come under intense attack by literary critics such as Hayden White and structuralist and poststructuralists philosophers such as Jacques Derrida. In 1990 I was invited by the Philadelphia Philosophy Consortium to exchange ideas with the Polish philosopher, Leszek Kolakowski, who had been a leading philosopher in Communist Poland, and had sought to move Marxism in a humanist direction. After going into exile, he had turned to a form of Catholicism that looked to mythical sources of historical knowledge in the place of rational inquiry. We were asked by our Consortium hosts to talk about the role of reason in historical study. An exponent of a radical postmodern position who served as commentator maintained that there are no criteria of historical truth, and attacked particularly my paper as beholden to what he called the blackmail that the heritage of the Enlightenment exerted on modern thought. At this point Kolakowski came to my aid, calling on his sad experiences in Poland where history served the purposes of the party and responded that without an effort to prevent distortions of the truth, history would degenerate into propaganda.

I discussed my Philadelphia talk with Winfried Hellmann, the editor at Vandenhoeck & Ruprecht in Göttingen, who urged me to transform my talk into a small book in German for his series of paperbacks including works on the theory of history. I agreed and wrote a text that was published in 1993 as *Geschichtswissenschaft im 20. Jahrhundert,* and that I subsequently rewrote in an expanded English language version, *Historiography in the Twentieth Century. From Scientific Objetivity to the Postmodern Challenge,* which was published in 1997 and re-issued in an expanded form in 2005. In many ways this was a sequel to my *New Directions in European Historiography* (1975). The former had dealt with the rise of social science approaches after 1945. The new book dealt with the challenge to these approaches by various forms of cultural history, and the question of objectivity in historical studies. In its most radical form, the possibility of truth is denied by the argument that language does not reflect reality but creates reality. History is thus seen as the product of language. Since language has no definite meaning, an infinite number of histories are possible, each with the same claim to truth. I conceived my book not merely as a survey of major trends in historical studies in the last third of the twentieth century, but also as a critique of these trends and therefore as contribution to the theory of history. I took seriously the challenge that the new cultural approaches to history posed to social science histories, as described in my earlier book, but also the limitations of this critique. I also recognized that subjective elements enter into all historical interpretation and that, as I already made clear in *The German Conception of History,* ideological elements enter even into those works that are most committed to objective approaches. While I agreed that, as postmodernists such as Derrida insist, all narratives, including historical narratives, must be "deconstructed" to make apparent the ideological components that distort them, I did not believe that historical studies could be reduced to ideology and that all historical interpretations have the same truth value. If this were the case, it would be impossible to disprove the Holocaust deniers. I also believed that in a complex modern world, there is a need for social science approaches which, however, must give greater consideration to cultural factors. I still believe in the importance and validity of rational inquiry. History *is* distinguishable from fiction. It may be difficult to establish the past as it really occurred, but it is often possible to establish through research what did not occur and thus to refute myths and propaganda. And this I consider one of the main tasks for the honest historian. I see the study of history as an ongoing dialogue. Few questions of historical inquiry can be answered definitively. However, while there will be multiple interpretations, these are not arbitrary but can be subjected to rational scrutiny. The book was reviewed very critically in the *American Historical Review* from a postmodernist position but has actually done quite well and has now appeared in eleven European and East Asian languages.

Shortly after the American edition appeared our Swedish friend Bo Stråth arranged an exchange between me and Hayden White at the European University Institute in Fiesole outside Florence, where we could discuss these issues in front of a larger audience. Jürgen Kocka published a German version of the exchange in *Geschichte und Gesellschaft* (History and Society), and Aaron Gurevich published a Russian version in the new journal *Odysseus*. In addition Chinese translations appeared in China and Taiwan, and an English text was published in *Rethinking History*.

In January 1997, I officially retired from the university in Buffalo, but immediately received an offer to teach a graduate seminar each fall in Buffalo for the next five years. I accepted because I valued the opportunity to work with students. I continued to have my office in the department. The arrangement continued for a sixth, seventh, and eighth year. I took on no new doctoral students but continued to work with those students who had begun their dissertations with me, and I also served on a number of dissertation committees. Thomas Behr, a devout Catholic, wrote on an important Catholic theologian and social philosopher in nineteenth century Italy. It may seem surprising that someone would work with me on such a theme, but I had been very interested in nineteenth century social Catholicism in France in connection with my early work on the Saint-Simonians. My three final doctoral students coincidentally worked on GDR topics: Gregory Witkowski on agricultural collectivization, Bruce Hall, a Mormon, who had come to me from Brigham Young University with an excellent M.A. thesis on the Mormons in the GDR, wrote on the small religious sects in the GDR; and Axel Fair-Schulz, an East German, worked on three intellectuals of Jewish background who after having fled from Nazi Germany returned to East Germany after the war. One of them was Jürgen Kuczynski. Fair-Schulz is now working on a history of the Kuczynski family from 1800 to the present, as a case study of a family of radical left intellectuals of Jewish background.

Two conferences were held at the time of my retirement, one in Leipzig and one in Buffalo. In early 1997, friends in Leipzig organized a small workshop for my seventieth birthday. The theme was how they would judge their earlier works after the events of recent years. Hans Schleier, Werner Berthold, Gerald Diesener, and Fritz Klein presented papers that were published as a small volume. The following year a larger conference was held in Buffalo, which brought together German and American colleagues. Helmut Böhme, with whom I had worked for many years on the Buffalo-Darmstadt exchange, came with his wife, as did Hanns Seidler, the chancellor of the Technical University of Darmstadt and a good friend, Klaus Bade of the Institute for Migration and Multiculturalism in Osnabrück, who had encouraged us to write our joint autobiography, and his close associate, Jochen Oltmer. Bade had invited Wilma and me in 1996 to give talks about our childhood and youth before emigration and the time immediately after our arrival in North America in 1938. The theme of the conference, supported by a grant from the German Academic Exchange Service (DAAD) with matching funds from the university in Buffalo, was the "Integration and Exclusion of Minorities in Germany and the United States." Manfred Berg from Berlin, who had written the first German work on the National Association for the Advancement of Colored People, spoke about whites in the NAACP, and Tony Freyer from the Law School at the University of Alabama, who had written the first important scholarly book on the Little Rock desegregation crisis, spoke about my role in the crisis. Our Canisius colleague Larry Jones edited the volume that was published by Berghahn Books in 2001.

In the fall of 1997, I visited Korea again for lectures. In early 1998 Wilma and I spent a month at the University of Aarhus in Denmark where I gave a number of lectures on current historiographical currents, lectured in Copenhagen and Odense, and spent a Saturday at a workshop with doctoral students from various Danish universities.

In February and March 1999, I spent five weeks as a guest at the University of New England in Armidale, New South Wales, Australia. John Moses had invited me to a conference on Germany and the First World War and I was then asked to conduct the first four sessions of the honors seminar on historiography. For Moses' conference I developed a paper that I had prepared for a conference that Gustavo Corni had organized in Trento, Italy, in October 1998 on the intellectuals in the First World War. The paper compared the role of historians during the First World War in Germany, Austria-Hungary, France, Great Britain, and the United States, discussing the manipulation of history in war and the responsibility or failure of responsibility of historians in such circumstances. I had first met Moses in early 1970 when he visited me in Buffalo on his way from Germany to Australia, after he had read *The German Conception of History*. Moses' grandfather, a Lebanese Christian, had come to Australia early in the last century. Moses received his doctorate in modern German history in Erlangen. He had been very impressed by Fritz Fischer's book on Germany and the outbreak of the First World War, agreed with Fischer's thesis and befriended Fischer. In addition to becoming a professor of history in Australia, he also became an Anglican priest, and as a scholar was interested in the chauvinistic and anti-Semitic role of the established Evangelical Lutheran churches in World War I and under the Nazis. For the past several years he has worked on a biography, now about to go to press, of Dietrich

Bonhoeffer, the dissident Protestant theologian who was executed by the Nazis. Moses and I have been good friends ever since we met many years ago.

We very much enjoyed the weeks we spent in Armidale, a small friendly university town in the highlands of Australian New England that reminded us of Fayetteville in the Arkansas Ozarks. I found my colleagues congenial and enjoyed the four historiography sessions of the seminar, one of which I devoted to the treatment of aboriginal peoples in Australian historiography. It was a wonderful summer in February and early March. I went swimming every day and we lived in the middle of the campus, in a park-like setting, in the caretaker's cottage beside the Vice Chancellor's mansion where Moses lived with his wife, Ingrid, the Vice Chancellor (equivalent to a university president in the US), whom Moses had married in Germany, had a meteoric career in Australia, after having started her higher education only after their two sons were old enough for her to do so.

There was, however, one unfortunate series of events. While we were in Armidale, an exhibit on the Righteous Gentiles, who had saved Jews during the Holocaust, opened in the local art museum, sponsored by the B'nai Brith of Australia and New Zealand. I had a very good conversation in the morning of the opening day with the president of the B'nai Brith of Australia and New Zealand, who it turned out was the best friend of my favorite cousin, Sidney Gore. Both had come to Sydney from Hamburg in 1939 at the age of eight. The B'nai Brith had asked that the public lecture on "Postmodernism and the Holocaust," which I was scheduled to give at the university, be part of their program at the art museum. I was invited to give the talk once more in Sydney. That evening two Jewish women from Sydney were to speak about Jewish religion at a church in Armidale, which does not have a Jewish community. John Moses, Wilma, and I attended. After the two women gave a very superficial talk on Jewish holidays and symbols, the first question related to the Israeli settlements in the occupied territories. One of the women announced that she would explain the Jewish point of view on the settlements and defended the policies of the Netanyahu government. I stood up and, carried away by my emotional reaction to what she had identified as the Jewish position, said that I too was Jewish and that she should be ashamed to speak of "the Jews" because many Jews and many Israelis would disagree with her. At the end of the evening I went up to her, apologized for having said that she should be ashamed, but said that I stood by the rest of what I had said. She pointed at Moses, whom she recognized, and told me that I had permitted myself to be used by "that Syrian." She continued that a lot of time and money had been spent on giving Australians in this community a good picture of Jews and that I had spoiled it. The next morning I was informed that my lecture in Sydney had been canceled. It was, however, rescheduled by the university. My cousin told me on the phone that the word was going through the Jewish community in Sydney that I had said that I was ashamed to be a Jew. Against Wilma's and my cousin's advice I decided to send a letter to the B'nai Brith to set the record straight. Instead of an answer, I received a registered letter from a Sydney law firm carrying the same surname as the woman, informing me that they had been instructed to take action in connection with the "defamatory material" in my letter to the B'nai Brith. "The totally false and defamatory statements in your letter included the following: 1. The accusation that Mrs. L. made a racist remark referring to Professor Moses as 'that Syrian.' You know quite well that Mrs. L. made no such remark ... and that your accusation is a pure fabrication."... 2. The statement that Mrs. L.'s presentation was 'simplistic and one-sided' and that it had a stridently nationalistic tone." The question raised about the settlements was "insulting when raised in the context of the Holocaust. You then followed her response with a violent anti-Jewish diatribe." I was asked to apologize for my allegedly defamatory statements within fourteen days and to provide the names and addresses of all persons who received copies of my letter or to whom I had made statements about the matter. I replied that I stood by my letter, that Mrs. L. had made the remark about John Moses as "that Syrian," and that I would only take back the characterization of her remark about Moses as bordering on racism. I heard nothing further from the law firm. I did get a letter from the president of the B'nai Brith, obviously embarrassed, in which he dissociated himself from the dispute.

To my great surprise I was informed in 2001 that the Board of Trustees at the University of Richmond had voted unanimously to offer me an honorary doctorate as a distinguished alumnus. As you will have read in an earlier chapter, I stuck out there like a strange bird. The school when I attended in the early1940s was associated with the Southern Baptist Church, and had resisted admitting black students for a long time. In later years the link with the church diminished and the school emerged as one of the best liberal arts colleges in the South. It was to be awarded the honorary doctorate not only for my academic work, but also for my efforts on behalf of racial justice. I had been invited already in 1994 to give a lecture there in a distinguished scholarly series, and at the time suggested that I deliver a more personal paper on my experiences as a young Jewish refugee at a Southern Baptist college. Now I proposed to talk on how I had seen the future of the world when I graduated from the University of Richmond in 1944, and how I saw the years since then in retrospect. The talk that I gave on October 3, 2001, barely three weeks after September 11, caused some controversy because of my critical remarks about American and Israeli policy.

In the 1990s, I had begun to work on a history of modern historiography, and signed a contract with a publisher. As I proceeded, I became increasingly unsure of the project. Much had been written on the topic. In 1999 a very good small book, *Modern Historiography* by Michael Bentley, appeared, which accomplished what I had intended. I began to feel that my original plan with its orientation on Europe and North America was too limited and that an inter-cultural history of historiography from a global perspective was needed. Such a history did not exist, at least not in Western languages. The various histories of historiography that had been written in the twentieth century concentrated on academic history, neglecting the fact that even after the professionalization of historical studies in the nineteenth century, a good deal of history was written by non-professional historians who often reached a wider public. While I did not agree with Hayden White that history was merely a form of imaginative literature, I saw a great deal of overlap, particularly in the nineteenth century, between the great works of historical scholarship, such as those by Ranke and Michelet, and literature; as a matter of fact their historical works were read by a broad public. I began to move from viewing history as an autonomous professional discipline to seeing it as part of a historical culture in which other expressions of historical consciousness played a role. Thus I was less interested in the great historians and in the great works of history that had been the concern of virtually all histories of historiography, including my own, although they were representative of the culture and time and provided keys for understanding them. Works in the 1980s that studied collective memories, like the French series, *Lieux de Mémoire* (Places of Memory) pointed in this direction. I thus saw the need to analyze the discourse that was dominant in a given epoch and society. I set myself two important limits. One was that I would focus on historical writing after all, realizing that such writing is an expression of a broader culture, but also believing that it is better to approach the culture through its parts than to drown in a fathomless sea. Second, I decided to begin my study in the late eighteenth century, as I would have done if I had followed my earlier more conventional plan, but for a different reason. In this earlier plan, I started as Bentley did with the late eighteenth century as the starting point of professional scholarship. However, I chose this starting point because until then there was little contact of historical traditions and practices beyond cultural boundaries, such as, for example Western, East Asian, South Asian, Islamic, and Sub-Saharan historiographies. Contact had begun much earlier in other areas, such as the economic penetration of the non-Western world. Before 1750 or 1800 the history of historiography is basically a record of separate traditions that have little contact with each other. After 1800 this changes. There is a steady influence of the West on non-Western historiographies. This is not a mere process of Westernization, as everywhere indigenous cultures respond differently. The beginning point of the study I conceived, therefore had to be the situation at the threshold of Western influences. Although there are marked differences there are also parallel developments and processes of modernization of historical studies in East Asia, India and in the Muslim world. After 1800, modernization takes on a predominantly Western face, but there are different forms of modernization in the West and in each of the non-Western cultures. There is thus no uniform process of modernization but there are multiple modernities. What I envisaged was not a well integrated, encyclopedic work but rather an extended essay, perhaps three hundred pages long, which presents less of a survey than a series of questions about how one can in fact write such histories.

I was able to convince my longtime friend Q(ingjia) Edward Wang to join me as co-author. Wang had written an important book, *Inventing China through History* (2001) on Chinese historical writing in the twentieth century, which dealt with the role of traditions of Chinese scholarship in the modernization of historiography in China. We complement each other well. Wang who received his MA in Shanghai and his doctorate in the United States, teaches in the United States.

He has maintained close contacts with his alma mater in Shanghai and with institutions in Taiwan, reads Japanese well, has written on the transmission of Western historical thought to China via Japan, and is well acquainted with Western discussions.

My migration from a focus on German national traditions of historiography to the comparative study of Western historical thought was similar to that followed by Jörn Rüsen on a much larger scale. I met Rüsen in 1971 at the very beginning of his career. We both shared an interest in the philosophy of history and specifically in the theory of historiography. Rüsen was much more deeply rooted than I was in the German tradition, which I saw critically. Consequently, although we became good friends, we criticized each other's work in book reviews. In the 1990s Rüsen organized a number of international conferences on historiography and historical theory, which moved fairly quickly from traditional German historicism in the early sessions and volumes to a broadly comparative intercultural perspective in later conferences and volumes. I attended several of these conferences. An early one dealt with the modernization of historical studies in the nineteenth century, identifying modernization with professionalization. History came to be regarded as a science as it became a professional discipline. I was asked very early to give a paper with the title, "Why Did History Become a Science in Germany Earlier than in Other Countries?" which I changed to "Did History Really Become a Science Earlier in Germany than in Other Countries?" In the paper I questioned the extent to which the highly ideological professional history in Germany could really lay claim to being scientific, and pointed to developments in nineteenth century French historiography that made a much greater contribution to new directions in the twentieth century than the German tradition did. In 1996 Rüsen organized a colloquium for which Peter Burke submitted for discussion ten theses on the characteristics that distinguish Western from non-Western historical thought, to which Chinese, Japanese, Muslim, Black African historians, and I responded.

As I began to work on my new project, I established closer contacts with East Asia, particularly with Professors Chen Qinang and Jiang Peng at the Research Institute of World History at the Chinese Academy of Social Sciences in Beijing whose work concentrated on comparative historiography. I served as a consultant for their projects. Chen invited me twice to China, in 2001 and 2003, both times to colloquia in Beijing and Nanjing. In 2001 I also presented my project at East China Normal University and at Fudan University in Shanghai. In 1999, Wang and I organized a conference on comparative historiography in Buffalo with Chinese, Japanese, Indian, Latin American, Australian, French, German, and American participants which resulted in a volume, *Turning Points in Historiography*,[1] that appeared in 2002 and was promptly translated into Chinese. In December 2002 Wang and I presented our project to a Chinese-German conference in

---

[1] Q. Edward Wang and Georg G. Iggers, eds/, *Turning Points in Historiograpju. A Cross Cultural Perspectibe* (Rochester, 2002).

Berlin organized by Jürgen Kocka at which also my Taiwanese students Chou Liang-kai and Chang Shideh participated.

In 2000 and 2002 we spent two months in Vienna. In 2002 I was a fellow at the International Research Center for Cultural Sciences where I organized a small international workshop to which I invited Sumar Sarkar from New Delhi; in the summer semester of 2002, I conducted a seminar on historiography as guest professor at the University of Vienna with several excellent students in the class. I am still in contact with two of them, Franz Fillafer, an Austrian, and Fotis Kaliampakos, a Greek. Fillafer at present has a doctoral fellowship at the Max Planck Institute for History in Göttingen, In 2002 and 2003, I participated in two conferences in Kofu, Japan to which Sato had invited me, and in the fall of 2004 I had the opportunity to discuss my work at the University of Iceland in Reykjavik and at an international conference on historiography at the Central European University in Budapest. My contacts with East Asia continue. The Chinese translation of *Historiography in the Twentieth Century*, based on the expanded English edition of 2005, has just been published, and the Chinese translation of our autobiography has been completed and is scheduled to be published later this year. In the summer of 2005, I spent ten days in South Korea where I discussed the progress of the intercultural history of modern historiography on which I am working, and I have also been invited by Prof. Sato to do something similar in Japan this coming December. In July of this year, I am to be awarded an honorary doctorate from the Technical University of Darmstadt, this time not for my role in the student exchange between Darmstadt and Buffalo, for which I was honored earlier, but also for my scholarly work.

One topic that constantly occupies us is where we shall spend our final days. The decision may very well dictated by circumstances not under our control, such as our health. At this point we are in remarkably good health, but at our age—Wilma turned eighty-five in March 2006, and I seventy-nine in December 2005—this can change. Right now we enjoy the best of two worlds. There is no question that we feel more at home in Göttingen than in Buffalo. We have many more friends in Göttingen, with some friendships like that with Ulrich and Irene Justus, who are among our very best freinds, dating back to when we first came to Göttingen in 1961, and also throughout Europe, including in Wilma's case the Czech Republic—than we have in Buffalo or in North America. There are many more persons in Göttingen with whom we can exchange ideas. We expect to be able to carry on much longer in our apartment on Schillerstraße than in the suburb of Amherst, N.Y., where we are dependent on our two cars and face the prospect that in the not distant future we will no longer be able to drive. I have already stopped driving at night.

In the 1960s and 1970s I was very active in the Draft Counselling Center in Buffalo and until 1975 was chair of the education committee of the NAACP. I am still a member of the board of directors of the Buffalo NAACP branch, but I am no longer able to make the contribution I made under very different circumstances in Arkansas and New Orleans. After many years, the historically African American Phi Beta Sigma fraternity that pledged me in Little Rock in the early 1950s rediscovered me and after initial hesitations again became an active member. I am hoping to establish closer contacts between the fraternity and the NAACP.

Unlike in Buffalo we have close contacts with the Jewish community in Gottingen. It had been dormant since the last Jews were deported from Göttingen in 1942. We have been members since it was revived in 1994. I attend services almost every Friday in the small liberal congregation that consists largely of recent immigrants from the former Soviet Union, many of whom receive social assistance. A positive development has been the contact the Jewish community has established with the local Muslim community. In fact, the Muslim community took the initiative. After two synagogues were bombed in Istanbul two years ago, the imam of the local Turkish mosque came to the Jewish Friday evening service with two of his congregants to express his sorrow. Since then a monthly roundtable has been established that includes Jews, Muslims, and representatives of the Protestant and Catholic churches. I am active in the group.

When we are finally forced to make a decision, we shall probably return to Buffalo. We miss our son Jonathan, of whom we see quite a bit when we are in Buffalo. We appreciate being close to Canada, the frequent trips that Daniel makes from Toronto to see us either alone or with Janet and one or more of our grandchildren. And then there are Wilma's two favorite cousins in nearby Hamilton, Ontario. Jeremy and Carol live farther away, in Minneapolis, but we get to see them several times a year, in Buffalo or in Minneapolis, and occasionally in Europe. In March of last year, Jeremy spent three weeks in Germany with Göttingen as his base, while on an assignment to write about the integration of new Jewish and Muslim immigrants in Germany. My stay in South Korea last June coincided with his participation in a conference in Seoul on alternative forms of journalism. Ultimately when we shall have to decide, the ties to our children will bring us to Buffalo, but even then we hope to maintain our contacts to Göttingen.

Chapter 11

CONCLUSION

WILMA

We have lived together for over half a century, and since our youth the world has changed very much. We have had to revise or drop some of our convictions, and others have been added. Private decisions, where to move, what positions to accept, we have always been able to make jointly, but this does not mean that we have liked or disliked the same people and circumstances. To Georg scholarly contacts are much more important than to me, and his are also much more numerous. At breakfast he often tells me of his dreams, in which usually people appear whom he knows professionally. He refers to many more people as good or very good friends. I am much more careful about using the word "friend", and use it only when we know much about each other, are very fond of each other, and want to, and can, tell each other everything that is important to us.

The differences between our ways of looking at life are obvious in this autobiography. We think differently and we write differently, but we also complement each other. We had very different childhoods and youths. I therefore found it easier to report about my childhood and youth than about my later life; with Georg it is the other way around. My scholarly works, especially about the Jews in Bohemia, stem from my interest in the world from which I came and are, to put it humorously, an extended *mishpochology*. Therefore there is no exact separation between the personal and the scholarly. Others may decide whether this was detrimental to scholarly objectivity.

Georg's relationship to Judaism is different from mine. It is important to him to observe the major Jewish holidays. Ever since I have known him, he hoped to find a Jewish community where he feels at home and can get involved. He finally found it in the newly revived one in Göttingen, which he attends almost every Friday night.

For me, religious services do nothing, especially since they are conducted for the most part in a language that I do not understand. Georg responds to such remarks of mine by pointing out that I have concerned myself a great deal with Jewish topics. This is true, but the works that I have focused on have almost always been Bohemian and secular, written almost a hundred years after Kafka referred to the "last end of the prayer shawl", and have had nothing to do with Talmud and with other sacred writings. For many years I have spared no effort, digging in archives and libraries to unearth details of the daily life of earlier generations: anecdotes, parodies, sayings, and clever replies from an environment that seemed increasingly to tolerate the Jews and yet made distinctions between Jews and others. These were distinctions that in my youth, if we were aware of them at all, dismissed as unimportant. We, the Jews I knew, felt safe in Masaryk's Republic. Many of the jokes that we had in ready supply concerned Jews who did not want to be Jews. When, on the other hand, someone claimed to be a "conscious Jew", which often was the case when there were clouds on our Jewish horizon, it made us sad. Whatever they meant, their embracing of their Jewish heritage amounted to "whistling in the dark" and did not influence their fate.

As for Georg's work, it also is not devoted to sterile objectivity. The pursuit of justice and a humane world are important to him. I do not think that such a world will ever exist. In retrospect I know that the Czechoslovakia into which I was born and that I have defended enthusiastically, was not a paradise for everybody. Not even Tomáš Garrigue Masaryk with all his excellent qualities could accomplish that, and the events since his death, there and in the rest of the world, have not improved the prospects for a better world.

Georg works almost constantly, on his scholarly projects or helping his doctoral students, even long after they have received their doctorates. He also helps other young scholars and devotes himself to social and political causes. He reads newspapers and professional literature in order to inform himself, and he swims for the sake of his health. Unlike me he seldom reads for pleasure, and he hardly ever watches a movie or a play. But, to be honest, I also only learned gradually to do things purely for enjoyment and not for a cause.

My head is full of stories that I read or heard from childhood on, pranks my father played on authority figures as an adolescent, parodies of German classical poems that my mother knew by heart, and funny episodes that happened before I was born. They portray a colorful panorama of life, probablt better in my memories than it was in reality.

Both of us of course welcome many innovations that originated in our lifetime, in medicine, in transportation, and in technology, which make daily life easier, and here and there instances of social progress. However, when I look beyond our daily lives, I see little reason for optimism. Can one be confident that there will one day be peace in the many regions shaken by conflict, and that the weapons of mass destruction to which an increasing number of irresponsible governments and persons have access will not be used? There is much aggressiveness in human nature, and it seems that the world is becoming increasingly dangerous.

September 11, 2001 has shown us clearly how precarious peace is. The Cold War has fortunately ended, but the gulf between rich and poor and the religious and cultural contrasts that should have no place in a modern and enlightened world have increased the general readiness to use force and terror. The contrast between the proverbial optimism of the Americans and their fear of further terrorist attacks is great and enables the Bush administration to violate civil liberties on a grand scale. The coup d'état that gave us a president who had lost the election has resulted in widespread fears about the stability of American democracy. September 11 seemed to be a good reason for a serious re-examination of the American policies that contributed so substantially to the enmity against the United States, but that has been hindered by the wave of patriotism that followed 9/11.

I think of our grandchildren and worry about the world full of fear and aggressions in which they have to grow up.

GEORG

Unlike Wilma, I had a very problematic relationship with my parents and was considered a difficult child. Only with Wilma at my side, was I able to gain the self-assurance that I lacked in my childhood and youth. On the whole I lived my life as I had hoped I would when I was young. I wanted to become a scholar and a teacher and I did. But scholarship never meant everything to me. Interpersonal contacts and involvement in social issues meant a lot to me and were always related to my scholarly activities. Therefore the years at Philander Smith College (1950–56) occupied a special place in my and also in Wilma's life, although they did not help our careers. Building bridges between white and black Americans, between the East and the West in the Cold War, and reconciliation between Jews and non-Jewish Germans had a special meaning for me.

In a talk that I gave when I accepted an honorary doctorate in October 2001 from my alma mater, the University of Richmond, I attempted to look back at the hopes and expectations I had for the world when I graduated at the age of seventeen in 1944. The balance I drew on the development of the world in the years between then and now was less positive than that of my own life. I had left the University of Richmond with great expectations; despite the war and despite what I already knew about the Holocaust. I was confident that after the war, advances would be made toward a more humane world. I expected progress in many political and social sectors, the realization of the four freedoms Franklin Roosevelt and Winston Churchill had proclaimed in the Atlantic Charter for the postwar world. And much actually became reality. In 1942 it seemed likely that Nazi Germany and Imperial Japan would dominate the world; by 1945 this danger had been banished. Germany, or at least the Federal Republic, became a stable democracy and a member of a European community of states. The picture of the world that most Germans had held changed, away from the militaristic, anti-Western, anti-Slavic and anti-Semitic attitudes that had dominated politics and public opinion in broad circles in Imperial Germany and still in the Weimar Republic and found their high point in Nazism. In its place most of the German population affirmed a civil society and embraced democratic Western values. It is impressive that the Germans were ready to surrender the D-Mark, which in the postwar period had contributed so much to German self-assurance, for the common European currency. This change in German consciousness is an important reason why I decided to again become a German citizen, although I kept my American citizenship and I consider both countries my home.

Also in America some of my hopes were fulfilled. When I came to Richmond in 1939 and to Little Rock in 1950, segregation was still strictly enforced. In the 1950s and 1960s the courts and Congress invalidated many of the laws on which segregation rested. There were also changes in outlook: the view, based on racial prejudices, that America was a white Anglo-Saxon—or Nordic—Protestant country gave way to a vision of a multi-ethnic, multicultural society. And indeed blacks, Asians, and Latin Americans play an increasingly important role today in the public and cultural life of the United States.

On the other hand, progress has also had negative sides. Through the process of globalization the countries of the world have moved closer together, but at the same time the gap between rich and poor has widened. The age of wars between major powers, which marked the world since the beginning of the modern age, appears to have ended. During the Cold War both sides avoided a direct military confrontation that could have led to total nuclear destruction. But violence has not decreased since 1945. Instead of major wars there have been many small wars in which ethnic and national conflicts were fought out for years in the Balkans, the Near East, Central Asia, Africa, the Indian subcontinent and Sri Lanka. During the Cold War, these were often surrogate wars, in which the Soviet and Western blocs gave aid to the opposing sides. The world watched without intervening as mass murder took place in Cambodia and genocides were committed in Rwanda and now in Dafur. The rapid pace of modernization in the context of technological development and globalization created new tensions. Poverty, and even more dangerous cultural discontent with the modern world gave rise to new forms of fundamentalisms, and not only in the Islamic world. The old colonialism was replaced by a global capitalism that increased the gap between rich and poor. But although economic factors play an important role in this process, the international and local conflicts cannot be adequately explained with Marxist categories. Cultural, ethnic, and religious motivations make resolutions of these conflicts extremely difficult.

The attack on the World Trade Center, in which three thousand innocent civilians lost their lives, was a horrendous crime. But it must be understood in the broader context of the political situations that have given rise to terrorism. Terrorism cannot be reduced to Islamic fundamentalism, although the latter plays a role. Whether in Chechnya, Palestine, Kashmir, Sri Lanka, Saudi Arabia, or Iraq, terrorism is fuelled by the desperate struggle of suppressed minorities against powerful political enemies. The attack against the World Trade Center was inexcusable as are the suicide attacks in Israel, Chechnya, and Iraq. Nor can they achieve their aims. There is a bloody cycle of state sponsored violence, terrorist response, violent state responses, and new counter violence. I think that America has drawn the wrong lessons from September 11. It injured American pride and our sense of security. It has been used as a means to manipulate broad segments of public opinion to support imperialist domination abroad and reaction at home. Terrorism can in the long run only be curbed if the political causes that contribute to it are addressed. It is deeply disturbing that this is not taking place.

I have never believed that progress was inevitable, but I was confident that in the end reason will win out, a reason at the core of which is the dignity and self-determination of human beings. In intervals of about ten years I wrote essays on the limits and contradictions of progress, always maintaining the hope that, in the words of the prophets Isaiah and Micah, the time would come when the nations "shall beat their swords into ploughshares, and their spears into pruning hooks: nation shall not lift up a sword against nation, neither shall they learn war any more. But they shall sit every man under his vine and under his fig tree; and none shall make them afraid." Perhaps human nature is such that this goal cannot be attained, and certainly modern technology and the manipulation of public opinion pose serious threats. The twentieth century, which began with such great hopes, turned out to be the bloodiest in the history of the world. Since the Reign of Terror in the Jacobin stage of the French Revolution we have had to witness again and again how radical utopias, such as the Soviet Union under Lenin and Stalin and China under Mao, which promised to liberate humanity, achieved the opposite result.

I have thus over time come closer to Wilma's pessimism. But I am still convinced that we must strive, even if by small steps, for conditions in which all human beings can live in dignity.

INDEX OF PERSONS

A

Abel, Lionel, 110
Abeles (later Abels), Jara née Brüllneierová, 15
Abeles, Elsa née Ornstein, 1–22 passim, 62
Abeles, Gerta, 62
Abeles, Karl, 1–22 passim, 62, 65, 92, 201
Abeles, Mina née, 3
Abeles, Richard, 1, 2, 4, 5
Abeles, Walter, 15, 16, 17
Abeles, (later Abels), Hugo, 16
Abella, Irving, 18
Adams, James Luther, 57, 107, 159
Adenauer, Konrad, 93
Adler, Alfred, 127
Adorno, Theodor, 111, 123, 125
Albrecht, Prof., 83
Allen, William S., 122, 140, 153
Allende, Salvador, 119
Althusser, Louis, 124
Anderle, Othmar, 91, 107
Ankersmith, Frank, 190
Aptheker, Bettina, 158
Aptheker, Herbert, 144, 159
Aquinas, Thomas of, 56
Arendt, Hannah, 54
Arieli, Yehoshua, 115–116
Aristotle, 51, 56
Arndt, Ernst Moritz, 159
Arndt, Siegfried, 162, 166
Arndt, Timotheus, 162
Arnold, Felix, 64
Arnstein, Martha, 11
Auerbach, Phillip, 93
Avineri, Shlomo, 115

B

Baker, Norman, 138
Baron, Hans, 107
Barraclough, Geoffrey, 91
Bartels, Horst, 163
Barth, John, 110
Barth, Karl, 41
Bates, Daisy, 72, 78, 80
Bates, L. C., 72, 80
Beale, Howard K., 83
Beard, Charles, 53, 148
Becker, Miriam, 119
Behr, Thomas, 192
Beneš, Edvard, 179–180
Bentley, Michael, 195–196
Berg, Manfred, 193
Bergstraesser, Arnold, 46, 47–48, 49, 50, 53, 57, 58, 59, 60
Berlin, Sir Isaiah, 90
Berthold, Werner, 144–145, 148, 149, 150, 151, 155, 158, 162, 163, 166, 186, 192
Bessmertny, Yuri, 189
Bismarck, Prince Otto von, 27, 97, 135, 155, 159–160
Blair, F. C., 18
Blascke, Karlheinz, 161
Blaská, Vlasta, 174
Blasky, Jakub, 174
Bloch, Ernst, 149
Bloch, Marc, 89
Block, Timothy, 120
Böhm, Ilse née Haberzettl, 9
Böhm, Michael, 9
Böhme, Heide, 193
Böhme, Helmut, 133–134, 188, 193
Boja, Lucian, 142
Bokemeyer, Irmgard, 168, 182
Bokemeyer, Michael, 168
Bonald, Louis-Gabriel de, 56
Bonaparte, Napoleon, 155
Bonhoeffer, Dietrich, 193–194
Bormann, Martin, 92
Borutin, Sidonie Nadherny, 47
Bouska, Carol, 179, 199
Bracher, Dietrich, 135
Braden, Carl, 75
Bramke, Werner, 164
Branton, Wiley, 79

Braudel, Fernand, 89, 98, 156
Brauer, Max, 91
Bray, Emily, 20
Bray, Fred W., 20
Brecht, Berthold, 52
Brecht, Stefan, 52
Brod, Elisabeth, 176
Brod, Leo, 176
Brod, Max, 171
Brod, Peter, 176
Brok, Bertik, 174–175
Burckhardt, Jacob, 126
Burke, Alice, 38
Burke, Peter, 197
Bush, George W., 202
Butterfield, Herbert, 89

C

Camus, Albert, 98
Carbonell, Charles, 142
Carlebach, Josef, 32
Carsten, Francis, 139
Castro, Fidel, 105
Chamberlain, Neville, 35
Chang, Shih-deh, 133, 141, 19
Chapman, Dale, 38–40
Cherry, Francis, 77
Cherry, Francis, 81
Chou, Liang-kai, 132, 141, 198
Churchill, Winston, 202
Clinton, William, 63, 71, 81, 112
Coates, Willson, 126
Coetzee, John, 114
Cohen, Gary, 175
Cohen, Robert, 123
Colley, 18, 21
Corni, Gustavo, 193
Coughlin, Charles Edward, 59
Creed, 21
Creeley, Robert, 110
Crenshaw, J. L., 71
Croce, Benedetto, 126

D

Dabney, Virginius, 42
Daladier, Edouard, 35
Danilewski, Nikolai, 88
Darcy, Henry, 132–133
Darwin, Charles, 125
Davis, Alison, 51
Davis, Angela, 158
Davis, Natalie, 189
Day, Dorothy, 61
Day, John, 89
De Bruyn, Günter, 151
Debs, Eugene, 81
Dejaeger, Lucien, 99

Dejaeger, Marie T., 99
Derrida, Jacques, 110, 191
Dewald, Jonathan, 181
Dewey, John, 54
Diesener, Gerald, 186–187, 192
Dilthey, Friedrich, 89
Djilas, Milovan, 172
Douglas, Paul, 69
Doolittle, Dr., 8
Dreyfous, George, 85
Droysen, Johann Gustav, 94, 97
Dubnow, Simon, 52
DuBois, W. E. B., 87, 133
Dunnington, Marie, 46
Dušek, Milan, 174
Dušková, Eva, 174

E

Eckford, Elizabeth, 80
Eckstein, Frank, 21–22
Ehrenfels, Christian von, 171
Eichholtz, Dietrich, 153
Eichmann, Adolf, 93
Einstein, Albert, 55, 171
Elders, Joycelyn, 71, 112
Elias, Norbert, 141
Eliot, Fran, 64
Eliot, Johan, 64, 79
Emanuel, Muriel, 176–177, Christa, 177
Emanuel, Ralph, 176–177
Engelberg, Ernst, 146, 154, 155, 159–160
Engels, Friedrich, 52, 123, 124, 126, 159
Enzmann, Hilde née Liebscher, 9
Ewbank, John, 65, 70

F

Faber, Karl-Georg, 142
Fair-Schulz, Axel, 192
Fanta, Berta, 171
Faubus, Orval, 77, 81
Faulkner, Hanna née Popper, 11
Faulkner, Hanna, 199
Febvre, Lucien, 89
Federman, Raymond, 113
Ferber, Marianne née Abeles, 1–22 passim, 177
Feuerbach, Ludwig, 125
Fichte, J. G., 159
Fiedler, Leslie, 110, 120
Fillafer, Franz, 198
Fischer, Alexander, 157
Fischer, Fritz, 90, 94, 133, 147, 160
Fischer, Grete, 171, 176–177
Fischer, J. L., 107
Fleak, Audrey, 68
Fleak, Harry, 68
Florsheim, Ruth, 141–142
Foucault, Michel, 110, 123, 125

Fox-Genovese, Elizabeth, 127
Francis-Joseph, Emperor, 100
Franco, Francisco, 53
Frank, Walter, 137
Frankl, Ludwig August, 169
Franz Josef, Emperor, 5
Franz, Günther, 96
Frederick the Great, 155
Freud, Anna, 122
Freud, Sigmund, 122
Freyer, Tony, 193
Freyová, Gretka, 174
Friedenberg, Edgar, 120
Friedman, Milton, 140
Friedmann, Fritz, 81–82
Friedrich, Dagmar, 168, 178, 182
Friedrich, Hannes, 168
Friedrich, Heide, 100–101, 168
Frisch, Michael, 114, 138
Fulbright, William, 81

G

Gall, Lothar, 157
Gamer, Helen, 45–46, 47, 48, 49, 50, 58
Gandy, Samuel, 67
Gargan, Edward, 106
Gay, Peter, 123
Gay, Peter, 28
Genovese, Eugene, 127, 128, 150
George, Stefan, 59, 107
Gerber, David, 187
Gerhard, Dietrich, 98
Geyl, Pieter, 90
Girard, René, 110
Glatz, Ferenc, 139
Globke, Hans, 93
Goerdeler, Carl, 90
Goethe, Johann Wolfgang, 21,
Goldmann, Lucien, 89
Goldstücker, Eduard, 176
Gore, Sidney, 194
Gottschalk, Louis, 57
Grabski, Andrzej, 142
Gramsci, Antonio, 123, 124, 127
Gredel-Manuele, Zdenka, 132
Groh, Dieter, 135
Grol, Regina, 118
Gronicka, André von, 45
Gruber, Marchet née Sehr, 4, 13, 17
Grundvig, Nikolaj, 56
Gumbel, Emil, 59
Gundolf, Friedrich, 21
Gurevich, Aaron, 187–189
Gurevich, Esther, 190
Gutman, Herbert, 127, 128, 150
Gutsche, Regite, 149, 159
Gutsche, Willibald, 147, 149, 153, 159

H

Haberzettl, Anna née Wittek, 9
Hall, Bruce, 192
Handlin, Oscar, 116
Harnisch, Hartwig, 185
Harris, Marquis Lafayette, 70, 71, 77–78, 79, 83
Hartmann, Moritz, 169
Hartmann, Nikolai, 98
Havránek, Jan, 175
Hayashima, Akira, 141, 188–189
Hayek, F. A., 59
Heberle, Dorothea, 169
Hegel, G. W. F., 52, 90, 98, 126
Heidegger, Martin, 125
Heimann, Eduard, 54
Heimpel, Hermann, 94–95
Heine, Heinrich, 51, 56
Heller, Peter, 122
Hellmann, Winfried, 191
Henschel, Dr. Hans, 119
Herder, Johann Gottfried, 97
Heuss, Alfred, 94, 95–96
Heym, Stefan, 154
Hintze, Hedwig, 151
Hirsch, Rudolf, 165
Hirsch, Samson Raphael, 24, 25
Hitler, Adolf, 16, 26, 35, 37, 45, 90, 92, 97, 184
Hogan, John, 86
Holtzclaw, B. C., 41
Hölzle, Erwin, 96
Hook, Sidney, 54
Horáková, Milada, 172
Horkheimer, Max, 111, 123, 125, 136
Horn, Rüdiger, 163–164, 166
Hourani, George, 131
Hroch, Miroslav, 175
Hrochová, Věra, 175
Hronek, Henrietta, 61
Hruška, František, 13, 107, 173
Hruškova, Ruža, 107
Hubatsch, Walther, 104, 136–137
Hübinger, Gangolf, 186
Hübner, Werner, 144
Humphreys, Stephen, 122
Hutchins, Robert, 49, 55, 59

I

Igersheimer, Josef, 24
Igersheimer (later Iggers), Alfred, 23–43 passim
Igersheimer (later Iggers), Lizzie née Minden, 30–43 passim
Igersheimer, Gerson, 24, 29
Igersheimer, Lina née Mela, 24, 29
Iggers (formerly Igersheimer), Lena, 35–36, 39, 177

Iggers, Adam, 178–179
Iggers, Daniel, 63, 64, 66, 75, 85, 86, 99, 103, 120, 12–130, 131, 150, 177, 178–179, 182, 199
Iggers, Jeremy, 63, 66, 67, 85, 86, 97–98, 99, 103, 119–120, 129, 131, 149, 150, 177, 178, 179, 199
Iggers, Karl Jonathan, 66, 99, 103, 130, 131, 177, 178, 179, 182, 199
Iggers, Kelly, 178
Iggers, Maggie, 178
Iggers, Sarah, 178
Ingster, Oljean, 154
Isaiah, prophet, 204

J

Jackson, Andrew, 95
Jacobeit, Wolfgang, 141
Jacoby, Russell, 127
Jahn, Friedrich Ludwig, 159
Jarausch, Konrad, 157, 187
Jarislowsky, Steven, 52
Jaroslav, Novák, 107
Jay, Martin, 124
Jech, Pavla, 174
Jech, Tomaš, 174
Jechová, Božena, 174
Jefferson, Thomas, 54
Jesenská, Milena, 172
Johnson, Alvin, 53
Johnson, Lyndon, 108
Jolles, Mattijs, 58
Jonas, Albert, 33, 34
Jones, Russell, 42
Justus, Irene, 198
Justus, Ulrich, 198

K

Kafka, Franz, 122, 171, 172, 176, 201
Kahler, Erich von, 59
Kahler, Gretl, 14
Kalimapakos, Fotis, 198
Kallen, Horace, 53, 54
Kalmar, Annie, 47
Kamm, Henry, 165
Kantor, Halina, 119
Kardiner, Abram, 54
Katsch, Günter, 144, 149, 166
Kaufmann, Felix, 54
Kellermann, Bernhard, 102
Kerman, Daniel, 130, 131–132
Ketter, Robert, 121
Killy, Walter, 101–102
Kimball, John, 64
King, Martin Luther, 109, 167
King, Virginia, 167
Kirschner, Aloysia (Lola), 171

Kitzberger, Vaclav, 3, 4
Klauber family, 5
Klečková, Viktorie, 13, 18
Klein, Fritz, 146–147, 149, 163–164, 192
Kleinfeld, Gerald, 152
Klinger, Ruth, 171
Klitzke, Gert, 155, 159, 162, 178
Klitzke, Waltraut, 155, 159, 162, 178
Knížková, Anita née Krucká, 12
Knoll, Erwin, 153
Kocka, Jürgen, 135–136, 138, 141, 142, 155, 157, 160, 184–185, 198
Kocka, Urte, 142
Kohn, Caroline, 99
Kohn, Josef Sdligmann, 178
Kolakowski, Leszek, 191
Kollwitz, Kaethe, 15
Kompert, Leopold, 169
Koptová, Anna, 9
Kossok, Manfred, 186
Kouříková, Iva née Běláková, 15, 108
Kovtun, Jiří, 179
Kraa, Dieter, 150
Kraus, Karl, 46–47, 60, 104, 120, 170
Kriedte, Peterm, 138
Krolop, Kurt, 176
Kube, Margot, 168
Kuczynski, Jürgen, 146, 153–154, 156, 157, 184, 192
Kuczynski, Rita, 157
Kuczynski, Thomas, 184
Kundera, Milan, 173
Kunstmann, John G., 50, 58
Küttler, Astried, 159
Küttler, Wolfgang, 152–153, 155, 159, 164, 166, 185

L

Laing, R. D., 27
Lamprecht, Karl, 187
Landmann, Michael, 107
Langer, Susanne, 54
Lasch, Christopher, 128
Lau, Erich, 28
Leaming, Hugo, 37–40
Lederer, Emil, 14
Lee, Min-Ho, 141
Lee, Robert E., 37
Lekschas, Jan, 163
Lenin, V. I., 189, 204
Lennard, Henry, 54, 55
Lenz, Jürgen, 151
Levi, Artur, 101, 184
Levi, Liesl, 101, 184
Levy, Ernst, 35
Levy, Gershon, 35
Levy, Lina Ruth (Maus), 35

Levy, Martha née Igersheimer, 25, 26, 35
Levy, Siegfried, 32, 35
Levy, Walter, 52
Ley, Hermann, 145
Lieber, Cantor, 29
Liepe, Wolfgang, 47
Lim, Song-woo, 132
Lochman, Vilém, 12, 13
Loesdau, Alfred, 148
Loewenstein, Bedrich, 108, 116
Loewith, Josef ("Pepi"), 16
Loewith, Minna, née Abeles, 199
Logan, Rayford, 86
Lorch, Grace, 77, 80
Lorch, Lee, 77, 78, 80
Loving, Prof., 40–41
Lozek, Gerhard, 148
Lubasch, Nancy, 42, 53, 55
Lucas, Prof., 41
Lüdtke, Alf, 138, 139
Lukács, Georg, 89, 123, 124
Lustig, Arnold, 15, 17
Lustig, Marianne née Oppenheimer, 15, 17
Luther, Martin, 135, 154, 155

M

Maistre, Joseph de, 56
Maizière, Lothar, 167
Mandrou, Robert, 89
Mao, Zedong, 126
Marcuse, Herbert, 111–112, 123–124
Markov, Walter, 148–149, 186
Marshall, Thurgood, 85
Martin, Karl Heinz, 26
Marx, Karl, 51, 52, 90, 91, 98, 123, 124–125, 126, 138, 152, 154, 155, 159, 189
Masaryk, Alice, 179
Masaryk, Thomas G., 49, 179, 201
May, Karl, 8
Mayer, Carl, 54
Mayer, Hans, 149
Mayer, Milton, 59
McCarthy, Joseph, 68, 76
McClellan, John, 81
McKenney, John, 81
McKeon, Richard, 51
McMath, Sidney, 81
Medick, Hans, 138, 139
Meinecke, Friedrich, 89, 97, 107, 137
Mela, Harry, 34, 35–36, 37
Mendels, Judy, 118
Mendès-France, Pierre, 99
Metcalf, George, 45, 50
Meyerson, Martin, 109–111, 121
Micah, prophet, 204
Michelet, Jules, 126, 196
Middell, Mathias, 157, 187

Miller, Adelheid, 119
Miller, David, 119
Minden, Ernst, 30–31, 35
Minden, Henry, 24, 25
Minden, Max, 24, 25, 31
Minden, Sophie née Feitler, 24
Mitchell, Samuel Chiles, 41, 42
Mitscherlich, Alexander, 116
Molktke, Helmut von, 111
Moltke, Konrad von, 111
Mommsen, Hans, 135
Mommsen, Theodor, 95
Mommsen, Wolfgang, 135, 142, 155
Morial, Ernest, 85
Morse, Wayne, 108
Moses, Ingrid, 194
Moses, John, 193–194, 195
Motzek, Herr and Frau, 29
Mühlberg, Dietrich, 156
Mukherjee-Bose, Supriya, 132–133
Mussolini, Benito, 124

N

Náprstek, Vojtěk, 172
Náprstková, Josefa, 172
Nelson, Ray, 68
Němcová, Božena, 9, 171–172
Netanyahu, Benjamin, 194
Nichols, Guerdon, 79, 80, 82, 83
Nichols, James Hastings, 56, 57
Niebuhr, Reinhold, 41, 5
Niethammer, Lutz, 139, 186
Nietzsche, Friedrich, 98, 122, 125, 126, 132
Nipperdey, Thomas, 102, 136
Nkrumah, Kwame, 132
Nothnagle, Alan, 165
Nothnagle, Almut, 165
Novick, Peter, 190

O

Oberländer, Theodor, 93
Opat, Jaroslavm 172
Ortved, Janet, 178
Österreicher, Olga, 6
Owsowitz, Michael, 120

P

Parker, Harold, 151
Pascal, René, 20
Pate, Clarence, 132
Pavel, Ota, 175
Pelzer, Inge, 8
Pestalozzi, Johann Heinrich, 33, 34
Peters, Jan, 185
Peterson, Walter, 133
Petzold, Joachim, 147

Piccone, Paul, 123
Pinochet, Augusto, 119
Pipes, William, 64, 75
Plessner, Helmuth, 96, 97
Pleyer, Kleo, 137
Ployhar, Jiří, 176
Pohle, Fritz, 26–28, 37, 91
Pók, Attila, 139
Popper, Alois, 3, 5, 6
Popper, Hedda, née Ecksteui, 3, 5, 6
Popper, Hugo, 3, 61, 65
Popper, Josef (Pepi), 3
Popper, Karl, 62, 90, 140
Popper, Martha née Ornstein, 3, 5, 10, 11, 61
Popper, Sophie née Grünhut, 8
Porter, 46
Possekel, Ralf, 164, 166
Post (Postnikov), F. A., 64
Preston, Alice, 63
Pulzer, Peter, 116

Q

Qi, Shirong, 140
Quitterer, Marie, 5

R

Rakous, Vojtěch, 8, 117, 169
Randall, John, 54, 87
Ranke, Leopold von, 89, 96, 97, 126, 196
Ránki, Gyorgy, 142
Reed, Adolph, 104
Regan, Peter, 113
Rehbein, Irmgard, 100
Reich-Ranitzky, Marcel, 28
Rein, Adolf, 96
Reinders, Robert, 86
Reiter, Micha, 177
Rettigová, Magdalena Dobromila, 171
Ribbentrop, Joachim von, 60
Ricardo, David, 125
Riemann, Renate, 100
Řihová, Máňa, 174
Ritter, Gerhard A., 135
Ritter, Gerhard, 90–91, 104, 137
Rockefeller, John D., 109
Roosevelt, Franklin Delano, 30, 45, 98, 202
Rosegger, Peter, 9
Roth, Jack, 99, 153
Rothfels, Hans, 57–58, 59, 60, 90, 132
Rothschild, Theodor, 33
Rozell, Forest, 72
Rudofsky, Friedl, 7, 9
Rüsen, Jörn, 153, 187, 197

S

Sabean, David, 139
Sabrow, Martin, 157
Saint-Simonians, 51, 54, 56, 57, 88
Salomon, Albert, 54, 132
Salz, Ludwig, 5
Salz, Wally, 5
Samuel, Ralf, 33
Sarkar, Sumit, 198
Sartre, Jean Paul, 98, 145
Sato, Masayuki, 188–189, 199
Schachermayer, Georg, 107
Schäfer, Peter, 158–159, 186
Scheel, Heinrich, 166
Schieder, Theodor, 141
Schiller, David, 129
Schindler, Oskar, 174
Schleier, Hans, 142, 144, 151–152, 153, 162, 166, 185, 187, 192
Schleier, Sigrid, 162
Schleissner, Karl, 14, 17
Schlenke, Manfred, 107
Schlözer, A. L., 138
Schlumbohm, Jürgen, 138
Schmidt, John, 67–68
Schmidt, Marianna, 67–68
Schmidt, Walter, 153
Schmitt, Elisabeth, 47
Schmitt, Hans, 104
Schmoker, Arnold, 15
Schmoker, Emil 15
Schnabel, Franz, 92
Schoenbaum, David, 116
Schöne, Albrecht, 102
Schorske, Carl, 122–123
Schramm, Percy Ernst, 95, 104
Schuder, Rosemarie, 165
Schul, Rosie, 33
Schultens, Howard, 162, 169
Schultens, Irene, 162, 169
Schultz, Helga, 156–157, 185
Schulz, Prof., 47
Schurmann, Franz, 52
Scott, Emma, 72
Seger, Olga née Abeles, 3
Seraphim, Hans-Gunter, 102
Servatius, Robert, 136
Seton Watson, Hugh, 104
Shao, Lixin, 132
Šiklová, Jiřina, 172–173
Silberhorn, Mrs., 10
Silbert, Morris, 20
Simon, Walter, 135
Simon, Yves, 56
Skilling, Gordon, 179
Smith, Adam, 125
Snell, John, 83, 86, 104
Soniat, Llewelyn, 85
Spengler, Oswald, 88, 107
Stalin, Joseph, 76, 126, 150, 204
Stein, Hans, 14

Stein, Karl Baron vom und zum, 57
Stern, Karl, 10
Stern, Leo, 143, 150
Stock, Ulla, 92
Stråth, Bo, 192
Strauss, Hanne, 119
Strauss, Herbert, 55
Strauss, Leo, 59
Streit, Clarence, 38–39
Strirba, 16
Sullivan, Louis, 99
Světlá, Karolina, 9

T

Talmon, J. T., 115
Teich, Mikolaš, 108
Teichova, Alice, 108
Thadden, Rudolf von, 96–97, 184
Thadden, Wiebke von, 96
Thälmann, Ernst, 149
Thomas, Norman, 59
Thompson, Daniel, 104
Thompson, Edward P., 123, 124, 127, 150
Thompson, Lyell, 66
Thompson, Marki, 66
Tichopad, Jaroslav, 4
Tillich, Paul, 54, 94
Tillmann, Heinz, 144
Tocqueville, Alexis de, 126
Tolle, Karl-Heinz, 100
Tolle, Marcelle, 100
Tomášková, Jana, 174
Topolski, Jerzy, 139, 146, 190
Tortarolo, Edoardo, 190
Toynbee, Arnold, 88, 107
Trautmansdorff, Karl von, 3
Troeltsch, Ernst, 89, 107
Troper, Harold, 18
Truman, Harry S., 68
Tsomondo, Micah, 132
Turner, Henry, 153

U

Ubl, 5

V

Valota-Cavallotti, Bianca, 142
Vann, Richard, 142

Veblen, Thorstein, 53, 188
Vierhaus, Rudolf, 137–138, 184
Vogl, Josef, Dr., 3, 21
Vogt, Hannah, 101, 184
Vogt, Josef, 107

W

Wainman, Charles, 37, 38
Wallerstein, Immanuel, 154
Walser, Martin, 101
Walthet, Peter, 132
Wang, Q(ingjia) Edward, 140, 196–198bs
Wanka, Leni, 4
Warburg, Max, 30
Weber, Marianne, 188
Weber, Max, 51, 54, 89, 91, 136, 152, 155, 188
Wehler, Hans-Ulrich, 135–136, 138, 142, 148, 160
Wein, Hermann, 98
Weinberg, Lore, 52
Westermeyer, Clifton, 79
White, Hayden, 126–127, 152, 190, 191, 195–196
Wieacker, Franz, 97
Williams, Thaddeus, 74
Wirth, Louis, 51
Witkowski, Gregory, 192
Wittram, Reinhard, 93–94, 96, 97
Wolle, Stefan, 166
Wondrasch, Josef, 3, 4, 5
Wondrasch, Marie, 3, 4, 5, 13
Wright, Robert, 133
Wunderlich, Frieda, 54

Z

Zachariah, Mr., 65
Zagorin, Perez, 127, 128
Zarembka, Paul, 124
Zástěra, Jaroslav, 12
Zetkin, Clara, 162
Zhang, Zhilian, 140, 142, 187
Zwahr, Alexander, 166
Zwahr, Annette, 166
Zwahr, Hartmut, 141, 155–156, 157, 158, 164–165, 166, 167, 186
Zwetschkenbaum, Elias, 4, 5, 8, 12, 13

Grade school in Horšovský Týn, 1931.

Hamburg elementary school, with Hitler's picture in the background, Fall 1934.

Wilma's parents, 1936.

Wilma with mother and Marianne, 1936, in garden.

First day in Canada, November 12, 1938.

Georg with parents and sister Lena, ca 1940.

Wedding picture, December 23, 1948.

Georg and Esperanto class, Philander Smith College, 1952.

Meeting of the American Association of University Professors chapter in Lander Smith College, 1952.

New Orleans peace demonstration, Spring 1963.

Lee Lorch's wife Grace with Elizabeth Eckford, whom she had just rescued from a mob, September 1957 at Little Rock Central H.S.

Wilma and Georg, Dillard University, 1959.

Wilma and the Czech author Ota Pauel, Prague, 1970.

Lecture in Beijing, 1984.

Wilma and Daisy Bates of Arkansas NAACP, ca. 1990.

Wilma, late 1990s.

Georg, late 1990s.

Wilma, Georg, and sons, 1994.

Georg and the three sons, ca. 2000.

Georg reading from their autobiography with Wilma, University of Vienna, March 2003.

Wilma and Georg, Esslingen, 2004.

www.ingramcontent.com/pod-product-compliance
Lightning Source LLC
Chambersburg PA
CBHW071340080526
44587CB00017B/2909